Consider Jesus

Lamar & Cos —

My brother and sister
on the way ...

Don Jacos

Dec. 7 2006

DAILY REFLECTIONS *on the* BOOK *of* HEBREWS

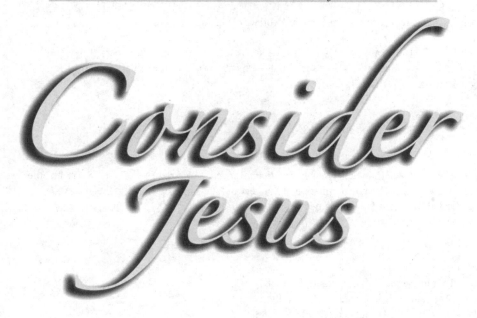

Consider Jesus

Donald R. Jacobs

Herald Press
Scottdale, Pennsylvania
Waterloo, Ontario

Library of Congress Cataloging-in-Publication Data

Jacobs, Donald R.

  Consider Jesus : daily reflections on the book of Hebrews / Donald R. Jacobs.

    p. cm.

  ISBN 0-8361-9347-4 (pbk. : alk. paper) — ISBN 0-8361-9348-2 (hardcover : alk. paper)

1. Bible. N.T. Hebrews—Meditations. 2. Jesus Christ—Person and offices—Meditations.

3. Devotional calendars. I. Title.

  BS2775.54.J33 2006

  242'.2—dc22

                    2006022685

CONSIDER JESUS

Copyright © 2006 by Herald Press, Scottdale, Pa. 15683

    Published simultaneously in Canada by Herald Press,

    Waterloo, Ont. N2L 6H7. All rights reserved

Library of Congress Catalog Card Number: 2006022685

International Standard Book Number: 0-8361-9347-4 (paperback)

International Standard Book Number: 0-8361-9348-2 (hardback)

Printed in the United States of America

Book design by Sandra Johnson

Cover by Sans Serif

12 11 10 09 08 07 06 10 9 8 7 6 5 4 3 2 1

To order or request information, please call

1-800-759-4447 (individuals); 1-800-245-7894 (trade).

Web site: www.heraldpress.com

To
Anna Ruth,
my wife, my companion
on the Way.

Consider Jesus

**In the past God spoke ... at many times and in various ways,
but in these last days, he has spoken to us by his Son (Hebrews 1:1-2).**

Welcome to the book of Hebrews, written to Jews who had embraced Jesus Christ as Messiah. What a rich heritage the Jews had, punctuated with inimitable leaders like Abraham, Moses, and David. Furthermore, they were custodians of a very precious treasure, the law, given by God himself to Moses. And they were entrusted with the priesthood that was designed to bridge the gap between God and people.

It is little wonder that the Jews who believed in Jesus Christ as the promised Messiah should have sought to blend their newfound faith in Jesus with their respect for the law, the priesthood and their renowned leaders. The author of Hebrews, while acknowledging the greatness of the Jewish heritage, spared no effort to lift up Jesus Christ as superior to the law, to the Aaronic priesthood, and to all of the leaders of the Jewish people.

I also have a godly heritage for which I praise God, but my faith in Jesus Christ must rise as a mighty mountain, far above all things. I need to listen carefully to the words of this letter for my own walk with God.

These reflections are extremely personal, often written in light of what was happening to me. You will find testimony and witness on almost every page. It is my sincere desire that you will have the same meaningful experience that I am having as I relate the eternal truths of this precious letter to my own walk with God. And may you be strengthened in your faith as you do what the Holy Spirit instructs to do: "Holy brothers, who share in the heavenly calling, fix your thoughts on Jesus, the apostle and high priest whom we confess" (Hebrews 3:1).

The Spoken Word, a Window to the Heart

In the past God spoke (1:1)

"God spoke." This morning I am distracted. I long to hear from someone I dearly love, just one word. The silence is painful. How do I know what is troubling him unless he speaks? I need to hear a word so I can see into his soul. I get frustrated when someone I love is silent.

"God spoke." I am thankful God spoke. As I look back over my seventy-plus years of life, I am truly pleased by what God did. He has done mighty things for me. My heart rejoices as I see him carrying the cross up Calvary's hill to make my salvation possible. He lovingly wooed me to his side. He prepares the way before me. Everywhere I turn, I see his tender care. What he did, does, and will do is enough to set the soul to singing.

But the most amazing thing is that God speaks. He is not a distant being shrouded in mystery, unknown and unknowable, way off somewhere. On the contrary, our God, the Father of our Lord Jesus Christ, figures out ways to speak to us. He delights to share his heart with those who love him. Our God is a self-revealing God.

"God spoke." And he continues to speak to this very day. He delights to open his heart of love to us.

O heart, rejoice and turn your ear to God.
Remember, God has spoken most eloquently
in his beloved Son, my Savior.

Jesus, God's Awesome Word

In the past God spoke (1:1)

I gave some good advice to someone yesterday. At least I thought it was good. It was what I considered my best advice. Now what? Honestly, I doubt whether that person, who was "fortunate enough" to receive my golden words of wisdom, will act on what I recommended. My words have very limited power. I can chuckle at that.

That is not true of God. When he speaks, something happens—always. The third verse of Genesis amazes us with how God said, "'Let there be light,' and there was light." He went on to create the entire universe by speaking it into existence. He willed it, then spoke, and it was. What is seen is there because God, the Creator, spoke it into being.

Darkness needs no creator for it is simply the absence of light. Likewise silence needs no creator. Creative power acts through speech. God's word is the way he channels his character, power, and wisdom. His word is the expression of who he is. In fact, it *is* who he is. When I hear and respond to God's word, any part of it, I am actually in touch with God.

My primary connection to God is through his word. When that word invades my life, when I embrace it and believe it totally, I experience the same power that created light and everything in his vast universe.

Lord, speak, your servant listens!
Break the silence in my soul.

God Still Speaks

God spoke ... at many times and in various ways (1:1)

My wife, Anna Ruth, and I went to Tanzania when we were in our mid-twenties because it seemed a good thing to do, and it was. I had no intention of serving more than one missionary term there. My plans were fixed. I saw my future on a lush green college campus in America, teaching my beloved subject, history. I was definitely a "one-termer" in Africa.

That all changed one evening. As I was enjoying the golden glow of the African sun setting over Lake Victoria, I heard the voice of the Lord. "This is your place, Don. Learn of me through these people." God spoke! I knew without a doubt that I was where God wanted me to be and that he was getting me ready to hear more through those brothers and sisters in the Lord.

That the holy, almighty, all-powerful God speaks at all is wonder enough. That he condescends to speak and walk alongside a halting missionary staggers the imagination. How can it be? It is by grace alone.

Those who love Jesus and are led by the Holy Spirit expect God to speak. The Bible is full of how God speaks to people. Why should it be considered strange? Our verse for today says, "God spoke." But we now have the blessed privilege of making it present tense: God speaks today, and the Holy Spirit makes sure I hear!

Why, heart, should you be so hesitant
about expecting God to speak to you?
Lord, speak, for your servant hears.

Jesus, God's Word

He has spoken to us by his Son (1:2)

"God said, 'Let there be light,' and there was light" (Genesis 1:3). What happened defies the imagination. At once, intricate, complicated electrical particles were aligned so perfectly that energy became mass, and mass became a form of velocity. I do not understand how that works. I bow the knee before God and simply adore and worship him.

All of this happened, of course, before there was a human scientist to examine it. Scientists pore over the mysteries of this universe, trying to make sense of it all. They find nothing new; they discover what has always been there and was spoken into being by the creative will and word of God.

I remember a time when I was baffled by the thought that Earth is spinning like a top. I've learned something even more astounding since—that our galaxy is moving away from all other galaxies at the rate of 2,600 miles per second.

Is the Word that commanded all that the same Word who said, "I am the way and the truth and the life" (John 14:6)? Does God's Word, Jesus, produce in me the same miraculous release of energy that created this awe-inspiring universe? If the same Word speaks to me, why am I such a limp, unbelieving Christian?

Lord Jesus, God's creating Word, speak into my life.
Re-create me.

All of God Is in the Word

Appointed heir of all things (1:2)

Jesus is heir of all things.

A filing cabinet by my desk holds our will. In it Anna Ruth and I give directions about how we want our estate divided. It is nothing more than a piece of paper until we die; then it will mean something.

When Jesus died, in effect his will could then be opened. As we read that will we discover that he possesses an inheritance that is no less than the fullness of the Godhead (see Colossians 2:9). He is now the heir of all things and at the same time the executor of the will of God. In a most profound sense, Jesus is the will and the content of the will.

God made Jesus heir because he pleased his Father completely. At the transfiguration, a voice spoke from heaven: "This is my Son, whom I love; with him I am well pleased. Listen to him!" (Matthew 17:5).

Then several agonizing weeks followed, culminating in Jesus' crucifixion and burial. To show his complete approval of this perfect obedience, God raised Jesus from the dead. Because God was entirely satisfied with the way Jesus emptied himself, God filled Jesus with his own fullness. By grace, I inherit all there is in Jesus.

Jesus, thank you for your willingness
to die on the cross for me.
Now fill me with my portion of your inheritance.

Jesus, Co-Creator

Through whom he made the universe (1:2)

For years, the people who thought about how the universe came into being (cosmologists) believed in the steady state theory, which says material has no beginning and no end but constantly re-creates itself. There is no place for God or Jesus in that.

Edwin Hubble, the astronomer for whom the famous telescope is named, observed that since galaxies are moving away from one another at a rapid rate, they must have been closer in the past. This gave credence to a creation event. Some cosmologists resisted this finding for years because it opens the door to consider a creator.

It is marvelous that the latest, most convincing science supports the biblical affirmation that God created the universe and all that is in it. He did it by his Word (Jesus)! How it all happened we do not know, but we do know that our Jesus, who walked the paths of Galilee and who stilled troubled waters, was intimately involved in bringing the universe into being. His imprint is indelibly pressed into all that is created.

The universe was not only made through the Word but even now it exists and operates according to the Word. Satan contests that. Our text is clear, Jesus, not Satan, created the universe, though Satan claims to control it. I was not made to worship Satan, nor was any other creature. When people elevate Satan to the place of God, the entire universe receives a jolt. It is truly "unnatural."

I was created to love Jesus.

Lord Jesus, rule my universe as you designed to rule yours.

God's Word Is His Only Son, Jesus

In these last days he has spoken to us by his Son (1:2)

One of my English teachers was so carried away by Shakespeare that he said, "This man was truly inspired." Inspiration is a mysterious thing. When I hear a moving Handel oratorio or a heart-touching Mass by Bach, I too recognize inspiration. Certainly those artists were inspired. But is that the same as the inspiration we receive when we hear Jesus' words?

We can assume that when God, our Father in heaven, inspires someone, the result will be to lift up Jesus, his only Son. Some inspiration is just an emotional response to a strong affection, such as being overwhelmed by the beauty of a butterfly. That is good. If, however, anyone claims to be inspired by God and then proceeds to attack Jesus Christ as he is revealed in the Scriptures, we have good reason to question the source of the "inspiration."

Our Muslim friends are convinced that the Qur'an is inspired—the word of Allah. It does speak of Jesus. The Qur'an refers directly to him more than thirty times. It portrays him as a major prophet of Allah and refers to him as messiah and healer. But it challenges the biblical claim that Jesus is the Son of God. In chapter 4 verse 171 of the Qur'an, we read, "God is much too glorious to have a son."

God speaks in many ways today. But he will never contradict the truth that lies at the very heart of the gospel: Jesus Christ is God in the flesh, and he died and rose again to give me eternal life. That echoes divine inspiration.

Tune my ears, O Father,
to hear and obey your Son,
Jesus Christ.

Jesus, the One and Only

Has spoken to us by his Son (1:2)

I hear the voice of God as I ponder the lives of Old Testament saints. God still speaks to me through them. I think of David, for example, whose life story is a revelation of God's heart. In addition, David wrote poems and hymns that lay bare God's mercy, grace, and love for all to see.

I do well to sit at the feet of those saints of old. They spoke of what had been revealed to them. Similarly, I get excited and challenged when I read the words of modern saints. I also find my spirit soaring when I discern a word of wisdom from the mouth or pen of a spiritual sage. It is so good of God to speak to me through many voices.

I thank God for these many witnesses. Then I read these eye-opening words: "In these last days he has spoken to us by his Son." Hush! The Son of God Almighty, the co-Creator of the universe is speaking. Now, submit everything others have taught or spoken to the scrutiny of what the Son says. In all things, consider Jesus.

One of my Bible students in Tanzania asked, "What is your key to interpreting the Bible?"

I thought a bit and then replied, "I try to read the whole Bible through the eyes of Jesus Christ. Where there are apparent contradictions and difficulties in the text, I look to Jesus Christ as the last word."

> *Jesus, I acknowledge with all my heart*
> *that you are the Word of God.*
> *My life and destiny hang on that.*

God's Word Is for Each of Us

To us (1:2)

At one of the first worship services I attended as a new missionary in Tanzania, a middle-aged woman was the center of attention. She brought with her a well-used basket holding bits of skin, bones, leaves, hair, and a cow's horn filled with tacky medicine. That was her security. With those medicines she would fend off witchcraft attacks of all kinds. Then she met Jesus, who showed himself so powerfully to her—more powerful than all the spirit doctors—that she knew he would be her new basket. She determined to embrace Jesus as her security.

Imagine me, a young American missionary who had no experience of such things, standing in the circle of African believers, rejoicing when Yakobo, the leading elder, struck a match to destroy the basket, the fetishes, and the medicines.

It impressed me that Jesus met this woman exactly where she was. She needed a power that could overcome the witchcraft, the sorcery, and the "demands" of ancestral spirits. Jesus, she discovered, is that power.

I continue to marvel as I move from culture to culture and from church to church. Each believer, each congregation, each culture echoes the prophetic words of Isaiah, "For to us a child is born, to us a son is given" (9:6). Yes, Jesus is for everyone in every need. But the wonder of it all is that he has spoken to me, just where I am.

Lord Jesus, break all binding powers in my life
as you did for that Tanzanian woman.
Speak into my life with transforming power.

The Son and the Father Are One

The Son is the radiance of God's glory (1:3)

A few weeks before he was crucified, Jesus led his three most intimate friends, Peter James, and John, up a mountain. Up there, on the mountaintop, his "face shone like the sun, and his clothes became as white as the light" (Matthew 17:2). A voice from heaven called out, "This is my Son, whom I love; with him I am well pleased. Listen to him!" (Matthew 17:5). Our text for today delights in the knowledge that "the Son is the radiance of God's glory."

Sixty years later that same John was passing through a dark valley. The Roman Empire had turned against the believers, and the blood of martyrs flowed. The church suffered a violent blow. John must have been dumbfounded as he pondered what it all meant. While he was praying on Patmos, it happened again. As on the mountain, he saw Jesus in glory and wrote, "His face was like the sun shining in all its brilliance" (Revelation 1:16).

John's brother, James, was also there when Jesus was transfigured. He wrote years later, "Every good and perfect gift is from above, coming down from the Father of the heavenly lights, who does not change like shifting shadows" (James 1:17). A brother in Africa interpreted "shifting shadows" to mean that there is nothing in God that can cast a shadow. There is nothing in Jesus that contradicts God. He is the radiance of God's glory.

> *Lord Jesus, I pray that when something in my life*
> *casts a shadow of doubt—rebellion,*
> *self-sufficiency, pride, whatever it is*
> *—please reveal it to me by the Holy Spirit*
> *so that I can plunge it into the cleansing fountain.*
> *I want to walk in your light constantly.*

The Son and the Father Are One in Character

The exact representation of his being (1:3)

I find it interesting that the Greek word translated *exact representation* can be translated "character" or "engraving." The master engraver makes two or more images exactly alike. To me, this means that even though the Father, Son, and Holy Spirit have different "offices," they are absolutely identical in character.

As I think about this, I need to put some things right in my own head. For example, when growing up, I thought I had a better chance of getting what I wanted from my mother than from my father. If I wanted something from Dad, I usually appealed through Mom.

Is it possible that I have carried this same idea into my prayer life? I feel that Jesus and the Holy Spirit are near to me; they understand my frailty. But I assume that the Father is stern and might be tempted to punish me.

Why is it that I think the Father is reluctant to listen to me? The truth is, the Father loves me just as much as Jesus does. The Father knows me every bit as well as the Holy Spirit does. Furthermore, the Father is just as eager to satisfy the desires of my heart as Jesus or the Holy Spirit. It gives me comfort and hope to know that when I see Jesus, I also see the Father and the Holy Spirit. I have some unlearning to do!

> *Blessed Three in One—*
>   *Father, Son, and Holy Spirit—*
> *I know that you love, you rejoice, you suffer,*
>   *you hope, you save, you sanctify, you fill my life as one.*
> *My desire is to be at one with you.*

The Word Sustains Everything

Sustaining all things by his powerful word (1:3)

As a student I was taught to believe that the universe is sustained by natural laws, which makes irrelevant the idea of a sustaining God. One of my teachers explained it this way: The universe is like a clock. God made every piece just as it should be and made it to interact perfectly with all other parts. Having put the pieces together, he took his celestial key, wound the clock, and then sat back to see it working. (Yes, I was a student when we still wound up clocks. This dates me, doesn't it?)

I thought that made sense. So the way to understand the universe is to figure out the natural laws that make it work. The key to knowledge is science! Religion is a private matter, I was taught, and should not be used to understand the real world, the world of nature. I was content with that.

As Jesus revealed himself to me, more and more, I had to rethink my scientific assumptions. How can I square my scientific beliefs with statements like today's text? Jesus sustains all things. It pushes my mind to the limit and beyond.

However, if I begin with the assumption that Jesus is God among us and that he is the same Jesus who undergirds the universe with his word of power, then all makes sense. Remove Jesus from the universe for one moment and all returns to chaos again.

Lord Jesus, here is my wee personal universe. Rule it!

Jesus Brings Cosmos by Dealing with Sin

After he had provided purification for sins (1:3)

God spoke to Adam and Eve: "You are free to eat from any tree in the garden; but you must not eat from the tree of the knowledge of good and evil, for when you eat of it you will surely die" (Genesis 2:16-17).

Until that time, at each stage in the creation saga God said, "Let there be . . . ," and it was. Now we hear him say for the first time, "You must not." He knew eating from that tree would harm them, so he lovingly but emphatically warned them for their own good. The fruit of that tree had a purpose, no doubt, but it was not meant to be eaten by humans.

Our physical lives are possible because the elements obey. Imagine the difficulty God would have if the oxygen he created refused to fuse with hydrogen. There would be no water.

Sin, in its simplest sense, is willful disregard for the Word of God. When I say no to God, I thwart his influence in my life. If I am to walk with God, sin must be dealt with.

When the creation begins to rebel against its Creator, what is there to halt total disintegration and chaos? I am part of the created order, and God is my creator. My task now is to submit my will to his so that he becomes my sustainer. Sin wrecks it all.

Jesus, my loving Creator,
bring order out of my chaos
by giving me a purified and obedient heart.

Jesus, the Key to Peace

After he had provided purification for sins (1:3)

Satan attacks God's word, always. We all know the story of how Satan appeared in the garden and proceeded to do what he always does. He attacked God's Word, and said, "You will not surely die" (Genesis 3:4). The choice was clear: Is the Word of God true or is the word of Satan true? How can it be that Adam and Eve chose to believe Satan? Is there any wonder that things went wrong? The creation was made to be ruled by God alone. Satan makes a mess of creation because he is not the creator.

The tendency to doubt the Word of God is a temptation that can lead to disobedience, the essence of sin. My problem lurks deep within me. I much prefer to control than to be controlled. I would rather be self-reliant than to rely on God.

God reminds us that the universe is sustained by his power. By rejecting him, I bring calamity on my own head. Sin has cosmic consequences. Note where the Bible places the ultimate responsibility. God simply stated a fact: "You shall surely die." He did not say, "I will surely kill you!" By deliberately shutting the will of God out of my life, I invite chaos, ruin, and death. It is spiritual suicide. Rejecting God equals accepting Satan.

> *Lord Jesus, you told us clearly*
> *that the words you speak are the words of the Father.*
> *My precious Savior, forbid that my will*
> *should prefer the word of Satan.*
> *Cleanse my heart, mind, and will of anything*
> *that resists your clear Word.*

The Word Is Approved by Heaven's Majesty

He sat down at the right hand of the Majesty in heaven (1:3)

Jesus sat down. In Tanzania, for a time we lived near the tribal court where the paramount chief heard cases. He liked to have a few trusted elders with him to help him make the hard decisions. They were usually wizened old fellows who sat sedately beside him as he judged. It was considered a great honor to sit beside the chief.

I see in that African court scene a hint of what I read here. Jesus went right through, breaking the power of sin by his redeeming work. He pleased the Father in every way. He obeyed to the end, to death on a common Roman cross. Having paid the price of love, he was raised from the dead and, with his blood, entered heaven as the slain Lamb of God.

Then Jesus sat down at the right hand of the majesty in heaven. Paul wrote to the Colossians, "For God was pleased to have all his fullness dwell in him" (Colossians 1:19). Jesus finished his work, as he announced on the cross. The work of redemption was accomplished. Now the door is wide open for all that believe to enter full salvation by the eternal sacrifice of himself.

So he sat down, like a trusted elder or person who has run an exhausting race or a victor after a battle. Praise God, Jesus needs to do no more than he has done to ensure my salvation and make provision for my daily needs. He did it all.

Jesus, take your rightful place in my heart as in heaven.
Sit down on the throne of my heart and rule.
I abdicate gladly.

Jesus Satisfies Heaven's Demands

At the right hand of the majesty in heaven (1:3)

It is right and proper that I sing in my heart, "Worthy is the Lamb that was slain." In Revelation I read, "Then I heard every creature in heaven and on earth and under the earth and on the sea, and all that is in them, singing: 'To him who sits on the throne and to the Lamb be praise and honor and glory and power, forever and ever!'" (5:13).

When I see him in my mind's eye, sitting there by his Father, my soul is at rest. Jesus, the glorified Son, pleases his Father entirely and the Father beams with delight. The Father breaks into singing along with all the voices in heaven and on earth that exalt the name of Jesus. If Jesus brings joy to the heart of God like this, what keeps me from joining the choir and singing with full voice, "I too am pleased with Jesus." That is the least that I can do.

As I read the book of Hebrews and other writings of the New Testament, I am astonished at the way the writers exalt Jesus Christ, seemingly without limits. I have made too little of Jesus. My comprehension of him is much too limited. I need the Holy Spirit to open my eyes to Jesus in all his glory.

Pause and ponder the astounding assertion of John 1:1: "The Word was God." The Word of God is a person. His name is Jesus of Nazareth. If the Gospel writers believed that about Jesus, why should I take a lesser view of him? I must continue to consider Jesus.

> *Jesus, words cannot describe you.*
> *You are the Word beyond words.*
> *Give me ears to hear nothing but you,*
> *now and forever.*

Jesus—The Name Above All Names

**So he became as much superior to the angels
as the name he has inherited is superior to theirs (1:4)**

Naming is important in many African cultures. Most parents there give names with meaning, such as naming a child after an event surrounding the birth, in honor of the family line or the father, and so forth. In those cultures a baby does not become a full person until he or she is named.

I recall hearing of one family that had a string of stillbirths. To stop the bad luck, they decided to refer to their next newborn as an animal to trick the spirits that they suspected had been killing their children. When the child was strong enough to survive, they went ahead and gave it a human name. That "made it a person."

Those who love Jesus give him names. Here are but a few: the Christ, son of Mary, Messiah, Healer, Savior of the world, Prince of Peace, Lamb of God, Rose of Sharon, Bright and Morning Star. We could go on and on. I assume believers are still giving Jesus names, such as my closest friend, my helper, my all in all.

I love the prophecy of Isaiah 9:6: "For to us a child is born, to us a son is given. . . . And his name will be called Wonderful Counselor, Mighty God, Everlasting Father, Prince of Peace." Peter proclaimed, "Salvation is found in no one else, for there is no other name under heaven given to men by which we must be saved" (Acts 4:12).

Blessed be your name, Jesus, Son of God. I name you Friend.

Jesus—Superior to the Highest Angels

**So he became as much superior to the angels
as the name he has inherited is superior to theirs (1:4)**

Some ancient Jews believed that the angels, heaven's ministering spirits, were arranged in hierarchies. These Jews described how the angels in the heavenlies were organized, who was the most powerful, and who was subservient. They tried to determine which angels might be assigned to particular people or towns. They also believed their elaborate classifications gave them some power over angels. The challenge for them was to learn the names of all the angels and their ranks in order to influence them.

I found the dark side of this in Africa. The demon cults named all the demons, and each name indicated its position in the hierarchy. Naming demons gave the practitioners a certain power over them.

Some well-meaning Jewish theologians considered Jesus to be the highest angel. But Jesus is not an angel. His name says it all. He is the Christ, the Son of God, Emmanuel. Jesus is not an angel among us, but God.

Why is it that when I utter the name Jesus, something happens? I do not know, but as one hymn says, "There is something about that name."

> *Jesus, help me to verbalize your name,*
> > *for when I say that name, I am closer to you*
> > > *and something blends my soul with heaven itself.*
> *As I live my commonplace day, prompt me,*
> > *Spirit of God, to say, "Jesus."*

Jesus—Not an Exalted Angel but God's Only Son

You are my Son; today I have become your Father (1:5)

"You are my Son." I have sometimes wondered why people find it so difficult to believe that Jesus is exactly who the Bible says he is. I think of our Muslim friends. They simply cannot comprehend that Jesus was always God's Son, from the beginning.

Then I have friends who gag on the thought that Jesus died for sinners. They dislike the idea that God could be involved in any way in the violence of the cross. Yet they admire Jesus' ethics.

While living in Tanzania we learned that many of our neighbors were absolutely convinced that if they abandoned their worship of ancestors and looked to Jesus as their only security, they would be doomed. They could not imagine life without the protection they received from their medicines and fetishes, all empowered by ancestral spirits. I have known some who were willing to trust Jesus for salvation but were not willing to trust him with their crops, herds, or lives. It is not easy to believe in Jesus.

I see that I just wrote three paragraphs about why "people" find Jesus hard to accept. Do I have myself convinced that Jesus is no problem to me? Do I actually believe every word Jesus uttered? Do I believe all the testimonies in the Scriptures that reveal Christ? I hope I do. But do I really?

> *Jesus, I need a daily conversion to enable me*
> *to embrace the truth about you.*
> *Open my heart's door to the One*
> *whom all heaven adores and praises.*

The Word Is from Outside the World

When God brings his firstborn into the world (1:6)

God brought Jesus here. Jesus is not a man achieving godliness. He is God coming among people, as a person, to save. Jesus is not an example of the best that a human being can become. He is God reaching down because he loves the world so much that he is prepared to pay whatever is required of him for their salvation.

I come from a denomination that places great emphasis on following Jesus. We shy away from theologies that emphasize salvation but not discipleship. One of our favorite little stories is about one of the brethren who was asked if he was converted, to which he replied, "It is best if you ask my neighbor if I am converted." He had seen too many people who claimed to be saved but continued to live like people of the world.

To be sure, we must bend all our efforts, focus all our attention, and channel all our energies into following Christ. But this does not bring us closer to God. Salvation does that. The atoning work of Christ brings us into a forgiven relationship with God.

Then it is our duty to stay there. Jesus told his disciples, "Remain in my love" (John 15:9). Fellowship with God is not a position I attain but a work of God's grace that I maintain by bringing every thought and act into obedience to my precious Lord Jesus. All my service for God and mankind flows from the atoning work of Jesus Christ.

> *My Lord, convince me again*
> > *that what I need is from above, not from the earth.*
> *You, Jesus, came to us from glory.*
> *You alone can save and transform us into new creatures.*

Angels Serve the Purposes of Jesus

He makes his angels winds, his servants flames of fire (1:7)

It was well after midnight. I was lost, completely lost, as I drove the empty streets of Geneva, Switzerland, without a map, in a rented car. Furthermore, I could not speak French. I found myself praying, "Oh, Jesus, can you get me out of this one?" Within a block of praying that prayer I spied a person standing on a corner, so I stopped.

I rolled down the window. He spoke perfect English. He not only told me how to exit the city but where to turn to get to the little town where I was headed. He also told me not to miss the little street that would take me to my destination, alerting me to a landmark where I should turn.

After I had all that written down I drove off. At once it struck me. How did he know? As I pulled away I perceived in my heart he was an angel. As I peered into the rearview mirror, I saw no trace of him. Did he slip down a side street? Maybe.

That was one of several times in my life when I was convinced the Lord sent an angel specifically to help me in a desperate situation. So when I think of how the people who received this epistle worshipped angels, I can understand.

Having angels serve us is downright awesome. But we must never forget that angels serve the Lord. They act at his bidding, not ours. Surely it is right to appreciate the work of angels. But we do not worship angels; we worship God.

Jesus, forbid that I should worship your ministering spirits.
Give me a single heart that worships only you.

January 23

Jesus' Reign Is Forever

Your throne, O God, will last for ever and ever (1:8)

One day during Haile Selassie's rule in Ethiopia, I sat behind him on the platform on Mesquel Square in Addis Ababa at a religious celebration. The square was ablaze with the marvelous blooms of a yellow mesquel daisy. It was unforgettable.

Not many years later, I passed that same square and was disappointed to see that the then-ruling Communists had quadrupled the size of the square and paved every inch of it. Not a daisy in sight.

The believers I met in Ethiopia had suffered a huge jolt when the Communists took control. Everything had changed. I felt sad for them. But as I fellowshipped with them in a secret place, I became aware how they had come to know the unchanging King—the King of kings and Lord of lords, Jesus Christ. Because they knew Jesus as king, the political turmoil did not upset them terribly but lifted them into a life of greater faith.

With all their churches closed and some leaders imprisoned, their numbers grew tenfold in ten years. They realized that God did not abdicate his heavenly throne, and he did not abandon the church. His reign is forever. The throne of God is established.

Jesus, you are my king because of who you are
and for what you did to bring me,
an alien, into your kingdom.
I have crowned you as king of my little kingdom.
I rest in the knowledge that you are righteous
in all your ways.
Calm my troubled spirit, Jesus,
when I in any way doubt that you are still there
on the throne, forever and ever.

The Son Is Greater

God has set you above your companions (1:9)

In any company, Jesus stands head and shoulders above all. The writer of Hebrews claimed that Jesus is far superior to the most exalted angels. Furthermore, even though he shares human flesh and blood, he is superior to all saints and to Abraham, Moses, and Isaiah.

The angel told the godly Zechariah that he would have a son in his old age. The son was to be called John and would be "great in the sight of the Lord" (Luke 1:15). Indeed he was great beyond words. John the Baptist brought many children of Israel to God through repentant faith and water baptism. Jesus himself said, "I tell you the truth: Among those born of women there has not risen anyone greater than John the Baptist" (Matthew 11:11).

When John was baptizing on the Jordan's bank, Jesus appeared, requesting baptism. John said, "Look, the Lamb of God, who takes away the sin of the world" (John 1:29). He knew full well that Jesus was the promised Messiah. He considered it a blessed privilege to announce Jesus' appearing. It is with joy that he pointed to his superior.

John said to his followers, "A man who comes after me has surpassed me" (1:30). As Jesus gained prominence in the land, John again said, "He must become greater; I must become less" (3:30). Jesus is truly above all his companions.

> *Jesus, I acknowledge with John the Baptist*
> *that you are God's perfect Lamb.*
> *Eternal thanks.*
> *May your presence increase in my life*
> *as my demanding ego decreases.*

Jesus, My Righteousness

You have loved righteousness and hated wickedness;
therefore God, your God, has set you above your companions (1:9)

Jesus loved righteousness. His reign is forever because he reigns in righteousness. There is nothing in his governance that is not right. There is no reason for a coup in heaven.

Today's text rings in our ears: "God has set you above your companions." We had nothing to do with that. We did not appoint Jesus to die for our sins on the cruel cross on Golgotha. We did not demand that Jesus serve as our intercessor. God did not take a poll to find if Jesus should be the Savior of the world. This is the work of God, who set Jesus above his companions, above all others.

The good news that has come to us is that God has purposed it all. He has performed it and it is now done. Our joy is to receive this news and then to proclaim it with all our hearts. What we proclaim is God's good news to needy people.

> *Now, my soul, if God has elevated the name of Jesus*
> *to be above every name, why should you hesitate?*
> *What are you waiting for, my soul?*
> *Do you think he is not who he says he is?*
> *Or is it because you want preeminence over some area of your life*
> *and you cannot trust him to be Lord in that area?*
> *Why not cast caution to the wind and do what God has already done?*
> *Give me the courage and the faith to set Jesus above his companions.*
> *Give me the heart of the Baptist, who had it right. "He must increase!"*

The Joy of Jesus

By anointing you with the oil of joy (1:9)

Oil of joy. I do not recall ever using skin lotion, so I was intrigued by how our Tanzanian friends adored it. After scrubbing themselves clean, they applied their favorite oils, which kept the skin soft and healthy. How good they must have felt as they left the lakeside after a refreshing bath followed by a good anointing, joyfully making their way home. Is that like being washed by the blood of Christ and being anointed by the Holy Spirit?

As I think of anointing oil, my mind goes to Aaron, Moses' elder brother, who once assisted the people in fashioning a golden calf to lead them because he assumed Moses had died on the mountain. A more terrible sin is hard to imagine. Aaron sinned mightily. All joy drained from his soul when he saw Moses reappear with the law.

Aaron must have often pondered his hideous sin. To his surprise, when the tabernacle was completed, God chose a most unlikely first-ever high priest—Aaron himself. On the day of his installation, Aaron stood before the people at the entrance to the tabernacle. He must have felt dreadfully inadequate. There he was first cleansed with blood from the altar, then anointed with an ointment prepared specifically for that holy purpose.

This describes for me the essence of "the oil of joy." Poured out freely on penitent Aaron was oil of divine grace.

> *Jesus Christ, my loving high priest,*
> *   you had no sin to wash away.*
> *Aaron did. Nevertheless, you received this "oil of joy."*
> *Now apply this oil to me. Lord Jesus, pour it on!*

Jesus Laid the Foundations, Created the Heavens

**In the beginning, O Lord, you laid the foundations of the earth,
and the heavens are the work of your hands (1:10)**

Is it true that Jesus laid the foundations of earth and heaven? I gasp as I read statements like this. In the Old Testament, God alone is the Creator. This verse clearly applies to Jesus.

Why should I be so amazed? Jesus is Emmanuel, God in the flesh, God among us. Why do I find it difficult to exalt Jesus of Nazareth like this? I suppose it is simply a lack of faith. Or is it a lack of knowledge?

It seems incredulous that our Jesus is all that the Bible claims he is. I have heard the statement, "Your God is too small." I can accept that. I am prepared to expand my view of God because, after all, he is God, is he not? I am prepared to glorify God to the high heavens and to give him praise forever and ever. My mind is capable of that. But to attribute to the man Jesus Christ all that the writer of Hebrews does is another thing. As a poet once wrote, "I stand amazed at the presence of Jesus the Nazarene." I am slowly learning that Jesus is far greater than I ever imagined.

To fully appropriate the glorious riches of grace in Christ Jesus, I must first know who he is. If Jesus is any less than the writer of this outstanding book portrays him to be, what follows makes little sense. If, on the other hand, I embrace everything this book reveals about Jesus, then all else makes sense. Remove Jesus, and all that remains is utter confusion and hopelessness. Place him in the center and we see the glory of God.

Jesus, give me faith to believe.

Jesus Is Forever

They will perish; but you remain (1:11)

When I first saw the Himalayan mountain range dominated by the towering summit of Mount Everest, almost eight miles high, I thought, "Now that is permanence!"

Not so fast. I learned that the summit of Everest is actually a sea floor, once covered with water, carrying to this day microscopic remains of sea creatures. That mountain summit was once under the waters of the sea! There goes my symbol of permanence. Nothing on this planet is permanent.

So I turn my eyes away from earth, to the skies. There I see permanence. I see the same stars, in the same locations, as the Egyptians saw six thousand years ago. People have been navigating according to those stars since antiquity.

Think those stars must have been there forever? Think again. We now know that our galaxy, the Milky Way, is moving away from all other systems at an astounding rate. Furthermore, stars, of which our sun is but one, are not permanent. They are collapsing and new ones are being formed as I write.

That about says it for the permanence of the earth and skies. Natural permanence is an illusion. The hallmark of everything material is unmitigated change. Only Jesus remains.

> *Jesus Christ, you are unchanging.*
> *I realize that I must look to heaven, not the heavens,*
> *   to find permanence.*
> *You are the same, yesterday, today, and forever.*
> *In you is no variance. You change not,*
> *   and I am yours—forever.*

Jesus Is Eternally Dependable

**They will perish, but you remain; they will all wear out like a garment
(1:11)**

I do not, for a moment, deplore change. In fact, I realize that the universe can hold together only because of constant change. The only reason I can breathe is because just the right amount of oxygen is available when I need it. That oxygen is distributed because many things are changing, constantly.

But the sobering thought is, that which changes also ceases. The writer of Hebrews used a powerful figure of speech. All that appears permanent is rather like a garment that is worn until it has served its purpose. It wears out, then is thrown away, never to be worn again. That is natural law. I would be foolish to trust my eternal destiny to natural law, which will serve its purpose and then be discarded. I can learn much from nature but it can never teach me about eternity.

No, God remains. When nature has fulfilled its purpose, God will roll it up "like a robe" (1:12). But he will never do that with me or you. He has given us eternal life through Jesus and we participate in his absolute permanence, so our destiny is assured. When the lights of Orion go out and when Mount Everest is rubble, we will not be amazed. When the foundations of the earth shake, we will applaud our God and we will enjoy eternal life forever and ever.

Thank you, Jesus, for clothing yourself in temporary human flesh
to win eternal salvation for me.
Because you did that, I can rise with you in fullness of life
to live in your glorious presence forever and ever. Amen.

Jesus Alone Sits at God's Right Hand

To which of the angels did God ever say, "Sit at my right hand"? (1:13)

This letter is addressed to people who had fallen in love with angels, like some people in our culture these days. This modern obsession with angels is both refreshing and dangerous. It is refreshing because it shows that western culture is becoming a little more comfortable with the supernatural. It is amazing that these days brazen, hardened, secular materialists sport little angel dolls from rearview mirrors. Angels are in.

The downside is that the idea of angels rushing about to get us out of difficulty or providing us with something for which we long can be advanced without any theological framework at all. Popular angelology, if it can be given that name, is based on the belief that there are nice spirits around that look after us. They are warm, fuzzy celestial friends who answer to our beck and call.

The Bible makes it plain that angels are ministering spirits sent by God. They are not autonomous nor do they appear when someone in need commands them. They do the will of God. The Bible gives us no basis for ordering angels about. Further, it tells us all we need to know about angels, which is very little. We add to that at our own peril.

> *Thank you, heavenly Father,*
> *for ministering to us human beings by means of angels.*
> *You know our needs better than we do,*
> *and you have ministering spirits to meet those needs.*
> *Forbid that we should make angels or any other creature*
> *the object of worship.*

January 31

Trust Jesus, Not Angels

**Are not all angels ministering spirits sent to serve those
who will inherit salvation? (1:14)**

Angels are undoubtedly real to true believers. In my own life I can recall specific times when I was either rescued or encouraged by an angel.

Many years back, I was doubting whether the Lord could help me through a very difficult personal problem. The Lord, who knew that, dispatched an angel to rescue me from danger when I was climbing Mont Blanc in France. When the visitation occurred I did not realize it at first, but immediately afterward I knew it was an angel. I then heard the clear voice of the Holy Spirit saying, "Do not doubt my ability to get you through the personal problem that you are facing. Did I not get you down off this mountain?" My faith was restored. I repented of my unbelief there on the spot, and a new sense of God's love came over me.

I rarely find it appropriate to call on God to send an angel to assist me. I seldom think to myself, "Now is a good time for God to send an angel." As a matter of fact, the angelic appearances that have occurred in my life were completely surprising—actually, startling.

Our Lord Jesus, angels are creatures. You are Creator.
Thank you for making the ministry of angels available to me,
but deliver me from focusing my attention on them.
They do not sit at the Father's right hand. You do!
I look to you to supply all my needs out of your fullness.

Salvation—Jesus' Precious Gift

Those who will inherit salvation (1:14)

"Jesus saved me. I know that and I know that he is sufficient for my present grief." Those were the words of Mera Kivengere as she gave her widow's testimony in Kabale, Uganda, beside the casket of her late husband, Bishop Festo Kivengere, my revered friend.

Mera had it right. Of all the good gifts of God's grace, the central one is salvation. All else flows from that.

I believe I will avoid many of the perils that beguile believers if I keep at the center the realization that I am saved because Jesus Christ made full atonement for me. God enriched me with many gifts, but salvation must certainly be the greatest. Sometimes I almost forget that I, a blatant sinner and rebel, am reconciled to God by the poured-out blood of Jesus Christ. God never meant that I should try to save myself.

How easy it is to focus on some effect of salvation, such as good works or some glorious experience. May I, like Paul, boast only in the cross of Christ.

The amazing picture in Revelation 5 makes it so clear: the crucified, risen Jesus Christ is the darling of all heaven and the archenemy of Satan. Shouldn't I, like all the hosts of heaven, ponder this source of salvation and respond with all my heart, "Worthy is the Lamb that was slain"?

May this hymn of praise be constantly on my lips today as it will be when all creatures acknowledge that Jesus is exactly who he said he is.

Lord, keep me focused on that which is the center of your focus,
the Lamb that was slain.

Jesus, My Moorage

We must pay more careful attention ... so that we do not drift away (2:1)

While visiting missionaries on their houseboat in Borneo, I sometimes jumped over the side into the broad river and enjoyed a swim. Once I was not careful and swam into a swiftly moving channel that soon carried me a good distance from the boat. I was alarmed. I had drifted into a strong current that carried me away.

I was simply drifting away. I think that is what the writer is referring to in today's verse. Drifting occurs when I am not paying attention. I never say to myself, "Today I am going to turn my back on Jesus and live my own life. I am going to drift away." No, I simply take my own way and slowly, slowly drift away, oblivious to my plight.

So, what do I do if I find myself far from the boat? First, I acknowledge that I have drifted from my first love, Jesus. Then I repent of wanting my way instead of his, which is what led to the current peril. Then I rush again to Jesus.

Fortunately I need not exert all my energy to make it back to the boat. The moment I repent, I am in the boat again. Drifting takes time. Restored fellowship with God is instantaneous.

Lord Jesus, may your Holy Spirit
make me aware of any spiritual drifting,
for my safety lies in being where you are.
Never, ever, let me just drift away.

Focus on Jesus

We must pay more careful attention (2:1)

Pay attention! As a teacher, when I wanted to make sure the students would not miss something important, I would say, "Now, pay attention." I don't know where that expression comes from, but it seems to work.

"To pay" is to make an investment. I "pay attention," for example, before I pay money for something. I want to know that my money is not going to be wasted. If I am so concerned about the few dollars I have that I focus my attention on some purchase, how much greater is God's appeal that I pay attention to my relationship with him?

I find that I can go through a day, even a week, without giving any serious attention to what I claim to base my life on—the good news of salvation and wholeness in Christ Jesus.

For example, as I write this, my sciatica is flaring up. What should I do, what pills should I take, how should I reorder my life so that I can live with the searing discomfort? I can go on and on like this without once considering what the gospel has to say about pain. I pay attention to the pain, that is for sure, but I do not pay attention to God's provision in times of distress.

> *Lord Jesus, you paid attention to your Father*
> *morning, noon, and night,*
> *while eating, sleeping, preaching, healing*
> *—in all ways and at all times.*
> *Your attention never wavered.*
> *Rivet my attention. I want to fix my eye on you.*

Jesus, the Old, Old Story

We must pay more careful attention . . . to what we have heard (2:1)

Here, the writer does not intend to give new insight into the Gospels. He simply begs his readers to put into practice what they already know.

It's said that Mark Twain made a disclaimer something like this: "It ain't those parts of the Bible that I can't understand that bother me, it is the parts that I do understand."

The story was told in my home community of a well-meaning agriculture officer who offered a notoriously lazy farmer some advice. Upon hearing the advice, the farmer said, "Thanks, but I already know how to farm better than I do."

Revived believers are those who put into practice what they know. Carnal believers often accumulate more and more knowledge but pay little heed to what they discover.

We must pay attention to what we already know. We all need wake-up calls. This letter to the Hebrew believers is such an alarm. "Pay attention to what you have heard." It takes a lifetime of obedience to put into practice what we already know.

Soul of mine, when you cry out for refreshing from heaven,
do not be surprised if you hear that still, small voice
reminding you to put into practice what you already know.

God's Message: Jesus

If the message spoken by angels was binding (2:2)

I sweated a little, not from the African heat, but because I was about to open a letter marked Office of the President of Tanzania. From the president? The letter took on a weight all its own. I had written to him, but did not expect a reply, not from the president. But there was the letter, in a small packet of mail. That letter from President Julius Nyerere did not really say much. Yet I remember the excitement of receiving it.

Hearing from a head of state pales in comparison to receiving a message from almighty God. Am I all atwitter when I get a message from God himself in Jesus?

Jews who were familiar with their texts believed that angels delivered God's law. The NIV calls the angels "myriads of holy ones" (Deuteronomy 33:2).

The Jews revered angels, as we have seen. The presence of angels reinforced the gravity of God's message. The law was "spoken by angels," and that emphasized its importance. The message of God's love was so important that angels delivered it.

Jesus, you held the law in high esteem.
You made it clear that you did not come to abolish the law,
but to raise it to a higher level
by writing it on the fleshly tables of our hearts.
You also made it clear that we are not saved by obedience to the law.
That is not its purpose. However, your newborn followers
do desire to live a holy life.
Jesus, may I have the same high regard for the law that you had,
knowing it was given by angels.

Jesus, the Law of God

The message spoken by angels was binding (2:2)

The law was, quite simply, a description of the way reality operates.

In his writings, E. Stanley Jones, the great missionary to India, reminds us time and again that the universe was not only created by God but also operates according to God's law. Jones contends that when we make false assumptions about how the universe operates, we set ourselves up for disaster. For example, God created the universe, and he sustains it constantly. But it simply will not work right if we try to substitute a man-imagined god, or no God at all, in the place of the living God. It is little wonder that the first word of the Ten Commandments is to resist the ever-present temptation to displace God with something else, for that which replaces God ultimately becomes a god.

Or take the command not to lie. Is it not self-evident that the universe simply could not operate on lies? Chaos would reign. The universe was created to operate on truth. Or consider the commandments against lust. If all people were driven by uncontrollable lust, what kind of world would this be? What would happen if everyone simply took what his or her neighbor has?

These words and guides are self-evident; they hardly need explanation. They describe, not an alternate way to live, but *the* way. While in Uganda I heard it said, "Even if you are not a Christian, it is best to live like one!" This was spoken in light of the spread of AIDS, but it is disarmingly true in any circumstance. Can I say that even nonbelievers would be happier if they lived like Christians? I think so.

Jesus, you are the truth. May I hold you in my heart always.

A Surprise for Angels

The message spoken by angels was binding (2:2)

In a way, I pity the poor angels who delivered the commandments to Moses on that fearsome, arid Arabian mountain. They must have been aware of the incurable perverseness in the human heart that would make it almost impossible for people to obey that wonderful set of immutable precepts called "the law." What sounded like good news to the angels came across as bad news to the Jews, who stopped up their ears, protesting that they had heard enough.

The first prohibition must have stung them to the heart: No other god. How could they obey that one? The memory of the golden calf was fresh in their minds. That very month they had already tried to replace God.

I find it consoling that God revealed two things to Moses: first, the law in all its stark authority and second, the institution of the priesthood with its sacrifices that made a way for poor, struggling people to experience the forgiveness of God. I like to think that the angels had a part in delivering both messages. In addition to the law, they finally could deliver a message of hope: God forgives penitent sinners.

In any case, the writer insists that the message delivered by mere angels is binding. The law is the law. The law stands for it is simply a description of the way things work. It can never be broken or changed, but it can be challenged and disobeyed.

> *My Father in heaven,*
> *I am convinced that every sentence of the law is true.*
> *Give me a heart of obedience to hear and to obey.*

Jesus Is Good News

**How shall we escape if we ignore such a great salvation? This salvation,
which was first announced by the Lord, was confirmed to us by those who
heard him (2:3)**

If what the Jewish hearers considered to be bad news was delivered by a host of angels, how much more seriously should we take the good news delivered by God himself?

The good news is called "a great salvation." God announced it. If God himself announces something, it must surely have ultimate validity. We should listen more carefully to the words of God himself, made clear by Jesus Christ, than to the message delivered by angels, no matter how great the angels.

This all might sound a bit strange to our ears because we know that both the law and the gospel came directly from God. The writer wants to shift the reader's attention away from focusing on angels, the carrier of the message, onto Jesus, the message itself. If the message of the law is binding, the message of grace is equally binding, if not more so. Grace is certainly much more glorious and welcome than the law.

*Lord Jesus, if someone else had announced the good news
of our salvation, I may or may not have listened.
But because you who have earned our salvation announced it,
how can I be so cold-hearted as to turn a deaf ear?
Lord, open my ears to hear your every phrase.
May I add my testimony to that of the millions of blood-bought sinners
who have confirmed by their faith and by their lives
that they not only received the message
but also embraced it and lived it.*

Jesus, Our Great Salvation

How shall we escape if we ignore such a great salvation? (2:2)

We hear our culture's mantras: Actualize your potential. Reinvent yourself. You can do it. We say to each other, "Be yourself, do not be cowed by anyone." Some even say, "Get in touch with god within you."

When salvation is offered, free and complete, in Jesus, why do we prefer to turn our backs on that unspeakable gift and opt for self-improvement? That is the mystery of the ages.

If salvation were sold like a membership to an exclusive country club, there would be no shortage of people who believe they've earned the right and would pay the price. How good the food tastes if you feel you've earned it!

Salvation is not offered to achievers but to believers and to people who are acutely aware of their unworthiness. The only door into eternal life is through that lowly one at the foot of the cross. The blood that was spilled there gives us merit, nothing else. As we come to Jesus, in the first instance and ever after, we relinquish every bit of self-effort and cast ourselves on his merits alone. Every follower of Jesus knows this very well.

> *My Lord, I need to recapture the thrill of the salvation*
> *I received at your hand by simply believing.*
> *May I never ignore my "great salvation."*

Saved by a Great Savior

A great salvation (2:2)

How far does this "great salvation" go?

The apostle Paul had the joy of seeing people of every description being saved. He wrote, "I am convinced that neither death nor life, neither angels nor demons, neither the present nor the future, nor any powers, neither height nor depth, nor anything else in all creation, will be able to separate us from the love of God that is in Christ Jesus our Lord" (Romans 8:38-39). I love my denomination, the Mennonite church. However, our emphasis on good works, good behavior, and good appearances can be a slippery slope to legalism. We demand high standards of our members. We want to keep sin out of the church. This is commendable but it can be a challenge.

A Mennonite pastor friend of mine sought advice from his bishop. The pastor was concerned because people with broken marriages, drug addictions and otherwise messed-up lives had begun to attend his church. The pastor asked the bishop for advice. With tongue in cheek, the wise bishop replied, "I suggest that you post a sign outside the church, 'No Sinners Allowed.'" That is one way! But the gospel is precisely for sinners.

We need to have rules and high expectations but we may never set a higher standard for conversion than God's. I suppose the highest standard one can meet is the broken and contrite heart that cries out for mercy.

Lord Jesus, break my judgmental heart
that I may embrace all penitent sinners
without regard to their past.

February 11

Speak Out for Jesus

**This salvation, which was first announced by the Lord,
was confirmed to us by those who heard him (2:3)**

My job is to confirm my salvation. How do I do that? One way is by testimony.

I got some well-meaning advice from African friends before returning to America: "When you meet new people, tell them that you are saved." That is what they do. They realize that the longer you put off giving witness, the tougher it is to do. They also know that the gospel becomes winsome and alive when people confirm it with their testimony. I must confess that I did not always follow this advice.

We also confirm our salvation by receiving it. Unfortunately, many people hear but do not obey. Some go so far as to admit that salvation "was first announced by the Lord," but for them, that is where the matter rests. Rather than obeying, they take refuge in their beliefs.

Many of my African friends were more open than I was about their witness. Their eagerness to share tended to put off some of us missionaries. One missionary sister could restrain herself no longer. "Why," she demanded, "do you have to talk about salvation so much?" One of the Africans reached down and embraced one of her little children and asked, "When this one was born, weren't you excited when you heard that first cry? You would have been concerned if the baby had not cried. We are simply announcing that we are born again."

Lord Jesus, free my tongue to testify to your saving grace.

Jesus—God's Witness

Confirmed to us by those who heard him (2:3)

Revival is sustained by testimony. When people are excited about the wonder of their salvation in Jesus Christ, the gospel spreads like wildfire. The opposite is also true. Where there is no testimony, there is only religion. When the Holy Spirit stirs believers, they witness. That is a universal gospel principle.

It is easy for me to sit here and write this. It is quite another thing to actually tell others about the hope that lies in me, about my faith in Jesus Christ, my Lord and Savior.

One reason is that all the forces of hell are ordered into action when people freely testify. The apostle John discovered that. In the preface to Revelation, he wrote that he was under arrest "because of the word of God and the testimony of Jesus" (Revelation 1:9). A more accurate translation probably is "testimony about Jesus."

Had the followers of Jesus been quiet about their beliefs, John would not have been on that dreadful island, a prisoner of Rome. But they were not secretive. When they were forced to declare their ultimate loyalty, they did not hesitate but claimed with conviction that Jesus is Lord. For that they were persecuted mercilessly. And for that John was on that lonely island.

> *Lord Jesus, I use this tongue of mine for many things.*
> *Teach it to exercise its most holy function,*
> *to bless your name forever and ever.*

Signs Point to Jesus

God also testified to it by signs, wonders and various miracles (2:4)

After a few years in Tanzania, I reluctantly joined a few believers who were praying for a person tormented by evil spirits. To my utter amazement the evil spirits yielded to the power of the blood of Jesus Christ. My first response was, "Praise the Lord!" My second response was, "I didn't know that was possible."

I quickly recalled Jesus' good advice, "Do not rejoice that the spirits submit to you, but rejoice that your names are written in heaven" (Luke 10:20). Nevertheless, I was amazed.

I am slowly learning that signs, wonders, and miracles are important, but they are not the reality. Jesus is the reality. It is tempting to seek reality in that which is passing. I suppose I am a bit like Thomas, who said, "Unless I see . . . I will not believe" (John 20:25). Having satisfied Thomas's need for proof, Jesus said, "Blessed are those who have not seen and yet have believed" (verse 29). One of them is me.

We are living in a Thomas era. Many people seek after signs, wonders, and miracles. When the Lord deems it appropriate, he does send signs. But he does it wisely lest we mistake the sign for the reality, lest we seek healing but not the Healer, lest we seek health but not the Life, lest we seek salvation but not the Savior.

> *Lord Jesus, bring just enough signs into my life*
> *that I will know of your constant care.*
> *Keep me from hankering after signs and wonders.*
> *Jesus is wonder enough.*

Father, Son, and Holy Spirit Work Wonders

**God also testified to it by signs, wonders and various miracles, and gifts of
the Holy Spirit distributed according to his will (2:4)**

The letter to the Hebrews does not provide us with a definitive theology of the Holy Spirit. However, the Spirit's ministry and witness shine through every paragraph.

In 3:8 the Holy Spirit warns believers not to allow their hearts to be hardened. In 6:4-6 the writer says that those who have been blessed by the work of the Holy Spirit in their lives must not fall away. Then in 9:8 we read that the Holy Spirit revealed that the way into the Most Holy Place is possible only by the atoning work of Jesus. In 9:14 the Holy Spirit enables Jesus to offer himself as the unblemished offering. In 10:15 we read that the Holy Spirit is pleased with the new covenant in Christ Jesus, and in 10:29 the Holy Spirit is referred to as the Spirit of grace. The Holy Spirit has freedom to work because of the atoning work of Jesus Christ.

Over the years, I have found that the major hindrance to the power and guidance of the Holy Spirit in the lives of people who are saved is sin, not lack of knowledge. I discovered that if I am doing my part of repenting of the negatives, the positive power of the Holy Spirit of God rushes in and does his blessed work.

Blessed Lord, thank you for the great Comforter,
the blessed Holy Spirit.
He is able to do his amazing work because Jesus paid the price
so that our sins can be forgiven.
I praise you, Lord, that the blood of Jesus and the Holy Spirit
blend so marvelously that I am set free from sin
to serve my risen Lord.

Jesus, the Gift and the Giver

Gifts of the Holy Spirit distributed according to his will (2:4)

One of the most convincing signs of salvation is that those who are saved receive gifts of the Holy Spirit. Today's verse is the only reference to gifts of the Spirit in this letter.

Paul wrote at length about gifts in his letters, particularly in Ephesians 4:7-13: "But to each one of us grace [*karis,* or gifts] has been given as Christ apportioned it. . . . It was he who gave some to be apostles, some to be prophets, some to be evangelists, and some to be pastors and teachers, to prepare God's people for works of service, so that the body of Christ may be built up until we all reach unity in the faith and in the knowledge of the Son of God and become mature, attaining to the whole measure of the fullness of Christ."

Ordinary human or natural gifts are not signs of the presence of the Holy Spirit. The gifts of the Holy Spirit are. I suppose the gifts of the Holy Spirit are those we would not have if we were not born again by the atoning work of Jesus and energized by the Holy Spirit.

I believe the Holy Spirit purifies natural gifts and gives spiritual gifts as he wishes. For example, I believe that I am naturally a teacher. As I place that gift on the altar and seek to be more Christlike in exercising it, the Lord gains glory and the church is edified.

> *Lord Jesus, use me as you wish.*
> *You are the distributor of the gifts.*

February 16

Jesus, My Most Precious Gift

Gifts of the Holy Spirit distributed according to his will (2:4)

What gifts of the Holy Spirit did I receive that are not necessarily "natural"? The gift of faith, surely, for that alone explains my openness to Jesus Christ. Without it, I could not understand who Jesus is, in actuality. The second gift is no doubt the presence of the Holy Spirit himself. But these two gifts are internal; they do not "show."

What are the external gifts? Here I find myself floundering a bit. Can I identify any gifts that I have that are so apparent they can only be explained as the mighty work of the Holy Spirit? I am not sure. I need to think about that.

Some churches emphasize the Spirit's gifts and look for them as evidence of a believer's salvation. These churches do not accept human, natural gifts as sufficiently authenticating. They are no doubt right. Because the New Testament records that speaking in tongues often accompanied the special outpouring of the Holy Spirit, some groups use that as the litmus test of an authentic baptism. I am not sure about that.

Is not the ultimate test of the baptism of the Holy Spirit a broken and contrite heart that recognizes sin quickly and repents at once? That spirit is required for the employment of all gifts, natural or spiritual.

Jesus, I bring to you my gift, a willing and ready spirit.

Jesus, Eternal Reality

It is not to angels that he has subjected the world to come;
. . . [God] put everything under [Jesus'] feet (2:5, 8)

Now and again I try to put things into perspective by asking, What is going to be around when everything vanishes? What will remain when nations are no more, even the hugely powerful United States of America? What will remain when the courts close their doors and all judges disappear? What will remain when philosophy, art, and culture are no more, when all musical instruments fail and every canvas is gone? What will remain when all legal tender vanishes, when ownership will mean absolutely nothing? What will remain when no humans inhabit this spinning sphere, this planet Earth? What will remain when the natural elements shudder, wobble, and disintegrate?

Atheists are convinced that nothing will remain. They wager everything on that. Life is meaningless, they claim. They like to think that when all things pass, only an empty nothingness will remain. Having no tomorrow, they have no claim on today. Nothing matters, really, because when matter is no more, there will be nothing at all.

Hebrews tells us, "Once more I shake not only the earth, but also the heavens . . . so that what cannot be shaken may remain" (12:26-27).

God is the eternal reality. All else will perish. I want to build my life on what will remain.

Lord God, may this assurance establish my soul every day of my life
so that I may focus on eternal matters.

Jesus, the Ultimate Authority

It is not to angels that he has subjected the world to come (2:5)

Believing that there is nothing beyond the material world can never satisfy my soul.

I believe that God—the Father, Son, and Holy Spirit—preexisted everything that we call "real." Before the world was created, God was. Consequently, when the world (cosmos) is no more, God remains. A French word for God is Eternale. I like that.

As a believer, I live my life in the light of the future. I believe that I will be with God when the world as we know it is no more. The universe is transient. God is eternal.

One's view of reality is primarily a matter of faith. The "Godless" view is based on the belief that there is no reality beyond the material universe.

Jesus came among us, making an extraordinary claim: "Anyone who has seen me has seen the Father" (John 14:9). He calmly revealed that he and God are one. Jesus does not just believe in God and introduce us to God. He is God. Furthermore, he invites all who deny that God exists to look at him closely, and they will indeed see God.

> *God, I see your hand at work on every page of the Holy Scriptures.*
> *I shape my vision of you as I read the ancient text,*
> *for it is breathed upon by the Holy Spirit.*
> *Every page enlarges my conception of who you are.*
> *Yet when I walk with Jesus Christ, your only Son,*
> *and see him ministering to all who believe,*
> *I am quick to acknowledge that I see you.*

Surpassing Love

What is man ... that you care for him? (2:6)

On my computer's screen saver, I have some breathtaking pictures from the Hubble telescope. Talk about awesome! The beauty and the enormity of our starry universe humble me. How many suns are there, and how many galaxies? The extent of it staggers the imagination.

In light of astronomical numbers, the human census seems insignificant. There are about 6.5 billion people alive today. That sounds like a lot, but it's a drop in the bucket compared to galactic figures. How many billions of galaxies are out there?

Why should God be interested in us at all? That is a fair question. The marvel of it is that we human beings seem to occupy God's thoughts all the time. Our salvation is so important to God that he emptied heaven itself to make it happen, by sending to earth his only Son to die an ignoble death on a cross between two thieves. That is how much God thinks we are worth. He values each human being.

Who can make sense of that? It is a mystery that can be solved only by contemplating a type of love that surpasses all loves.

Lord, I have no idea why you care for us humans.
But if for a moment I doubt my worth in this universe,
I need only ponder what my salvation cost you
—the most precious thing you had, your very own Son,
who died for me.

Jesus Elevated Mankind

What is man ... that you care for him? (2:6)

The unbeliever asks, "Who is God that I should pay any attention to him at all?"

The believer turns the question around, asking, "Who is man, and why should God bother about his unruly creatures who scamper about the earth?" The believer then pauses and asks, "Who is this God who loves so much?"

I recall a Ugandan friend, William Nagenda, sharing a dream he once had. In it, he saw a distressed shepherd who had lost a sheep that was named William. The shepherd asked his father if he could leave the herd to his care and try to find William. The father agreed, and the shepherd left the flock. As the day dawned the shepherd returned, bleeding and exhausted, carrying a sheep on his shoulders. "I found your sheep that was lost, Father," he said.

"But you are bleeding and sore," his father replied.

"I know, Father, but this is William. It was terribly difficult, but William is worth it." Nagenda pointed to that dream as a turning point in his life. Having been plagued by a lack of self-worth, he was comforted by the idea that he was worth it!

How much was William worth? How much am I worth? What is man that you care for him? The answer is to be found at Calvary. I am so valuable to God that Christ died for me. Can I ever doubt my worth? Can I possibly repay God for what he has done for me? Never. That kind of love astounds me. My mind falters, but my heart is warmed. I hear Jesus, my good Shepherd, tell his father, "This is Don, Father, I found him and he is worth it."

Awaken, soul, and sing his praises forever.

Jesus Displaces Self

You made him a little lower than the angels (2:7)

"You can do it!" That phrase sums up the worldview of our western culture. "You are in charge." "You can make it happen." "It all depends on you."

Our secular philosophers declare that mankind has now come of age, so we need not rely on anyone but ourselves. Religion played a part in human development, they assert, but we are now "grown up" and have no need for belief in God. We must take full responsibility for our lives.

The pride behind this idea is frightening. It asserts that we no longer need help. The so-called Enlightenment, which made these assertions, was more than two centuries ago. So what happened? The great advances in science, much applauded by Enlightenment philosophers, enabled people to kill one another in ways beyond belief. "You can do it" is true. In our pride we can destroy one another and our planet in ways never dreamed of.

Modern philosophers think that this philosophy of self-determination is a new idea. In reality, it is as old as mankind because we have always wanted to move God right out of our lives and plant ourselves as the center. Remember the first temptation: "When you eat . . . you will be like God" (Genesis 3:5).

God created the universe and all that is in it. The universe was not fashioned to be run by Satan or any other creature. When I try to run my life without regard to God, I reintroduce chaos.

> *I readily admit, my Lord, that when I try to run my universe*
> > *I mess it up;*
> *when you run it,*
> > *I have peace in my soul.*

Delivery from Despair

Yet at the present we do not see everything subject to him (2:8)

By ourselves we can never, even in our most "exalted" moments, display the character of God. It is simply impossible. The only way out of our dilemma is by relying entirely on Jesus Christ. He does not stand at the edge of the deep pit we were in and yell down to us, "Get yourself out of there. You can do it!" He knows very well that we cannot possibly get out. Religious philosophers invent promising ladders as a way out. But all such ladders fail.

Jesus did not advise us to construct a man-made ladder as a way of escape, nor did he throw us a rope. He actually entered our pit, lived as we live, and was one of us. He then took on himself all of our sinfulness and died to it on the cross. He is now inviting us to trust him fully so that the power that raised him from the dead might deliver us from the despair of the pit. Praise God for this marvelous way of escape!

Lord Jesus, I am eternally thankful that you did not falter
when you were sorely tempted.
I shudder when I see you carrying that heavy cross to Golgotha,
because that was not your cross; it was made for Barabbas.
He was to be crucified that morning.
You were willing to take his place.
As you died on Barabbas' cross, so you died on mine.
How you, Son of God and Son of man,
could pour out your lifeblood for me, I simply do not know.
But I receive it by faith.
Because of you, I am saved now and forever.

The Patient Victor, Jesus Christ

Yet at the present we do not see everything subject to him (2:8)

I thrill to the sound of Jesus' voice when he gathered his disciples in Galilee just before his ascension: "All authority in heaven and on earth has been given to me. Therefore go" (Matthew 28:18-19).

Having completed his work on Calvary, Jesus received "all authority." If that is the case, why did Jesus not cast Satan from the earth then and there? Jesus announced his victory over Satan. He delivered the mortal blow to old Screwtape. Why not destroy him outright?

The author of Hebrews did not press that question but simply acknowledged that "at present we do not see everything subject to him." He knew that the answer as to why Satan still roams the earth is lodged in the heart of our loving God.

What did happen when Jesus gave himself as a living sacrifice for sin? John wrote, "The reason the Son of God appeared was to destroy the devil's work" (1 John 3:8). And Paul insisted that when Jesus gave his life as the eternal sacrifice for sin, he "disarmed the powers and authorities" (Colossians 2:15). The author of Hebrews wrote, "Since the children have flesh and blood, he too shared in their humanity so that by his death he might destroy him who holds the power of death—that is, the devil" (2:14).

Jesus, you are the victorious one; you conquered me.
And you will continue to conquer
until your Father says the time has come.

Jesus Disarmed Satan

Yet at the present we do not see everything (2:8)

Jesus defeated Satan.

The Bible uses strong phrases when it says Jesus "destroyed the devil's works," "disarmed Satan," "destroyed Satan who had the power over death." It sounds like a completed job. "If that has happened," we might correctly ask, "then why is our world so full of evil?" That's what the author is talking about in today's verse.

At the cross, Jesus inflicted a mortal wound on Satan, from which he will never recover. By giving his life as the perfect sacrifice for sin, Jesus broke Satan's primary weapon, fear of judgment. Jesus dispelled the fear of death because a way was found to forgive sin. That is the reason we sing praises to our Lord, for he did not flinch but gave himself as a lamb without spot or blemish and sealed the victory.

Meanwhile Satan, alive but mortally wounded, brandishes desperately the weapons he has left. When people receive Jesus and live in the power of his resurrection, they experience, often to their surprise, that Jesus Christ has power over Satan and his hosts. Those who reject Jesus Christ have no resistance at all against Satan.

> *You know full well, my Lord,*
> *that I am absolutely helpless against Satan.*
> *Strengthen me with Calvary power to overcome his attacks.*

Jesus Glorified

But we see Jesus . . . crowned with glory and honor (2:9)

We can concentrate our attention on one of two things: on this world with all of its confusion or on Jesus, who is crowned with glory and honor. We should consider Jesus.

All natural religion has self at the center. The desire to survive and prosper is common to all peoples. We fashion idols or gods or ideologies, hoping to enhance our chances to prosper. Hinduism and Buddhism are full of such idols. We in the west do exactly the same thing, but we would never think of calling them idols or gods. They are thought of simply as "life goals." When we establish these goals, we appeal to every conceivable power on earth and in heaven to aid us.

I suppose it all comes down to whether we believe that Jesus will be and do all that he promised. Will our hero be victorious? If we see that our hero has broken through the enemy lines and bids us follow, we rejoice, renew our hope, and run to him.

At times I push Jesus aside and try to run my own affairs. When I become worried or angry or critical, it is a sure sign that I have put myself in the center.

> *Lord Jesus, forgive me when I take my own way.*
> *I recall my vow to you that I will make you central all my days.*
> *As I repent of my self-centeredness,*
>   *my relationship with you is restored;*
>   *the blood of cleansing has done its work again.*
> *May I see you, Jesus, crowned with glory and honor in my life*
>   *as you are in heaven.*

Jesus Died That I Might Live

Crowned with glory and honor because he suffered death (2:9)

I think I am like most people. I want resurrection power but I do not want to bow as a sinner before the cross and die to self. Jesus was not a sinner, but he knew that the only way to resurrection was through death. "For the joy that was set before him [he] endured the cross" (Hebrews 12:2). I am prepared to work hard to earn my salvation, but I am definitely unwilling to die for it. Yet that is exactly what I must do.

In order to enjoy the salvation Jesus earned through death I receive that salvation in the same way, by dying to self. Salvation costs me nothing but death to self. That is a high price for a human being to pay. I suppose this is why so few people avail themselves of Jesus' saving work.

When I read today's verse, I must remind myself it is about God. Who can even begin to understand the mystery of his grace? I stand amazed at the cross of Christ. What is actually happening there? I read that "greater love has no one than this, that he lay down his life for his friends" (John 15:13). In reality, Jesus had very few friends as he hung on that cross. He is not dying for his friends only, but also for his enemies. He is dying for those who are killing him. The blood he is shedding will wash away the sin of the Roman soldier who cries out for forgiveness, just as it washes my own soul as I repent.

> *My Jesus, that is love beyond degree.*
> *It is a good thing that I do not need to understand it*
> *before I believe it!*

Jesus, Perfected Through Suffering

**In bringing many sons to glory, it was fitting that God
. . . should make the author of their salvation perfect through suffering
(2:10)**

We stand before the mystery of human suffering. The Bible gives no apology for it. Jesus suffered to give us eternal life. But what about our suffering, which seems to produce nothing but pain and bitterness?

The question of suffering is perhaps the most asked question of all time. Our text insists that God created everything and sustains everything through the word of his power. Good. I like that. But if God is as good as he said he is, then why, some ask, do we see so much suffering in the world?

The Father of our Lord Jesus suffers, but the unregenerate mind cannot conceive of a suffering God. When nonbelievers see suffering, they assume that God does not care. Or they solve the dilemma by declaring that there is no God.

When natural disasters or acts of terrorism occur, people wonder where God is. The answer is simple: he is suffering with the afflicted. Our God, the Father of our Lord Jesus Christ, perfected his Son through suffering. There is no doubt that God suffers—far more than we do.

> *Lord, I weep as I see Jesus suffering in my stead.*
> *I praise you, Father, for it is through that suffering*
> *that I can experience eternal joy—healed by his stripes.*

Jesus Suffered for Me

Perfect through suffering (2:10)

Jesus did not suffer because Satan held him hostage. He suffered because our sins were on his bleeding back.

Seven hundred years before the cross, Isaiah saw the suffering servant and knew exactly what people were going to say as Jesus hung there: "We considered him stricken by God, smitten by him, and afflicted" (Isaiah 53:4). They thought surely God was punishing Jesus for something he had done. Their own scriptures read, "He that is hanged is accursed of God" (Deuteronomy 21:23). Seen through Jewish eyes, the one on the cross surely must have broken the law in some way and was suffering the consequences for that disobedience.

They were right in believing that sin must be punished. They carried that over to the cross. They thought God was punishing Jesus for claiming to be the Messiah.

Look again, all who would ponder the divine mystery. He is not suffering the consequences of his own sin, for he was sinless, "but he was pierced for our transgressions, he was crushed for our iniquities; the punishment that brought us peace was upon him, and by his wounds we are healed" (Isaiah 53:5).

Isaiah saw the suffering of Christ as the key to understanding salvation. Through obedient suffering, Jesus purchased my salvation. The mystery is solved. God "did not spare his own Son, but gave him up for us all" (Romans 8:32). God suffers.

Lord Jesus, you did it all for me and for all
who read these amazing words.

March 1

Taking Jesus Literally

Perfect through suffering (2:10)

As I delved into theological reading in my early twenties, I was convinced that I must fix my eyes on the life and teachings of Jesus. This made sense to me as an Anabaptist, for our religious tradition has always emphasized the fact that Jesus' teachings are to be taken literally. I believe that to this day. I was and am convinced that Jesus' way is the right way.

He is the answer to war, for example. I remember how scandalized I was when I realized that the great wars of the twentieth century were essentially Christians slaughtering other Christians. Would it not be a huge step forward if all Christians in the world would simply refuse to kill one another? That may not be the answer to war, but it would certainly help. It is good to take Jesus literally.

I felt then that Christians should focus on ethics and not on the esoteric religious ideas of Jesus dying for my sins and that sort of thing. As I look back, I do believe that I felt that the cross was too easily taken as an excuse for slovenly ethics. In order to have believers act more like Christ, I would have welcomed a cross-less gospel, or at least denied the blood atonement. I saw too many hypocrites to suit me.

Now I am in my mid-seventies. As the old hymn says, "The cross has a wondrous attraction for me, for 'twas on that old cross that the dearest and best for a world of lost sinners was slain." I am drawn again to ponder the cross of Christ as the key to life.

My blessed Lamb of God, forbid that I should ever apologize
for your cross of shame.
For there my life was transformed.

60

God's Child Because of Jesus

In bringing many sons to glory (2:10)

In my mind's eye I see my ancestors in a long line stretching back across the ages to our primal parents. I am linked to all of them through the DNA of sin, which prefers my own way to God's way. This perversity is built in. The parade of mankind passes. They all carry a banner, "My way, not God's." Each generation has its own problems to overcome. But sharing a similar spiritual DNA, they are unable to attain peace with God on their own.

Mankind cannot alter that spiritual DNA. Scripture tells us that everyone, like sheep, gets lost. Even the greatest of the saints fell into sin of one sort or another. All the blood sacrifices put together did not change the spiritual DNA of one person. The law did not change the DNA, nor did the old covenant that God made with his people. Human institutions try to limit the harm done by that harmful but powerful spiritual DNA. Some, such as the judiciary and the police department, work hard to control sinful activity. Even the great Greek philosophers could not break free from the self-centered nature of their spiritual inheritance. Socrates solved his problem by killing himself.

The heredity that the writer of Hebrews is talking about is spiritual heredity, which resembles natural heredity but with one huge difference: spiritual heredity can be altered by a spiritual DNA transplant.

Jesus Christ, thank you for making it possible
for your Holy Spirit to dwell in me,
not to control the old DNA but to replace it.

God's Son Because of Jesus

In bringing many sons to glory (2:10)

When people are "made sons" (or daughters) by civil adoption they maintain their DNA. But when Jesus brings "many sons to glory," he implants in them a new spiritual DNA. The Bible has many ways to describe this. Jesus described it to Nicodemus as being born a second time. Jesus also speaks of giving us eternal life. He is this eternal life. Our native spiritual genes lead to spiritual death. The life Jesus plants in us leads to life.

The Bible also speaks of Christ being reborn in us and that his presence in us is nurtured by the ministry of the Holy Spirit. This transaction was so real to Paul that he could explain it in only one way: "For to me, to live is Christ" (Philippians 1:21). This is not the transformed life; it is the transplanted life.

At times, I envision myself as a compulsive sinner with Jesus at my side to tone down the volume of my sinfulness. In fact, Jesus changes me fundamentally by becoming the dominant presence in my life. The Trinity aids me in my determination to be more and more conformed to Jesus, who is now at home in my soul. Jesus is Emanuel, God in me. Instead of being ruled by my sin nature I conform to Jesus who is in me. That is the ultimate heart transplant.

Jesus, you did not come to advise me but to replace me.
Give me simple faith that understands that awesome truth.

Jesus, the One for Whom All Creation Exists

For whom, and through whom everything exists (2:10)

Why is there anything? This was the question that my fellow students at the university never asked, probably because they knew it had no answer. They kept plugging away at their little projects that kept them busy while the big question of purpose went unanswered.

I can understand that, because the human mind, no matter how brilliant, could never come up with the answer that we read about here, that everything is by Jesus Christ and for him.

When you think of it, it is a colossal stretch. The Jews had huge problems with it, and the Greeks scoffed at the notion that Jesus of Nazareth could possibly be the "First Cause": their way of describing God.

I discovered that many African cultures have a vague idea that there is a creator God somewhere but "it" is unknown and unknowable. They are content to let the matter rest there.

Then we hear a statement like this from a New Testament writer: "For by [Jesus] all things were created: things in heaven and on earth, visible and invisible, whether thrones or powers or rulers or authorities; all things were created by him and for him" (Colossians 1:16). Now, *that* is radical thinking. It borders on the unbelievable.

> *Lord Jesus, is this possible? Is it true?*
> *Is this the solution to the age-old riddle of purpose*
> *   —that you are the reason for everything?*
> *May I join your amen choir? I believe!*

I Am Jesus' Brother

So Jesus is not ashamed to call them brothers (2:11)

Throughout my life I faced the choice of either standing alongside fallen brothers and sisters or abandoning them. To be honest, if it did not cost me anything I was there for them. But if I thought eyebrows would be raised if I continued a relationship with such a person, I hesitated.

I should have been more courageous in relating to the hurting ones. The Holy Spirit reminds me that it is only by God's grace that I have not fallen as they did, for the potential is there. I am a debtor to grace. When I ponder the cross, I see Jesus standing by me. Those sins that are nailed to that cross are my sins. He identifies with me to bring me to God.

The apostle Paul admitted that of all the sinners who ever lived he was the greatest. I do not think for a moment that Paul was exaggerating or trying to impress. When he was suspended between earth and sky, that is what he discovered about himself as he focused his eyes on the Holy One (see 2 Corinthians 12:2-6). Seeing Jesus crucified strips me of all my pretense. I discover that other sinners are my brothers and sisters—like me, covered by the atoning blood.

> *Thank you, Jesus, for showing me*
> *that I am a sinner like everyone else.*
> *But thank you most of all for preparing, by your sacrificial death,*
> *a robe of righteousness that covers me and all who believe*
> *—your brothers and sisters by redemption.*

Brother Jesus

Jesus is not ashamed to call them brothers (2:11)

Why should Jesus stand by me? I am so unlike him that I can only cringe as I consider my desperate state. Is it possible that Jesus can somehow change my sinful nature? Can he make a way for me to daily crucify the rule of sin in my life? Praise be, he not only can, he did. As Mary's son, he is well aware of the weakness of the flesh.

The story is told of a man who was found hunched over a drunken woman along a roadside in England. Seeing this well-dressed fellow picking up the woman, a passerby asked, "Do you know her?" The man answered, "She is my wife."

The faithful husband gave not a thought to his own reputation when he saw his beloved wife drunk, once again, lying in a ditch. He lovingly took her home.

Is this not my Jesus? He is not ashamed to call me his brother, because he knows of the power of his atoning blood. He stands by me. I can and will be changed into his likeness.

> *Jesus, you are despised by the world today.*
> *Forbid that I should be ashamed to call you my brother.*
> *I am such a friend of the world*
> *that I am tempted to be ashamed of you.*
> *Cleanse me of all timidity when it comes to acknowledging you*
> *as my all in all.*

Jesus, Our Singing Messiah

In the presence of the congregation I will sing (2:12)

What a picture. Here is Jesus, the Holy One, the Son of God, the co-Creator of the universe, singing his heart out, not in heaven, but among fallen sinners.

"But, Jesus," we might ask, "aren't you ashamed to be identified with this bunch of incorrigible sinners?" His reply: "They are trophies of the powerful grace of God. I poured out my life for them. Look again at the cross, where my blood flowed out as the fountain for sin and for cleansing. These repentant sinners rejoice in their life-changing salvation. Why should I be ashamed of them? To be ashamed of them would be to despise God's grace. Ashamed to be their brother? Not a bit of it. In fact, I love to sing the songs of Zion with them. My greatest joy is to stand with these blood-bought, grateful sinners and there, for all to see, I embrace them as my true brothers and sisters. Think it not strange that I delight in calling them brothers and sisters. It is for that reason that I poured out my life, to bring many children to glory."

The day is coming when Jesus will join this choir of brothers and sisters from all nations, tribes, tongues, and cultures, praising God with all his heart because his atoning work has accomplished exactly what was required to bring sons and daughters into the household of faith.

The next time I gather with brothers and sisters in my congregation, I will use my holy imagination to see Jesus Christ standing there with us as we praise his name. As he embraces each of us with all of our problems and hopes, he draws us into his presence and then turns his eyes toward his Father and says, "Here am I, and the children God has given me" (2:13).

Jesus, I am both humbled and gladdened by your love for me.
Thank you for making a place for me in that choir of joy.

Jesus Sang

In the presence of the congregation I will sing (2:12)

I recall another time when Jesus sang—in the upper room. He took the bread and the wine, proclaimed his death, and then "when they had sung a hymn, they went out to the Mount of Olives" (Mark 14:26).

What hymn did Jesus select? The hymnbook of that time was the book of Psalms. Maybe it was number 23: "Even though I walk through the valley of the shadow of death . . . you are with me" (verse 4). Or was it 34: "The Lord is close to the brokenhearted and saves those who are crushed in spirit" (verse 18).

Or it is possible that Jesus chanted from Isaiah 53: "He was despised and rejected by men, a man of sorrows, and familiar with suffering. . . . We considered him stricken by God . . . and afflicted. But he was pierced for our transgressions, he was crushed for our infirmities . . . and by his wounds we are healed" (verses 3-5). Jesus is our song. He is hymn enough.

Jesus, I am both humbled and gladdened by your love for me.
That you would invite me to stand beside you in the heavenly choir
　　　is just too lofty a thought for me.
I gladly take my place beside you,
　　　however, unworthy as I am, and sing my heart out with you.
Give me a heart to praise you forever and ever.
You have made them to be "a kingdom and priests"
　　　to serve our God, and they will reign on the earth.

Jesus' Adopted Children

Here am I, and the children God has given me (2:13)

Anna Ruth and I left the United States to serve in Tanzania in 1953. At that time we had no children. While living on the shores of beautiful Lake Victoria, the Lord blessed us with two, Jane and David. What joy they brought to us!

In retrospect, I think of Anna Ruth's mother not being able to hold the children of her only daughter. Her telegrams of congratulation and her many letters left us knowing that she accepted the fact that she could not be there, but the longing to embrace those little ones burned in her soul.

Then, after six years, it was time for furlough. Jane was four and David was two. Imagine the thoughts going through our minds as we stepped off the plane in New York City. Jane and David were soon in Grandma Charles' arms. Anna Ruth and I almost burst with gladness. "Grandma," I said. "These are the children God has given us. They are your grandchildren." All of the grandparents joined in the happy moment. Each embraced Jane and David with hearts full of thanksgiving.

In my mind's eye, I see Jesus approaching his Father, surrounded by happy, chatting, thankful children, saying, "Here I am, Father, with the children that you gave to me. Embrace them, Father God, one at a time. Each is precious. I know each by name. I have kept every one. I proudly present them to you. They are covered with my righteousness. Receive them. They are ours."

> *Our Father in heaven, how can we express our thanks*
> *for being called your children?*
> *Certainly by doing what you asked us to do—love you,*
> *love one another, and spread the gospel.*

Jesus, God's Condescending Grace

Since the children have flesh and blood, he too shared in their humanity
(2:14)

The man-made religions of the world reflect the human longing to be like God. They assume that by dint of discipline and thought people can actually rise to an understanding of God.

The gospel is not about people rising to God but about God becoming man. Jesus came down and "shared in their humanity."

It all started with God's love. He knew the wretchedness of the human condition. Originally he created people to enjoy his fellowship. They did not value that very highly. It seems as though they preferred to hang out with Satan.

How could that be? Had I been in God's shoes, believe me, I would have disowned them in an instant. But that is not God's love.

This is how God's grace works. Even before the foundation of the world, in the councils of heaven, a way was sought to repair the damage, long before it happened. The only possible answer that would be consistent with God's eternal justice and mercy would be for God to share "in their humanity," to live as a person and, in the end, to die as Son of man on a Roman cross. Love beyond words. I do well to consider Jesus.

> *My God, I discover that the story line of the gospel*
> *is certainly not human beings going up,*
> *but you always coming down.*
> *The way of your grace is always to condescend in order to save.*

Jesus Died to Save Me

**Since the children have flesh and blood, he too shared in their humanity
(2:14)**

This is why the gospel is good news to the brokenhearted and fallen ones. They discover that in their wretchedness, God in Jesus Christ is standing beside them, ready to save.

It is also why the gospel is bad news to the proud and self-sufficient. They are insulted to think that they cannot take their destiny into their own hands. For them the cross is foolishness.

For those who know the incurable rebellious nature of their own hearts, the poured-out life of the Son of man is the most amazing discovery imaginable. Is it possible that God loves me so much that he was willing to go through all of that just for me? If I were the only rebel in the universe, couldn't God simply make an exception for me and just pronounce me forgiven? As I ponder this, I realize that God cannot simply say, "Don means well and I love him, so I'll forgive him for his sins and sinful nature. That will show him how much I love him."

Impossible. The only basis on which God can forgive me or anyone else is by the atoning work of Jesus. I am not forgiven because God loves me but because Jesus Christ did what he did to carry my sin on his lashed shoulders that horrible but wonderful day as he made his way to that accursed tree outside Jerusalem.

*My Lord, Jesus, it is on the basis of your poured-out life,
your shed blood, that God is able to forgive.
That is what makes the gospel such compelling
and glorious good news.*

Jesus Kills Death

**So that by his death he might destroy him who holds the power of death
(2:14)**

Satan has many powerful ways to keep people in his debt. Life in Africa made me aware that the devil had one ploy after another to keep people bound to him. The most obvious was the way he impersonated "ancestral spirits." People feared ancestral spirits yet believed they needed the spirits' help to prosper in this life. That suited Satan just fine. He exploited this to the full, promising people power if they would submit to the will of the ancestors. He empowered what some call "witch doctors" to represent the ancestors. So people brought their sacrifices and went away with spiritual power. In this way Satan maintained a stranglehold on them.

The worst form of this was witchcraft that threatened harm and death. Satan's ultimate card is the fear of death. He employs it to enslave people. Only Jesus can sever Satan's strongest rope, the fear of death.

No matter what our culture or religious upbringing, death strikes terror. It frightens us for many reasons, one of which is that we know we are sinners, whether we admit it or not. We read in 1 Corinthians 15:56 that "the sting of death is sin, and the power of sin is the law."

Lord Jesus, knowing that my sins are forgiven by your atoning death,
I slip Satan's noose.
I no longer fear meeting you on the day of judgment.
I see it now—Satan has no power over those whose hope is in you,
God, my redeemer.
Glory!

Jesus, the Mighty Conqueror

That ... he might destroy ... the devil (2:14)

We need to tarry at the foot of the cross where God dealt Satan a deathblow. Something powerful happened when Jesus, God's spotless Lamb, gave himself as the eternal sacrifice for sin.

Paul wrote in Colossians 2:15, "And having disarmed the powers and authorities, he made a public spectacle of them, triumphing over them by the cross." That triumph was complete; the mortal wound was inflicted. Satan will never recover from that wound.

Why, some ask, did God not consign Satan to the fire of destruction then and there? I well remember a pastor friend of mine in Tanzania asking this question. Satan was making the pastor's work difficult, playing havoc in the lives of the sheep of his flock. Things would have been much easier for him if old Screwtape had not been around to destroy everything good. Did God miss a good chance to rid the world of Satan when Jesus gave his life a ransom for sin? God knows.

The good news is that in Christ Jesus, Satan loses his power and ultimately will be cast into the lake of fire. On the cross, the prophecy of Genesis 3:15 was fulfilled: "Eve's descendant (Jesus) will crush the devil's head, even though the devil will strike his (Jesus') heel" (my paraphrase). The wounded heel is healed, but the crushed head will never get well. The tail might still wag, but for believers there is no poison in the fangs.

> *Lord Jesus, the problem of evil has stumped philosophers and kings.*
> *Thank you for revealing to me, a simple person,*
> *that when you poured out your life unto death,*
> *you broke, for me, the power of Satan.*
> *I face a defeated foe. I will praise you, Jesus, my Lord,*
> *for that salvation forever and ever.*

Jesus Banishes Fear

Held in slavery by their fear of death (2:15)

Fear often complicates the business of dying, especially if a person carries unconfessed sin. That is the point here.

Fear is a God-given gift. It keeps us from doing stupid things. It is a good thing, for example, that I fear damaging heat. Otherwise, I would burn my hand terribly on the stove. Fear of God is a primal fear, a good fear, for it helps us to live up to the standard God has set. Because of the fear of God, some people become followers of Jesus Christ, for he promises to cover us with his righteousness so that we are acceptable in his awesome presence. That kind of fear is good.

On the other hand, fear can drive us to think and do things we would not do with a clear head. It can result in violence and killing. I have been lecturing these days on the disturbing reawakening of ethnic conflict all over the world. Arabs fight Jews. Kurds fight Turks. Hutu slaughter Tutsi. Basques fight Spaniards. Irish Protestants fight Irish Catholics. The list is endless.

I was asked, Is the reason for all this the desire for one group to dominate another? After much thought, I have come to the conclusion that the strongest motivation for ethnic violence is not the desire to dominate but fear. Each group fears for its life. Fear of what might happen drives people to do terrible things. Fear has torment.

> *My Father in heaven,*
> *I fear you as a son fears a loving, compassionate father.*
> *May that fear draw me closer to you.*

The Fear Problem

Held in slavery by their fear of death (2:15)

As people are caught up in the accelerating fear syndrome, they often slip their moorings from sanity.

Adolph Hitler claimed that he so feared for the German people who lived in surrounding nations that he invaded one country after another to "rescue" them. His tortured logic led to a situation that spun out of control, but it all started from a fear of what others might do to "my people."

Kosovo, where Serbs and Turks live side by side, has become a horrendous battleground. The Turks fear that Serbia will dominate them again. The Serbs fear that the power they have regained will be taken from them.

People everywhere are plagued by the fear that they will be overpowered. Some husbands fear that their rights will be eroded. Some wives fear that they will be dominated.

How about me? I fear what people think. I fear the weakening of body and mind as I grow older and see my friends' declining health. Fear follows us like a pesky phantom.

Jesus spoke often about the fear problem. Why do you fear? he would ask. It's a penetrating question. Jesus knew the answer. We fear because we hold on to things that are insignificant in the new kingdom. We cling to trivia and neglect solid truth.

> *Praise you, Jesus, for inviting us to be born again,*
> *to be translated from the kingdoms of this world,*
> *where personal and group preservation*
> *is our primary concern,*
> *to the kingdom of heaven,*
> *where we cling to you and you alone.*
> *I am discovering that this is the only way to truly banish harmful fear.*

Family Tree

He had to be made like his brothers in every way (2:17)

I grew up in a big family—seven boys and four girls. There wasn't much angelic about any of us.

Each had good and bad points. One brother could sell almost anything, but I thought he worked too hard. Another was as bright as could be, but was plagued with a quick temper that got him into trouble. Another loved nature. He was more comfortable in nature than with people. Yet another could do anything, but I thought him overgenerous. One loved people and basked in their favor. Another one was a born manager, so he felt frustrated when he could not "manage" Mom or Dad or me.

I knew my brothers inside and out. They were my textbook on human nature. Nothing surprised me in the way they behaved. That was just the way they were. Praise God, eventually each of them made a substantial contribution to the kingdom of God. They brought their humanness to God and he used them mightily.

None of these wonderful brothers—or sisters—were angels. We all knew that. Jesus did not come to save angels. He came to save people like me and my own family.

Thank you, Jesus, for coming to save sinners, ordinary human beings.
To do that, you became a human being—fully human yet fully God.
As you walked the dusty paths of Palestine,
no one would have mistaken you for an angel.
You were Mary's son. You were like your brothers in every way,
except you had no sin.
Thank you for desiring to be my brother.

Jesus, My Brother

He had to be made like his brothers in every way (2:17)

"He had to be made." Those are forceful words. He had to be made like me in order to save me. Was there not an alternate way that would have been loss costly?

Did the counsels of heaven explore all options? Why not have God declare a general amnesty proclaiming all sinners forgiven? That should do the trick. Why not send a respected angel to preach powerfully to people? Would people listen to angels? Why not send a revised set of commandments that people could easily obey? Why not destroy Satan at once? Why not bring down the curtain on the whole cosmic drama by destroying everything?

I imagine all options were considered. In the end, no other way was found to save me. The Son of God had to be made like those whom he would save.

"He had to be made." I can scarcely take this in. How can the One who fashioned the universe submit to be fashioned as a human being? What love! What grace! I marvel at the thought. He became like me so that he might remake me to be like him.

Jesus was not a man who attained the status of divinity. He was God who condescended to take on himself the nature of a human being in order to deliver me from the reign of Satan.

> *My Lord Jesus, that thought is too great for me.*
> *I have no way to comprehend that kind of love,*
> > *but with both hands outstretched I receive it.*
> *Thank you eternally for being my brother, my best brother.*

Jesus, Our Great High Priest

In order that he might become a merciful and faithful high priest (2:17)

Israel had innumerable priests but only one high priest at a time. On him was the awesome responsibility to appear in the most holy place once a year, bearing the atoning blood for all Israel's sins. It must have been a frightening moment when he lifted the veil and then haltingly entered the awesome place where God dwelt in his Shekinah glory, above the mercy seat. The high priest feared for his life. Would the blood of mere animals cover an entire year's worth of sin for all the people? It was not easy to be the high priest.

Legend has it that the experience was so fraught with fear and dread that the other priests tied a rope to the leg of the high priest when he went in. They assumed that the wrath of God would strike him dead on the spot if there was something wrong with the sacrifice. With the rope they could drag him out if God was not pleased. Not only would that be the end of the high priest, but Israel's sins would remain unforgiven for another year. Would God's mercy be exhausted this year? Who would dare to be Israel's high priest?

> *God, how can sinners ever come into your presence and live?*
> *It is surely because you accepted the atoning work of Jesus*
>   *as absolutely complete.*
> *My sins are judged in Jesus and are forgiven by him.*
> *Thank you, God in heaven, that for me, a sinner,*
>   *the gospel has come as the most welcome good news.*

Jesus, Our Advocate with the Father

In order that he might become a merciful and faithful high priest (2:17)

All human attempts to build a tower to approach God have the stamp of Babel on them. Human towers are built from the bottom up. We feverishly pile brick on self-righteous brick, hoping to approach God in that way. Only a moment's reflection brings us to our senses on that one.

I once heard of a whimsical dream in which a person, having died, appeared at heaven's gates. The keepers told him that a thousand points were required for entrance. "No problem," thought the fellow, who was known for his exemplary life. "I was baptized at twelve, had perfect attendance at Sunday school for years, and I was a good boy."

"Great," was the response, "that is one point."

So the chap went on. "As an adult I was married in the church, never missed a Sunday except for sickness. I sang in the choir, served on three boards, gave at least 15 percent of my money to charity."

"Great," came the reply, "that is another point. Now you have two."

"I paid my taxes, loved my nation, voted conscientiously, organized community activities, and chaired the Rotary Club."

"Great, that is another point. Now you have three."

"Before I died, I gave half of my estate to a Christian college and made sure all of my children and grandchildren were provided for."

"Great, that is another point, now you have four. Only nine hundred and ninety-six to go."

Oh, Lord, deliver me from all self-righteousness,
so that I can rely completely and only
on your most enduring grace.

Jesus' Gift to Us—the Atonement

That he might make atonement for the sins of the people (2:17)

When I consider the atoning work of Jesus, it is like opening a Christmas package from home. While in Africa, we often received parcels from America. I still remember those exciting Christmas Eves when we opened those packages of candy bars, old-fashioned bologna, new books, and music records from family and friends "back home."

That is a little how I feel when I open the divine packet called the atonement. What priceless treasures I find in that gift of gifts. One of the most precious things I find there is forgiveness for sins. To carry the guilt of unforgiven sins plagues any sensitive human conscience. Our consciences remind us time and again that we are incurable rebels.

One of the modern ways to ease the pricking of the conscience is to deny that God exists at all. Then the only thing that is real is the material universe. The universe is self-contained, self-controlled, self-renewing, and autonomous. That leaves God out of the picture. The problem is solved. I am guiltless no matter what my troubled conscience says. A good therapy session will settle my nerves. No God, no sin, no life after death, no problem. I care about nothing, really, except what makes me and others happy.

> *God, I believe that you created the universe and that it operates*
> *on the basis of your nature.*
> *Your most outstanding work was the atonement.*
> *May I build my entire life on what you created.*

Jesus, Our Atonement

That he might make atonement for the sins of the people (2:17)

People who hold to a materialistic view of the universe consider morality as man-made. There is no "truth," just science and discoveries.

For such people, the concept of atonement is a lot of fuss about nothing. But for the person who experiences the convicting power of the Holy Spirit, the atonement is more important than the rising sun, and more powerful than a galaxy of supernovas, for it holds the promise of a restored relationship with God.

I am convinced that conviction of sin does not come from logic. Logic most often tries to convince me that I should carry no guilt. Conviction of sin comes only by the Holy Spirit.

Belief in the atoning work of Jesus is a gift of God's grace. The hymn "Amazing Grace" has it right: "'Twas grace that taught my heart to fear and grace my fears relieved."

The human heart does not fear God naturally, nor does it naturally run to God for forgiveness. Both are gifts of grace, administered by the blessed Holy Spirit. Without the aid of the Holy Spirit, no human heart can fully realize the nature of sin and the wonder of the atonement.

> *Lord, I know the convicting power of the Holy Spirit.*
> *I praise you for it, because it tears away all pretense.*
> *I am a sinner in need of mercy and grace.*
> *Thank you for making full atonement for my sin.*
> *Through the blood of Jesus I am "at one" with you.*

Jesus Allows Testing

He was tempted (2:18)

I have been musing over three words: *testing, temptation,* and *sin.*

Testing. We make dozens of decisions each day. Each decision is a test of whether we are serious about following Christ. God is hoping that we will pass the daily tests. Such testing is common to all people. We should be making our decisions based on our calling and vision. Testings keep reminding us of the importance of keeping priorities straight.

Temptation. When testings challenge our faith, they become temptations. For example, it might be that I know that God is asking me to give money to someone. The test is whether I am going to write out that check or not. When I hesitate and think about the pros and cons, the test turns into a temptation. I may be tempted to give nothing at all, even though I know that God wants me to, or to use some excuse to rationalize myself out of what I know God clearly wants. As these thoughts, worries, and concerns swirl about my troubled head, I am tempted.

Sin. If at the end of all my thinking I decide to do what I know God does not want, that is sin. To renew fellowship with God I must admit that I yielded to temptation and ask him to take my sin to Jesus for cleansing. Then I am free.

> *Jesus, though tried and tempted, you did not sin.*
> *May it be so with me. If I fail, God forbid,*
> *please give me a repentant heart.*

Jesus Stands with Me in Testings and Temptations

He was tempted (2:18)

In my mind's eye I see Jesus speaking with impetuous Peter.

Peter was confused. He had promised to remain with Jesus during those dreadful days of his scourging and mockery. But Peter failed. Instead of standing with Jesus, he denied that he ever knew him at all. Jesus was aware of what was transpiring in Peter's heart and knew of his many weaknesses.

Jesus also knew that Satan had set a trap for Peter. Peter could not see it because he was fearful and confused. Jesus could have arranged circumstances in such a way that Peter would not have been in that judgment hall that night among Christ's enemies. But Jesus allowed him to pass through a living hell for a purpose Peter could not then see. He turned to Peter and said, "But I have prayed for you, Simon, that your faith may not fail. And when you have turned back, strengthen your brothers" (Luke 22:32).

Those words have been a great encouragement to all the Peters in the world ever since. Had he not passed through that fire of testing, he may not have learned the deep, deep lessons of divine forgiveness.

Jesus never leads us into temptation. But he often allows us to pass through times of testing in order to purify our souls and give us deeper insight into the marvels of his grace and love. Satan wants to destroy us. Jesus wants to save us. It is as simple as that.

Lord, increase my faith.

Jesus Suffered Temptation

Because he himself suffered when he was tempted (2:18)

Was Jesus really tempted like I am tempted?

Is it possible that "God in human form" could experience the onslaught of all the forces of Satan? Today's text answers with an emphatic yes. Not only was Jesus tempted like an ordinary mortal, as the Son of man, but he was also tempted as the Son of God.

Why should Satan not tempt Jesus? Satan was well aware that if he could get Jesus to disobey his Father in heaven for but one instant or in one area of his life, Jesus would be disqualified as a perfect sacrifice.

If Satan, the deceiver, could lure Jesus, the Lord, to deviate from the will of his heavenly Father, there would never be an answer for sin. Had Jesus failed, there was no other plan. God had no other son to send. So it is little wonder that Satan marshaled all the hosts of hell to concentrate all their fury and deception on the Son of man.

That is precisely the picture. John the Baptist no sooner announced that Jesus was God's Lamb, here to take away the sin of the world, than Satan pounced on Jesus. For forty days Satan appealed to every human instinct to try to make Jesus sin. Jesus was tempted as a human.

> *Thank you, Jesus, for rebuffing every satanic assault.*
> *You dealt Satan a mighty blow in the wilderness.*
> *It is little wonder that the enemy of our souls set traps*
> *   of every description for three full years,*
> *   culminating with the temptation to avoid death on the cross.*
> *Thank you, Jesus, for obeying your Father to the end.*

Jesus, Our Enabler in Temptation

**Because he himself suffered when he was tempted, he is able to help those
who are being tempted (2:18)**

The writer of Hebrews insists that Jesus "suffered" when he was tempted.

We know that he felt the full blast of Satan's hatred. Satan set every snare that he had to trap him. Jesus was not only tempted like we are, but his temptations went far beyond ours, and his sufferings were certainly more intense. It is impossible for us to imagine the nature of Jesus' temptations. He endured all the temptations common to mankind, but as Son of man and Son of God he tasted temptation that we can scarcely understand.

Jesus taught his disciples to pray, "Lead us not into temptation, but deliver us from the evil one" (Matthew 6:13). That prayer came from the heart of one who knew temptation intimately. Jesus' sustained oneness with his Father enabled him to be victorious over Satan. By faith, he obeyed his Father and believed that his Father was able to defeat Satan.

Now Jesus invites us to live in him, to have unbroken fellowship with him, so that in the hour of temptation we will overcome.

> *Jesus, forbid that I should ever try to fight temptation*
> *by my own power.*
> *I am not able; you are able.*

Jesus Is Able

Fix your thoughts on Jesus (3:1)

I love to read and ponder the prophets—Isaiah, Jeremiah, Ezekiel, and the others. They open for me a window into God's heart.

They tell of the love of the covenant-making God. The prophets stir my heart, for they reveal to me the God of mercy and truth, the God who gives himself for his people. I bathe in the refreshing streams of prophetic writing.

The people who received the letter to the Hebrews also adored the prophets of old. Its writer lifted up the prophets in the first two chapters of his letter and then made an amazing declaration: "Jesus is able." He is reminding me that even though the prophets spoke the truth, they cannot help anyone to overcome. They fulfilled their purpose. They warned, taught, consoled, inspired, and encouraged, but they could not produce life.

His readers looked to the angels for help. That was better, in a way, than expecting help from the likes of Moses and Isaiah. People who research such matters tell us that angels fascinated the imagination and the theology of many New Testament believers, as already noted. Angels can help but they cannot save.

> *Jesus, enable me to fix my thoughts on you.*
> *For when I consider you, the prophets and angels fit into place,*
> *as does everything else.*
> *May I not be distracted by even beneficial witnesses,*
> *for I know they themselves have their eyes riveted*
> *on the Savior of the world, Jesus Christ.*
> *They encourage me to do the same.*

Jesus, God's Greatest Thought

Fix your thoughts on Jesus (3:1)

The New Testament speaks of angels. They are, indeed, ministering spirits. I have become increasingly aware of the work of angels. But I must never seek the aid of an angel. Angels are not autonomous; they must be sent. If I come to depend on angels instead of on the One who provides for my needs—at times through angels—I am setting myself up for frustration.

Having said that, I praise God for the ministry of prophets and angels. Where would I be without them? Be that as it may, I know in my heart of hearts that there is, in fact, only One who "is able." His name is Jesus Christ.

Why should I get so excited about the means of grace? If I am not careful, I fix my eyes on the means and neglect the way, Jesus Christ. For example, I hold some men and women in high esteem, some living and some who have gone to glory. For example, for years I have read Charles Spurgeon and Oswald Chambers almost every day. It is good for me to learn from these men of God. But I know that I see in them only reflected radiance. The source of all radiance is the One on whom the Shekinah glory fell on that sacred mountain, Jesus Christ. When I fix my thoughts on him, I am in contact with eternal life. He alone is able. I hear from heaven, "Listen to him."

Father, forbid that I should fix my attention on the gift
instead of the giver of all gifts.

Jesus, My Example

Fix your thoughts on Jesus, the apostle and high priest whom we confess
(3:1)

In time, people resemble what they fix their thoughts on.

I still shudder when I recall the day Anna Ruth and I, while walking the streets of Calcutta, decided to stand in line with Hindu worshipers to pass by a grotesque black goddess being extolled that day. It was bedlam like I had never seen. As we were jostled by the frenzied worshipers, we felt a strange presence. Over a loud speaker, we heard a harsh demand, "You white people, take off your shoes!"

I do not remember if we did or not. But the crowd soon pushed us along until we stood in the presence of the hideous idol. Others were throwing money and food to the priests who surrounded the goddess. They became fiercely angry when we gave nothing. As we emerged from the temple and out onto the street again, I thought, "Every one of those people did exactly what their goddess would do." That is how it appeared to me. They had become just like their idol. The spirit of the man-made idol possessed them.

I have been reflecting on how I am influenced by what fascinates me. I am convinced that I become more and more like my heroes. So I had better choose my heroes with care!

> *Lord Jesus, as I fix my eyes on you,*
> *I reflect your virtues in my own life.*
> *Praise God! You live in me,*
> *changing me ever so slowly into your image,*
> *from glory to glory.*
> *Jesus, keep changing me as I keep my attention*
> *focused on you—only.*

March 29

Jesus, Apostle and High Priest

Fix your thoughts on Jesus, the apostle and high priest whom we confess
(3:1)

I need a hero. God knows that, so he tells me, "Fix your thoughts on Jesus."

God wants Jesus to be my one and only hero, for he knows that people become more and more like their hero. In some ways I will never be like my hero. Jesus is the Lamb of God. I can simply acknowledge that and praise God for him. I cannot be a "little" Lamb of God. But I can do my best to imitate him in ways that are possible for me. My bedside book, *The Imitation of Christ* by Thomas à Kempis, is a great help to me in this.

Is Jesus my hero? Do I pin all my hopes on him? Do I believe that he loves me eternally? Am I convinced that my hero, Jesus, will fulfill every promise that he has made? Am I convinced that he has no peer?

God in heaven has pinned all his hopes on Jesus. That is the kind of trust that the Father has in his Son. If Jesus falters, there is no plan B. Am I like God in this regard?

Many heroes attract our attention. We should have but one. Jesus was not simply one of the apostles, but the apostle and the one great high priest. As John put it, Jesus is "the One and Only" (John 1:14).

> *Lord, give me constancy and perseverance as I fix my eyes on Jesus,*
> *with not even a glance for any other,*
> *so that I can grow into his likeness.*
> *For I know that I will increasingly resemble the One whom I worship.*

Jesus Obeyed and Saw Wonders

He was faithful to the one who appointed him, just as Moses was (3:2)

Before the writer of Hebrews established the reasons for the superiority of Jesus over Moses, he acknowledged that both Jesus and Moses were full of faith. For the Jews, Moses was the greatest, and his greatest virtue was his faith in Yahweh.

Because of his love for his people, Moses decided to forfeit all the privileges that went with being the son of Pharaoh's daughter, just as Jesus did when he laid aside his privileges and gave himself without reservation to winning our salvation. Truly, Jesus was faithful, as was Moses.

Moses learned that it did little good to tell God that he believed in him. He proved his belief by stepping out in faith. He soon discovered how costly it is to be faithful to God. At the same time he discovered that God's almighty power is released in a remarkable way when people decide to simply obey.

Moses went far beyond his own experience and knowledge. He quaked with fear as he followed God. He could go on only as he renewed his trust in God. But look at what happened when Moses abandoned his own will to follow God: Israel was delivered.

As Moses walked with God, extraordinary things happened. A nation was shaped.

My God, forbid that my indecision to follow you
should stand in the way of others getting blessed.

Jesus, My Faithfulness

He was faithful to the one who appointed him, just as Moses was (3:2)

I began my walk with the Lord when I made a conscious decision to abandon the demands of self and follow him no matter what. But that was only the beginning. I am discovering that ongoing faithfulness requires unbroken fellowship with God on a daily basis. I cannot simply slip into a gear called faithfulness and ride merrily to glory. I can remain faithful only as long as the Holy Spirit has dominance in my life.

Faithfulness is costly. Jesus calls it *the cross:* "If anyone would come after me, he must deny himself and take up his cross and follow me" (Matthew 16:24).

I am thinking back over my own sixty-year pilgrimage with the Lord. I would not be honest if I were to gloss over the many deaths I had to die as I walked with Jesus. As a missionary, I had to die to one privilege after another for the sake of the gospel.

The flip side of the cross is that those things to which I died had become hindrances to my freedom in Christ. So in retrospect, instead of remembering the pain of dying to self, I feel the exuberance of new life in Christ, unfettered by those "privileges" I once held dear.

Lord Jesus, the faithful Son, be in me "faithfulness" to God,
which is possible only through the grace that you supply.

Jesus, Greater Than Moses

Jesus has been found worthy of greater honor than Moses (3:3)

Jewish history is full of influential people, but the Jews of old honored none more than Moses. Through him God revealed the law, which is nothing less than a window into the heart of God. That law formed the moral and legal basis for every Jew.

They recognized Moses as the greatest judge who ever lived. Before a Jew acted he would have asked himself, "What would Moses do?" Moses was just that influential in the life of every Jew. In short, all law and order issued from the writings of Moses. That put Moses in a category all his own.

Not only did Moses lay the moral and legal foundation for the nation, he also instituted the God-prescribed religious system with its tabernacle, priests, sacrifices, religious holidays, and rituals.

So every time a Jewish man or woman brought a sacrificial dove to the priest or when the entire nation gathered for a week of repentance, culminating in the Passover, they did exactly as Moses prescribed. He was the constant, pervasive influence in everything, the highest authority on all matters religious, legal, behavioral, or national. Is it possible that someone greater than Moses should appear?

Praise God for Jesus, who, while resembling Moses in many ways,
is far greater, for he is Son of God and Son of man.

Jesus, More Greatly Honored Than Moses

Jesus has been found worthy of greater honor than Moses (3:3)

No person in Jewish history exceeded Moses.

It was he who called the Jews out of the sufferings of Egypt and forged that "mixed multitude" into a nation called Israel. To be sure, the patriarchs Abraham, Isaac, Jacob, and Joseph were honored. But none dominated the nation's life and experience like Moses.

I find myself getting excited about Moses. What a man! How could he do it all? While leading more than three million people through the wilderness for forty years he found time to shape, if not actually write, the first five books of our Bible. The writing is superb and the poetry, like the hymn he wrote shortly after the Exodus, sparkles like a jewel.

All I have ever admired and wanted to be I see in that greatest of the great, Moses.

At the very heights of my feelings about Moses, I hear a calm, assured, persistent voice say, "Jesus has been found worthy of greater honor than Moses." Can it be? It can be, because Jesus is no less than the only begotten of the Father and the one and only Son of man. Moses was great, but Jesus is of another genre entirely.

Lord, my heart needs a hero. I have many, including Moses,
but I want to fix my eye and my heart
on the One who is most honored in heaven,
Jesus Christ of Nazareth.

Jesus Is Absolutely Unique

Jesus has been found worthy of greater honor than Moses (3:3)

I recall an African sermon in which it was said, "When the sun comes up, its light overcomes the moon and stars."

That's what occurred on the mountaintop where Peter, James, and John were dazzled by Christ's splendor. There stood their friend, Jesus, with Moses on one side and Elijah on the other, engaged in serious conversations concerning his coming death on Calvary's hill, dreaded but necessary.

I imagine I hear Moses and Elijah saying, "Lamb of God, we know in part the horror and dread you feel as you face the ignominy of carrying in your person what you detest the most, sin. But Jesus, that is the only way. We have confessed our sinfulness but those sins remain against us. We offered our sacrifices, hoping that one day the Lamb of God will carry our sins to the place of judgment where the wrath of God will fall upon all sin.

"So, Jesus, set your face as a flint to go to Jerusalem as a lamb goes to the slaughter, yielding your will constantly to the will of your Father. All eyes in heaven are on you, Jesus. Please, do not falter. Satan will try you severely. Resist him with all your divine might."

Jesus never wavered, even though he cried out in the garden, "If there is some other way." There is anguish in that groaning. What he was facing was terrifying. But Jesus learned again what he already knew: there is no "other way." He paid the price.

Thank you, Jesus, for fixing your eyes
on the great salvation that your death would win.
You endured the cross to set me free.

April 4

Planned and Built by the Trinity

God is the builder (3:4)

I find it exhilarating to jump in and help with a project. I recently spent a few hours mixing mortar and laying blocks for our daughter and son-in-law's house expansion. I was rather proud of myself that I could lay up blocks rather plumb and level. I had built part of a wall, and I hope I will always remember the blocks I laid in it.

But no one else will remember that. No one will rush to the spot where I made my little contribution and admire it. Rather they will say, "Larry, the builder, did a marvelous job here." I simply had the rare privilege of laying a few blocks.

To paraphrase today's verse, "Those few blocks were laid by me, but Larry is the 'builder of everything,' even my bit."

Moses had a huge role in building the nation of Israel. His fingerprints are everywhere. Likewise Elijah lit up the pages of the Bible with extraordinary miracles. Both laid their blocks faithfully and well.

All God's servants throughout history contributed to the magnificent building that we now occupy. Each is quick to point out, however, that the architect and builder is the Triune God—Father, Son, and Holy Spirit. At best we are all privileged partners in God's glorious project, building his kingdom on the earth.

Lord, may I build in the same way, laying my blocks with care.

Jesus, the Master Planner

Every house is built by someone, but God is the builder of everything (3:4)

The first two chapters of Hebrews acknowledge the contribution played by angels, those faithful ministering spirits. Nevertheless, angels join Moses and Elijah in gratefully acknowledging that the "builder of everything" is God. To be sure, the work accomplished by God is magnificent, but far above all is the glorious, magnificent God himself.

Creation is a prime example of God's handiwork. All creation bears the stamp of God's wisdom and knowledge. Take our planet as an example. What would it be like if the moon were a thousand miles nearer or farther from the earth? The earth depends on the gravity of the moon to regulate the tides that govern its weather. The moon is exactly where it must be, in its special orbit, and is precisely the right size, otherwise life as we know it would come to an end.

The psalmist had it right: "The heavens declare the glory of God. . . . There is no speech or language where their voice is not heard" (Psalm 19:1, 3).

All of nature reminds us of our creator God. We admire nature, but nature is not God. Nature is the work of God. We see the fingerprints of God as we ponder the universe, but God is as far above the creation as the builder is above what he or she is building.

> *Lord God, enable me to marvel at the works of your hand,*
> *but forbid that I should forget for a moment*
> *that you are high and lifted up,*
> *exalted over all.*
> *You alone are worthy of worship.*

We Are Christ's House

And we are his house (3:6)

Having lived for twenty years in houses provided by the mission board, Anna Ruth and I were excited when we purchased our own home. Not that the other places weren't nice. We enjoyed every one of them, from the quaint thatched-roof round cottage at the Katoke Teachers College on the western shores of Lake Victoria to the comfortable cement-block house in Nairobi, Kenya. We tried to keep those mission houses in good repair, a job I enjoyed. But I always knew I was repairing someone else's house.

What a difference when we bought our own property in Lancaster, Pennsylvania. We planted trees and made gardens, even dug out a little pond for fish, in the glorious liberty of ownership. We added a sunroom and moved internal walls. We could do that because it was ours.

As I write this I find my spirit soaring because I know that Jesus owns me. I am his house. He must feel as I did when I obtained full rights of ownership to our house. He need not consult anyone or get permission from anyone, not even me, before he makes changes in me, his house. He knows best and will do what is best for me. I am one of the many, many precious houses he will use for his glory as he works out his purposes on the earth.

Jesus, I am your own house. Do with me what you wish.

Christis Faithful

But Christ is faithful as a son over God's house. And we are his house (3:6)

Jesus cares for his house, night and day, summer and winter. He is faithful as an owner, as a repairer, as a protector. He is faithful as he oversees me, his house, and as he oversees his beloved church.

Jesus was faithful when he bought me. He paid off the mortgage. He fully paid all the liens that the enemy had against me. That happened when he gave his life willingly on the cross beyond the city wall. As long as there was a mortgage, there was co-ownership with Satan. Jesus canceled what I owed, and now he is the sole owner.

Jesus is faithful in his use of the house. He can help himself to his property—me—because he has sole ownership of me. He does not ask the house what changes to make, nor does he consult me. He is absolute master of it and does what is best, according to his wisdom.

God owns me. That is a glorious truth. It thrills me to know that I am God's property. But I see here a more extraordinary thing. Not only does he own me as a landlord, so to speak, but he surprises me by desiring to move in and live in my house. I become his habitation.

This is a truth too grand for me.
I simply accept it and praise you, almighty God,
that Jesus desires to live in me.
Lord, inhabit me entirely, every room,
and rule your house with truth and grace.

Hold on to Jesus!

If we hold on to our courage and . . . hope (3:6)

It is easy to hold on to courage and hope when blessings fall like spring showers. Even a timid grip is sufficient then. Praise God for times like that.

However, that kind of grip is not what the Holy Spirit has in mind here. It is more like gripping the rope lest you fall over a cliff or clutching for dear life the hand that is rescuing you from drowning. Hold on with all your might, in spite of the illogic of it all. Hold on even though the prospects of rescue seem futile. Hold on when others around you are losing their grip. Hold on when you feel helpless and hopeless. Hold on just a little longer, even though each moment seems an eternity. Hold on when doubts begin to creep in, doubts about God's love and his ability to save. Hold on when it seems as though Satan is gaining the upper hand.

I can imagine the strength of Peter's grip when Jesus rescued him from drowning. A few years ago I was in a spiritually boisterous sea when I cried out, "Save me, Lord, or I will surely perish!" I had nothing to hold on to but Jesus himself. I could not even hold on to his promises, for they seemed to be violated.

I prayed, "But for you, Jesus, I am done. There is no good thing in me that deserves your favor. I plead only your loving grace. If I perish, I will perish gripping your hand." Slowly, I felt his grip tightening on my hand. I heard him saying, "I am gripping your hand. I will never let you go."

Praise God, Jesus gripped my hand tighter than I could ever grip his, and he held on in spite of all!

Thank you, Jesus, for holding on to me
when I fear my hold will slip.

Jesus Breaks the Proud Heart

Today, if you hear his voice, do not harden your hearts (3:7-8)

A heart that is hard against God is in big, big trouble. That was Israel's sin.

We read in 2 Kings 20 that the Syrians convinced the Jews that, though Yahweh is the God of the hills and mountains, Baal rules the plains and the valleys, where people plant their crops, hoping for a harvest. So the Jews built altars to Yahweh on the mountaintops, but when it came time to plant in the rich soils of the valleys, they called on the local gods of fertility, Baal and Ashtoreth. This frustrated God so much that the only solution seemed to be to destroy idol-worshipping nations.

What does this say to me? I am writing this on Monday morning, after a blessed time of communion with our congregation on Sunday. It was a mountaintop experience. Now I am in the valley, which is full of challenges. I open my mail and find some unwelcome news. I get agitated and depressed. What should I do? I feel a bit of panic. Stop a minute, soul. What did you hear yesterday on the mountaintop? Have you forgotten so quickly?

When you are in the valley, look to God whom you met on the mountaintop, not to trivial powers that are impotent in the valleys of life.

> *Lord, why is it that when I think of how you saved my soul,*
> *I readily lift up my hands in holy reverence*
> *and sing those nice songs about faith and trust,*
> *only to sink into unbelief*
> *when faced with a challenge in the valley?*
> *I am guilty of the sin of Israel.*
> *I find it a challenge to trust you, Lord.*
> *Reveal yourself to me on the mountain,*
> *and please also manage my affairs in the valley of everyday living.*

Jesus, the Lord of Today

Today, if you hear his voice, do not harden your hearts (3:7-8)

This chapter contains a refrain: "Today!" Repent today. Encourage one another today.

I know from experience that it only takes a day to get a hard heart, sometimes less. I need only a small thing to trigger it, some harsh word, some rejection, a disappointment. Before I know it, I am floundering in unbelief. My heart gets hard as rock in a day or even less.

I am discovering that faith produces more faith, that thanksgiving produces more thanksgiving, that hope multiplies hope, and that joy leads to more joy. The opposite is equally true: doubt breeds more doubt, fear multiplies like cancer cells, splitting to produce more fear. Hardness becomes a rock.

The secret is to fix my thoughts on Jesus. He never acted on the basis of fear or self-interest. Satan trained all his munitions on Jesus for forty days in the wilderness, hoping that Jesus would seek self-interest or self-actualization. Jesus won the victory by saying no to self and yes to God. That struggle was even more intense in Gethsemane. Jesus' cry pierced the night air and resounded through heaven and hell: "Not my will, but yours be done" (Luke 22:42). That is brokenness beyond human understanding.

I owe my salvation to Jesus' courageous belief.

> *You overcame, my Lord,*
> *because your faith was as God's precious and unique Lamb,*
> *who alone takes away the sin of the world.*
> *Praise the Lord, you chose to believe!*

Jesus, Heaven's Most Convincing Sign

For forty years [they] saw what I did (3:9)

I took a course once called Christian Evidences. I filled page after page with notes on "evidences" of God in nature, in the human conscience, in history, and so on. I concluded that I am surrounded by evidence of God on every side. Further, if that is true for me, it must certainly be true for everyone. Why, then, do so many people reject God?

I suppose one reason is that an unbeliever can come up with an impressive list of "evidence" that "proves" there is no God. It does not take a genius to deny the existence of God.

So why is it that, in light of the same evidence, some believe and others do not? Mystery indeed.

"For forty years [they] saw what I did," said God. The hand of God was more obvious for that generation than almost any other. They saw the plagues, the miraculous salvation of those who put the blood of a lamb on their doorposts, and the public demonstration of God's power as three million helpless refugees crossed the Red Sea and the mighty armies of Egypt perished. Manna from heaven, water from a rock, cure for deadly snake bites, the gracious giving of the law on Sinai, and the promise of sins forgiven and of new life through the sacrifices and priesthood—they saw firsthand what God did, but failed to trust him with their lives. Seeing is not believing. Only those who believe can truly see.

> *Lord, I am guilty of that same flaw.*
> *What more could you have shown me to make me a believer?*
> *The problem is me.*

Jesus Helps Me See

For forty years [they] saw what I did (3:9)

An Egyptian god in the desert? Fashioned by Jews? There it was, for all to see. And all saw it! How could it be that they conspired to replace God with an Egyptian idol, a golden calf?

The writer of Hebrews put his finger on the reason for unbelief. He called it a rebellious spirit. Might that explain why Adam and Eve believed the voice of Satan, which questioned the veracity of God's word?

Deep inside the human heart lurks a spirit of rebellion. We prefer to make or be our own gods rather than bow the stiff neck in deference to almighty God, whose evidences fill the universe.

Words cannot express the awe and gratefulness in my own heart as I recall, as best I can, the mighty works of God in my life. I have less excuse to believe than did the Jews because I have seen God at work in my life, not for forty but more than sixty years. As I ponder the way God has worked for me and in me, patterns emerge. I see divine providence in the minutest things and the grandest. What additional evidence do I need to cast my all on Jesus Christ? I gladly give Jesus the reins of my life.

I must say, the most convincing evidence I have of God is that he has given me the desire to believe. That is the work of God that makes all the difference to me.

*Thank you, Jesus, for being my eye to see the Father
and to rejoice in his presence.*

Jesus, the Way to Rest

Their hearts are always going astray, and they have not known my ways ...
They shall never enter my rest (3:10, 11)

An African friend of mine owed a shopkeeper money in our little town of Musoma. It must have been long in arrears, because every time my friend passed that shop, he panicked. To reduce the distress, he began to pass regularly on the other side of the street. As time went by, he found it best to avoid that street altogether.

This made life difficult because he had to buy items from stores there. To make matters worse, his friends, who needed goods from town, often asked him to buy things for them there too. Being a man of standing in the community, he could not tell them of his dilemma. He felt cornered. As time went on, he feigned sickness rather than go to town. He even went to the expense of sending someone else to do his shopping.

Life got very complicated for this poor fellow. There was only one thing to do: go to the shopkeeper and confess that he had broken his promise and then take the consequences. In desperation he did so, and was forgiven. Together they worked out a repayment plan that he could handle.

The next day my friend went to town as a new person. The first thing he did was walk down the forbidden street and greet that storeowner. He was a free man. He was at home in Musoma once again.

> *Lord, I see that it is impossible for you to grant me peace*
> *if I refuse to repent of my sin against you.*
> *You canceled my debt at Calvary; now I owe you my love,*
> *my worship, my life.*
> *That is true rest.*

'Believe me'—Jesus in John 14

See to it, brothers, that none of you has a sinful, unbelieving heart (3:12)

Before I was converted, I knew nothing of skepticism. I was simply indifferent, as I recall. Life was a lark then, and I lived for the moment. I was like a ship in the great blue sea, sailing along without compass or destination, sometimes heading north, then south. It made no difference. I was not a skeptic or a cynic, simply indifferent. Why worry about anything? That was my philosophy.

Then on my "road to Damascus" Jesus met me. In an instant, I became a believer. In a flash, life had a purpose. Everything came into focus around him. That lasted for months. Then I discovered something about myself. I am a skeptic. This character trait in me came to life after I discovered belief. I was drawn to Greek skeptics, French skeptics, and American skeptics. They taught me how to think "logically."

That childlike faith I once knew was greatly diminished. I liked being a skeptic because it marked me as a superior person, unlike those who are gullible. I was not aware of the fact that skepticism smothers faith.

But, praise God, Jesus Christ appeared to me once again in Tanzania. After a great struggle, I became a simple believer once again. That cynical, skeptical streak lost its power. It is not that I never have a cynical thought, but I recognize it now as unbelief.

> *Jesus, you always believed.*
> *Since you have taken up residence in me,*
> *   be my believer for me.*

April 15

Jesus, Never Cynical

Encourage one another daily, as long as it is called Today (3:13)

A good antidote for cynicism is to encourage others.

When I begin to doubt or to lose faith, the best thing I can do is encourage someone else. Sure, when I am down, I need a word of encouragement myself. That helps. But I find that nothing braces my own spirit more than when I sincerely encourage someone else. It reorients me. Come to think of it, I cannot encourage and be a cynic at the same time. When I encourage another, I am actually expressing and deepening my faith. So the more I encourage others, the more firmly I root faith in my own spirit.

It does little good for me to say, "When I feel better about things, I will bless others." Such an attitude confirms me in my unbelief and starves others of blessing that they rightfully expect from me.

When I do not feel like blessing anyone, it helps me to honestly admit that to the Lord. "Jesus, I have the grumps so badly that I am no good to anyone. I do not want to bless anyone! How can I bless another when I am dry as toast? That is the truth, Lord."

Having said that, I see the sinfulness of my attitude. I know what to do with sin. I rush to the cross of Christ with it, confess it, and deposit it there where the blood of Christ cleanses it. Skepticism loses its power at the cross, for Jesus had every reason to be cynical, but he never stopped believing.

Lord, give me the sincere desire to bless others,
for as I bless, I believe, and my faith deepens.

April 16

Jesus Always Encourages

Encourage one another daily, as long as it is called Today (3:13)

A few years ago at church, I was struck by how well the young man at the piano kept time, though he was just a beginner. Unlike other young pianists, he did not hesitate when he missed a note. He did not fiddle around trying to get it right, but just went on, not skipping a beat.

I have no training in these matters, but I felt that the first prerequisite for a budding pianist would be a sense of time. I knew that my young friend would ultimately get the notes right. That takes practice, but a good sense of timing is a gift.

After the service, the Holy Spirit urged me to encourage him, which I did. To my delight, he has become a marvelous pianist. His father later confided that my few words of encouragement made a huge difference.

When I encourage another, led by the Holy Spirit, it has a significant effect—on me and on the one I bless.

Now I must learn to do that daily. When the Holy Spirit says, bless that brother, bless that sister, I had better do it then and there. I probably will not feel like doing so later on.

Jesus, you always believed. I know that.
Please, Lord, forgive me of my sin of unbelief.
Break my hard heart.
Whether I feel like it or not, I will bless others.
The blood of Jesus cleanses, and behold,
I am blessed all over again and the blessing flows
over into others' lives.
Lord, forgive me for my self-centeredness;
give me the heart of an encourager.

Jesus, Our Faithful Captain

Whose bodies fell in the desert (3:17)

It is one thing to leave Egypt, the land of bondage, and quite another to enter the land of promise. It takes a different kind of faith to enter into rest than to flee the bondage of Satan.

As the children of Israel ate their final meal as Egyptian slaves, they had only one desire—to get out of that place of bondage. Then marvelous things began to happen. They experienced the power of almighty God as they applied the blood of sacrificial animals to their doorposts, an act that saved them from suffering the death of their firstborn. They crossed the mighty Red Sea by faith, buoyed by the leadership of Moses, Aaron, and Miriam, and encouraged by the thousands who fled bondage with them. They were free at last.

It must have been exhilarating to stand on the eastern shore and sing with Miriam the joyful words of deliverance: "The horse and its rider he has hurled into the sea" (Exodus 15:1). The mighty arm of God had delivered them. As they moved out of Egypt, they were full of faith.

Then what? They suffered a greater plague, one of unbelief. Could not the God who broke the power of mighty Egypt provide bread and water for them? Could he not protect them from their enemies? Could he not ultimately subdue the lesser powers of tribal Canaan?

Lord, am I guilty of this same lack of faith?
Am I hesitating at the border of some land
that you want me to enter because I have been inflicted
by the plague of infernal unbelief?

Jesus, Our Sustainer

Whose bodies fell in the desert (3:17)

With their own eyes they saw God disarm the mightiest army in the world of that era. They saw it and even sang songs about it. But they failed to maintain that faith. On their desert journey they cowered in the face of enemies much weaker than fabled Egypt.

Their lack of faith was their undoing. Our text is actually a question: "Whose bodies fell in the desert?" The answer is obvious and the reason indisputable. They are the ones who had seen God's very strong arm saving them, but "they were not able to enter, because of their unbelief" (Hebrews 3:19). They did not enter into the land of promise; we see their bleached bones scattered in the wilderness, lying on hot sands.

I am pondering Psalms 78:40-42 in the King James Version: "How oft did they provoke him in the wilderness, and grieve him in the desert! Yea, they turned back and tempted God, and limited the Holy One of Israel. They remembered not his hand, nor the day when he delivered them from the enemy." They limited God by their unbelief. Is not God all powerful?

Is not this my own story? Do I not limit the Holy One of Israel by my reluctance to believe? The power of God is constant, but it is released to me and others by faith. My unbelief does not limit the power of God, but it limits his freedom to use that power to do his marvelous work for me.

Lord Jesus, you always sought for those who would believe.
May I lay aside all doubt and unbelief and with all my heart
trust you completely for everything forever.

Jesus, God's 'Yes'

Those who disobeyed (3:18)

I am wondering how disobedience and unbelief are connected. When I use the words in a positive sense—obedience and belief—I can see the connection. I obey because I believe. I will not obey someone whom I believe does not have my welfare at heart. Why should I obey someone whom I am convinced does not care for me at all? Or, flipped the other way, why should I not obey someone whom I believe has my welfare in mind and is able to help me?

The first act of disobedience in the garden of Eden stemmed directly from unbelief. God told our primal parents not to eat from a certain tree, "for when you eat of it you will surely die" (Genesis 2:17). Satan challenged that. "You will not surely die" (3:4), the deceiver told Eve.

Satan threw the gauntlet, "Believe me or God." Adam and Eve chose to believe Satan and disbelieve God. That decision changed more things than we know. The entire revelation of God, all of Scripture, tells the story of how God painstakingly devised a way to reverse that horrid tragedy. The solution was Jesus Christ, who always said yes to his Father in heaven.

Satan employed all his strategies on Jesus to get him to doubt God's word. The good news rests on the fact that Jesus pleased his Father in every regard. Jesus knew what Satan was after. Satan wanted Jesus to doubt God, but Jesus never doubted the words of his Father.

So, all of life boils down to the simple question, "Do I believe God or Satan?" The answer to this question will determine whom I will obey.

Lord Jesus, I believe you with all my heart, so I obey freely.

Jesus, Our Willingness to Obey

Those who disobeyed (3:18)

Satan spares no effort to plant doubts about God. He knows that when we begin to doubt any aspect of God's character, we are open to lies. Satan is subtle in all his ways.

His questions and assertions are so sensible. See if these sound familiar:

> If God loves you, as you once thought, then why is he allowing this?
> If you want to be truly free, take charge of your own life. Be a slave to no one.
> Especially not to Jesus. It is just fine to be religious, but make your own religion.
> The biggest hypocrites on earth are Christians. Their faith is all a sham.
> God is tolerant, but Jesus and especially his followers are intolerant.
> The way to end all war is to abolish religion once and for all, for religion is the basic problem.
> If God is God, then explain evil. Why does he allow it?

Satan is well aware of what is going on and has darts of doubt that he is deft at throwing. He seldom presents himself as the one who is more helpful than God. All he needs to do is plant doubts concerning any aspect of the character of God. If he can do that, then he has people eating out of his hand.

> *Lord Jesus, you have stolen my heart and affections.*
> *When temptation to question my faith strikes,*
> *disarm the enemy by increasing my faith in you,*
> *my Savior, my Lord, my refuge and friend.*
> *I recall what you said to Peter*
> *when he was in a sea of doubt and confusion,*
> *"I have prayed for you . . . that your faith may not fail."*
> *Lord, pray that prayer for me today.*

Jesus, the Answer to Unbelief

They were not able to enter, because of their unbelief (3:19)

The letter to the Hebrews is steeped in Old Testament imagery.

For the wandering Jews, Canaan promised to be the land of rest from their circuitous meanderings, which took them nowhere and depleted their resources. The wilderness provided no rest. To be sure, they ate heavenly manna and drank from the miraculous rock, but they were not settled. They could not build their houses, plant their crops, and rear their families, for they had not yet entered the land, the place of rest.

They knew that God had prepared a place of rest for them, the Holy Land. Why did they hesitate? I read somewhere that, had they traveled directly from Egypt to Canaan, it would have taken less than a month. What kept them from pressing on to inherit the land? It is all wrapped up in a word *unbelief,* as today's verse points out.

That is a sobering thought. As I reflect on areas of restlessness in my own life, I need to stop and ask what hinders me from entering into rest on this point? For example, I recently retired and am beginning to realize how much I came to depend on others to give my life structure. While I rejoice in the freedom retirement gives me, it has a way of unsettling me, making me restless. Without structure I am adrift. I must be careful that I do not strive to be somebody or to do something heroic, but to rest.

Lord, forgive my error.

April 22

Jesus, the Way to Rest

They were not able to enter, because of their unbelief (3:19)

I am discovering that I have been finding more rest, or security, in my supporting community than in Jesus. This is coming clear as I move out of those secure structures because of retirement.

I will never again have the support of people I enjoyed for the past thirty or more years. So what will I do? Will I look for another group to structure my life? Will I resign myself to aimlessness because I have no one to set my course? Is it possible to be productive without external supervision? Like a butterfly, I might just flit from one flower to the next, not able to rest on any.

I am depending on a system to give me rest. At the heart of it all, I find that I need peer approval more than I realized. Remove peer approval and I am like a flapping fish out of water.

Is it possible that I need the approval of people more than I need the approval of Jesus, my Lord and Savior? Do I find people more trustworthy than God?

Do I really believe that God will leave me in the lurch? Maybe, if I am honest. Why is it so hard for me to believe that Jesus is my structure and my most trusted peer?

> *Lord Jesus, you are not only the way to rest,*
> *you are also rest itself,*
> *for you rested entirely on your Father in heaven.*
> *Forgive my unbelief. I choose to believe. You are structure enough.*

Jesus Is the Way to Rest

Now we who have believed enter that rest (4:3)

It is hard to believe.

I have high regard for Albert Schweitzer, the renowned missionary to Africa who wrote *The Quest of the Historical Jesus,* first published in 1906. Schweitzer lived in a day when the techniques of internal and external textual criticism proved to many that Jesus was a myth. He set about to find out if Jesus was fictional or if he actually lived on the earth. He concluded that Jesus was a historical character. Good for you, Dr. Schweitzer.

But that is not the whole story. After proving that Jesus lived, Schweitzer concluded that Jesus had a serious personality flaw, he unfortunately had what Schweitzer described as a messianic complex.

Why is it so hard to believe in Jesus just as he is revealed in the Bible? Jesus knew. I recall his words when the crowds asked him enthusiastically, "What must we do to do the works God requires?" Jesus startled them with his answer, "The work of God is this: to believe in the one he has sent" (John 6:28-29). But we humans want to prove our worth, not just believe.

As a new, struggling missionary in Tanzania, I faced many doubts about Jesus. I finally came to the point where I determined to believe in Jesus as revealed in the Bible. I cannot begin to describe the change that came over me. The tables were turned. Instead of me challenging Jesus, he challenged me.

> *Thank you, Lord, for giving me the grace to believe,*
> *for then I entered into rest in a profoundly personal sense.*
> *Lord Jesus, may I ever and always find my Sabbath rest in you.*

April 24

Jesus Said, 'I Will Give You Rest'

There remains, then, a Sabbath-rest for the people of God (4:9)

As the Jews rested on the Sabbath, so do I rest on Jesus Christ, my Sabbath, every day.

The letter to the Hebrews opens by reminding readers that Jesus is greater than the angels. It goes on to show that he is greater than Moses. In this section, the letter exalts Jesus above Joshua, the leader who brought the children of Israel into the Promised Land, where they were to experience rest. It was a daunting challenge. Life in Canaan turned out to be anything but restful. The Canaanite tribes despised the Jewish "intruders."

The human soul longs for rest in a restless world. God, who planted this yearning in the human heart, promised rest. He set aside one day of seven as the Sabbath. It was the last day of the week—rest after work. The church starts the week with the Lord's day. They *begin* the week with rest. I prefer it that way myself. In any case God promises rest.

God prescribed specific times for rest in the Old Testament, such as the weekly Sabbath, the sabbatical year, and the year of jubilee, when debts were canceled and mercy ruled the day. The land, the cattle, and the people enjoyed rest. At least for that year.

God wants us to rest from our labors and to turn our attention to him, the source of all blessing. He wants us to find our rest in him.

> *Lord, you know how much I long for rest.*
> *You also know what disturbs my rest.*
> *Subdue the enemy, restlessness, in my life.*

Jesus Said, 'You Will Find Rest for Your Souls'

There remains, then, a Sabbath-rest for the people of God (4:9)

Sabbath days, festivals, and feasts of celebration punctuated Israel's religious life. Yet after each event the Jews returned to the hurly burly of daily life, as restless as ever.

The Bible attributes this restlessness to their failure to believe that God would care for their every need. In the wilderness, that famine of the heart remained even as they enjoyed the daily manna. They soon learned that the arrival of the law did not help at all. In fact, it added to their frustration and made them even more restless.

God promised that the Jews would find rest as they crossed over Jordan to their new home. Joshua did his job, depositing the Jews in the Promised Land, but he could not give them rest and peace.

Now there is a new Joshua among us, Jesus Christ, who says, "Take my yoke upon you and learn from me, for I am gentle and humble in heart, and you will find rest for your souls" (Matthew 11:29).

Human beings need be restless no longer. Jesus could promise rest because he knew that he was about to inflict a deathblow to Satan at Calvary. The very power that conquered Satan is the power that is mine if I believe. Jesus Christ is my rest.

> Lord, I know that in believing in you and what you have done for me
>   I find rest.
> When I begin to believe in my own ability to overcome Satan,
>   I lose my peace because, instead of resting, I am striving.
> When I doubt your love and grace, I slip back into the restless state.
> When I believe, then I am at rest.

Jesus, Rest from Depending on Works

**Anyone who enters God's rest also rests from his own work,
just as God did from his (4:10)**

Followers of Jesus are to be holy and should do good works, so we go about serving others in the name of Christ. That is right and proper. But we must be careful lest we drift into a works-oriented view of discipleship, which places us back under the old covenant and obligates us to try to please God by our obedience to the law and by our good works.

This is a snare into which conscientious people often fall. As an example, an elderly friend of mine, a bishop now departed, was saddled with the chore of enforcing the rules of the church. He had vowed years before at his ordination to uphold all the rules and regulations of the denomination. On his deathbed, he thought he had failed and was terrified by the thought that he must now answer to God. So he called the brothers to his bedside to help him find peace with God. They reminded him that he was saved by grace, not by works that he had done. Why then should he fear?

I understand that before he died he found peace with God by reaffirming what he knew all along, that we are saved through grace. Begone the dictum "saved by grace and kept by works."

Lord, I have given my life to serve you faithfully.
Teach me to know that my faithfulness does not save me.
I can never in a thousand lifetimes of self-sacrifice earn your favor.
I am saved to do good works, not saved by good works.
Lord, settle me in this foundational truth.

Jesus, the Word

For the word of God is living and active (4:12)

For me, words are linked with people. People are what give meaning to words. For example, if I read the words, "You will never know that Jesus is all you need until Jesus is all you have," I am somewhat impressed. But when I am told that these are the words of Mother Teresa of Calcutta, who gave her life to help those who are dying, I stand in awe. Her entire life empowers these few words.

The Hebrews knew this from the beginning. They made no distinction at all between the character of Yahweh and the words of Yahweh. When God said, "Let there be light," they knew it would create light because they knew Yahweh. Had Gabriel the archangel said that, nothing would have happened. Angels do not have it within their power to create anything.

The apostle John wrote, "In the beginning was the Word." This was not a new idea to the Greeks. Their philosophers taught that Logos (the eternal word) preexisted everything. John affirmed that, but moved on to declare, "The Word was God" (John 1:1).

The Word is God's word. The Word cannot exist without a person to speak it. So the Word rests on the character or the power of the One who speaks it. The Word became flesh—Jesus.

Our God, I suppose original sin is rejecting your Word.
In the wilderness you spoke clearly to your people.
They heard but did not heed.
They failed to fully embrace it and shape their lives around it.
Thank you for this warning to me to hear, believe, and obey.

Jesus, the Great Revealer of Truth

The word of God . . . judges the thoughts and attitudes of the heart (4:12)

Like many believers in my culture, I have had my share of problems with the Bible.

When I was a new believer at age sixteen, I placed my life under the spotlight of the Bible. Asking no questions, I just applied the Scriptures to my life. Every sentence had some meaning for me. Our little student prayer group had one goal—to let God change us from inside out according to the powerful, authoritative, penetrating Word of God. We had little interest in opinions. We went willingly to God's MRI and even more willingly dealt with the cancer that it revealed—diseases like pride, laziness, selfishness, critical spirit, things that warred against God.

A few years later, during the heyday of biblical criticism, I began to change ever so slowly. I was still a believer, but my reading and theological reflections forced me to face the general mood of the times, which raised hosts of questions about the Bible. Many of the theologians I read poked huge holes in the Bible. I began to wonder where it was leading. Was there anything that I could depend on? Many theologians found delight in subjecting the Bible to literary and historical criticism, but they seldom stretched themselves out to discover their own diseases. That is what happens when we tamper with the Word of God. We are tempted to stand as judge over the Bible instead of allowing the Bible to judge us.

> *Lord, I see it now.*
> *You pushed me into the place where I cried out,*
> *"I do believe; help me overcome my unbelief!"*

Jesus, the Word

The word of God . . . judges the thoughts and attitudes of the heart (4:12)

I was not settled in my own mind about a great number of things in the Bible. Like many in my generation, there was a disconnect between my view of the world and the view of the world found in the Scriptures. The Bible did not seem to be good science. The way I dealt with this was to think of God as a good communicator. He must have known that the Jews were steeped in superstitions, so he just went along with that in order to be understood.

That solution served me quite well, I thought, until Anna Ruth and I answered the call to serve as missionaries in East Africa. There a series of events pressed me to rethink my views of the Bible. It began with a new vision of God as holy and of myself as a sinner. I realized that I had allowed sinful attitudes into my life that blunted the power of the Holy Spirit.

Almost ten years after I was converted, I was in a far country. God knew that and set about to bring me back to my first love, Jesus, my Savior and Lord. I was overjoyed to catch an entirely new vision of the cross of Christ and found there the answer to my longing heart.

After that the Holy Spirit began to probe me, "Do you believe that the statements of Jesus in the Bible are his statements?" Ouch! I have learned that many of God's people have come to this point of crisis.

> *Lord, you know that I hesitated at first*
> *because I found the world you talked about*
> *a very strange world to me.*
> *But you enabled me to lay down my defenses and simply believe.*
> *You made me a believer. All glory to you.*

Jesus Removes Masks

Nothing in all creation is hidden from God's sight (4:13)

I have lots of masks. One of them has a huge smile painted on it. I put that on when I am in the dumps. People like me should never be in the dumps, right? We should be praising God constantly, shouldn't we? So, on goes the mask. It makes me feel a bit more secure.

I know there is a much better way to get a smile back on my face. I simply turn to Jesus with my hurts and wounds and confess the sins that bring on unbelief or self-accusation.

I am learning that it is absolute nonsense to wear a mask before God. He is never fooled. I am also learning that he is not interested in giving me one mask to replace another. He goes right to the heart of the issue. He is not at all interested in superficial remedies. His Word exposes the root cause in such a ruthless fashion that it almost feels like God is rejecting me. But that couldn't be further from the truth. It's actually proof that he loves me and will allow nothing to come between us.

I also have a nice religious mask, the one I am tempted to put on when I am around "saints" or when I am teaching or preaching. That mask has a halo on it. I love that mask. But it is not me. The real me has my eyes, my nose, my mouth, my everything. The real me is a grateful, transformed, redeemed sinner, made a saint by the wonder-working power of the atoning work of Christ. That is a me I can live with.

Jesus, I bring all my masks to you. I need them no longer.

Jesus, My Light

Nothing in all creation is hidden from God's sight (4:13)

I can be changed only when I am willing to live in the light, with God and with people, without a mask.

I think of Jesus as he entered Gethsemane. The disciples saw him overcome with sorrow. It was so evident and profound that they feared that he might die of that sorrow. Jesus refused to put on a smiling mask when his heart was breaking. We have no way of comprehending the weight of that sorrow.

He knew in his heart of hearts that he dreaded the prospect of going to the cross as God's Lamb. "My Father," he said, "if it is possible, may this cup be taken from me" (Matthew 26:39). There is no mask there. Jesus was pouring out his heart, telling his Father exactly how he felt.

I do not think it is always helpful to put on a show, so to speak, to let the world know that I am happy, frustrated, distressed, or sad. It is not always a good thing to blare out exactly how I feel. But it is even more dangerous to tell myself, "I feel this way," when I do not. The most helpful thing is for me to admit how I feel, even if I am embarrassed by it. It is good to own my feelings. That is the beginning of changing how I feel. Denying how I feel about something is walking in darkness.

"Nothing . . . is hidden from God," we read. So why should I try to hide something from myself?

> *Lord, when you were sad, you expressed that sadness.*
> *When you were full of joy, it showed.*
> *Help me to be as honest as that.*

Jesus, Our Great High Priest

**We have a great high priest who has gone through the heavens,
Jesus the Son of God (4:14)**

We have a high priest.

As I think of the role of the high priest in the old covenant, I try to put myself in his shoes. He had to be from the tribe of priests, the Levites, a group set aside to link people with God. They were not allowed to own land. God appointed them to administer the cities of refuge, places to which people guilty of inadvertent manslaughter could run and be protected from their accusers. But the Levites' major official function was to serve as priests. They offered sacrifices to God for the sins of the people. They did this by turns. As sinners themselves, they offered sacrifices for themselves first, then for the people.

Because the priests were to represent God among the people, they had to study to find out who God is and what he does. They pored over the Scriptures. A good priest would spend as much time pondering the nature of God as he did attending the rituals of sacrifice and making offerings for the sins of the people.

In short, a good priest knew the heart of God—his holiness, his justice, his love, his mercy, and his grace. He also knew what was in the hearts of the people. That must have been a stretch—to affirm the character of God while at the same time sympathizing with human weakness and yearnings. Can anyone ever do that perfectly?

Lord Jesus, you are my high priest.
Even though you are from the kingly,
*   not priestly, tribe, you are a true Levite.*
You know the heart of God and you know mine.
Your grace brings me to God.

Priest and King

We have a great high priest who has gone through the heavens,
Jesus the Son of God (4:14)

God established the priesthood as the primary way to administer grace to his people. As already noted, he chose the tribe of Levi, a comparatively large tribe, to stand in the gap between himself and the people.

One might expect that the people would choose and appoint priests to represent them before God. That is not what happened under the old covenant. God chose the priests and appointed them to represent him among the people. Then from among all the priests he appointed one to a special role, to represent all the priests. The high priest represented the entire nation on one hand, God and all of heaven on the other.

The first to fill this awesome role was Aaron. To be sure, Aaron knew the people, perhaps too well. He went along with their demands for a leader to replace Moses. Aaron also knew the character of God, at least to some degree. So Aaron was qualified to be God's appointed high priest. This points to Jesus Christ.

Jesus was appointed as the eternal high priest. His job was to stretch out two hands, holding God's hand in one and the peoples' hand with the other. That forms a cross.

You, Jesus, are uniquely qualified to be my high priest,
for you know the extent of my need
and you know the heart of God.

Jesus Went Through the Heavens

**We have a great high priest who has gone through the heavens,
Jesus the Son of God (4:14)**

I recall my first official visit with Tanzania's President Julius Nyerere. I was bishop of the Tanzania Mennonite Church at the time. As I waited with others outside his office, the door opened and a smiling Nyerere said, "Come in, bishop." I tell you, there is a huge difference between sitting with those who are waiting and being inside with the president himself.

Jesus went in. Having shed his life's blood, he appeared in glory to present himself to all heaven. He had arrived. At once the hosts of heaven gathered about this most sacred sight, Jesus Christ standing there, victorious, God's atoning Lamb that was slain. He did it! All heaven shouted, "Worthy is the Lamb."

It remained for Jesus as high priest to go through the veil and present his own blood before almighty God—"He entered the Most Holy Place once for all by his own blood" (Hebrews 9:12). The Bible does not record God's words when Jesus entered, but we know without a doubt that he received Jesus with heavenly joy, for then it was possible for him to forgive sins.

The excruciating work of obtaining eternal redemption for us was done. Jesus entered into his rest. Jesus, bless him, "has gone through the heavens." And all the hosts of heaven added their amens to the song, "Worthy is the Lamb."

We hear not one dissenting voice in heaven or earth or under the earth, or in the sea.

*Jesus, thank you for going through that curtain of separation
into the blazing presence of the Holy God,
by your blood for me.*

Jesus, the Breaker of Barriers

We have a great high priest who has gone through the heavens,
Jesus the Son of God (4:14)

What good is a high priest if he never goes through that curtain? Today's text declares that our great high priest "has gone through the heavens."

Micah foresaw the Son of God as a breaker of walls: "The breaker is come up before them: they have broken up, and have passed through the gate" (Micah 2:13 KJV).

I like that picture of Jesus breaking down the walls that separate the sinner from God. He continues to break down walls by the power of his atoning blood.

On their annual entrances, Jewish high priests may have tarried before the altar for a moment and then rushed out. But Jesus went in and stayed in. He entered without fear, knowing that his atoning work fully satisfied God.

The high priests were greatly relieved when they emerged alive from the awesome holy of holies. They were never quite sure if they were doing everything just right in preparing the offering. They knew if they emerged alive it was a sign that God accepted the sacrifice. Contrast that with Jesus, who remained inside forever because his atoning work was perfect. He knew that.

> *As I think of this, Jesus, I would not have you stay*
> *in the outer court of my life;*
> *instead I invite you to break every veil*
> *that hinders your full access to my life.*
> *Jesus, please "go through" me, every area, every part.*
> *I need you to break down every barrier between me and God.*
> *Come in and never leave.*

Jesus Is God's Son

Jesus the Son of God (4:14)

I confess that I can read today's verse without the slightest astonishment. Why doesn't it startle me like it did the readers of this letter? I must tell myself emphatically that this is the most consequential phrase ever uttered by lips or heard by ears.

Jesus is not one of God's sons; he is God's only son. There simply is no other. He is the only one who was Son of God and Son of man.

We in America are very much aware of terrorism. This fear causes some to rethink who Jesus is. Is he unique? The implication is that if Christians would just relax and admit that there are many ways to God, then the major grievance that Muslims have against Christians would be removed.

As I listen and watch the western media, I am led to believe that it is just fine to talk about God in our culture, because God-talk is inoffensive except, perhaps to atheists. But it is impolite and untactful to speak of Jesus Christ, because just to mention the name of Jesus is considered to be divisive.

People ask me, Are not God and Allah the same? The question could also be asked, Are not the Buddha and God the same? The idea is, if they are all the same, then why make a fuss over Jesus? Each religion has its prophets. God has many sons, they say.

The Gospel writers echo the song of heaven. Worthy is Jesus, for he alone was slain to deal with the cosmic problem of sin.

> *Son of God, your very existence enrages the wrath*
> *of unbelieving mankind.*
> *My heart is fixed. You are "Jesus, the Son of God."*

The Son Reveals the Father

Jesus the Son of God (4:14)

Jesus came to abolish the idea that God is unknowable. Jesus tells us exactly what God feels, thinks, and does. He put it simply, "The words I say to you are not just my own. Rather, it is the Father, living in me, who is doing his work" (John 14:10).

The words and work that Jesus mentioned are the centerpieces of his service, the atoning sacrifice through which God now offers forgiveness of sin and new life through the Holy Spirit to all who will believe. That is straight from the heart of God. The atonement is God's greatest thought and his greatest gift to mankind.

Remove the incarnation and the atonement from the Christian faith and what is left? The dread of a God who is unknowable, all-powerful, unpredictable. That is hell on earth.

I have noticed that, like Islam, the major Christian heresies invariably attack the incarnation of Jesus and his blood atonement. Each generation sees a new assault on the heart of the gospel, which is that Jesus is God's only begotten Son and that he died to atone for my sin. They all claim to have a new insight that enables them to acknowledge Jesus Christ as an important person while denying the incarnation and atonement.

> *Jesus, give me compassion for those*
> *who feel obligated to destroy you.*
> *Help me to see them as candidates for your all-sufficient grace,*
> *which will change everything for them as it has for me.*

Jesus, God's Maligned Son

**Since we have ... Jesus the Son of God, let us hold firmly
to the faith we profess (4:14)**

The warning we see here in the book of Hebrews is as timely today as it ever was. To "hold firmly to the faith we profess" means to hold on to Jesus as he is set forth in the Scriptures and as the church has known him for many centuries.

It is not easy to buck the tide. The easy way is to cave in and lose hold of Jesus Christ because of external pressure.

How thankful I am that I had the privilege of walking beside modern heroes of the faith. Archbishop Janani Luwum springs to mind. We were attending a conference together in 1975 when he confided to me that things were not well in Uganda. Yet he was planning for a conference to commemorate one hundred years of Christianity in that beautiful land. Janani invited me to attend and fastened a little pin on my collar to remind me of the event.

Within months President Idi Amin turned his irrational wrath on the church, accusing it of undermining his power. Amin commanded Janani to appear before him. Janani confronted Amin in the name of Christ, and he paid for it with his life.

I was deeply saddened to hear of Janani's death, but I was not surprised. I knew he had a firm grip on Jesus. He died rather than loosen that grip. He died holding on to Jesus, as Jesus held on to him.

The pin Janani gave me still reminds me of the cost of following Jesus.

*Lord, teach me to live as Janani died,
holding firmly to Jesus Christ.*

Hold on to Jesus

Let us hold firmly to the faith we profess (4:14)

In the French Jura mountains lies a magnificent waterfall. The best way to get to it is through a pedestrian tunnel. That should be no problem, but it is no ordinary tunnel. For some reason it has a bend in the middle. As you enter, you can look back and see the light but not ahead. Until you pass the bend there is no light where you are going. So it is necessary to walk in total darkness for a while, unless you have a light with you. That is when it is important to hold on to Jesus.

In our journey, now and again we are called on to pass through tunnels like that. God wills it so, in order that we learn to rely on his power, not our own. Every disciple of Jesus Christ passes through pitch dark tunnels when it is only Jesus and me, so to speak.

Jesus is no stranger to tunnels. Calvary was a bend in his tunnel. "At the sixth hour darkness came over the whole land until the ninth hour. And at the ninth hour Jesus cried out in a loud voice, . . . 'My God, my God, why have you forsaken me?'" (Mark 15:33-34). Thick darkness. Alone. Dreadful.

Jesus died alone so that as we pass through our tunnels we will never be alone. He is with us there.

When darkness descends on me, Lord Jesus,
and I can see no light, please grasp my hand tighter.
Together we will walk into the light of day.

Jesus, My Sympathetic High Priest

**We do not have a high priest who is unable to sympathize
with our weaknesses (4:15)**

When Moses tarried on the mountain, the people became restless because they thought they had lost their leader. They assumed that after forty days up there on a barren mountain called Sinai, he was surely dead. Aaron, their temporary leader, knew exactly how they felt. When they proposed making a gold calf, an Egyptian deity, Aaron went along with the idea, though he knew better. His sympathetic nature became his weakness. His sympathy blinded his eyes to the sinfulness of it all. It is good to sympathize with people, but it can also be dangerous.

Because he lived in the flesh, Jesus, our great high priest, knows our weaknesses and sympathizes with us in a way that no human can. He knows exactly how it feels to be a frail human being. But his sympathy never indulges sin. Were he to simply turn a blind eye to our sin because of his sympathy, we would be doomed. His sympathy opens the door to hope because he has provided, in his atoning blood, the way to live with weakness without sinning.

A few years ago I found myself in such deep sympathy with a person that I lost perspective for a bit. My sympathy was blinding my eyes to see the only thing that would help, the cross of Christ. I remembered the advice of a wise brother, "Push people up against the cross where they can get the help they need."

Jesus, your sympathy never makes an excuse for sin
but provides a way to be set free from sin.
Thank you, Lord, for that.

Jesus, My Confidence

Let us then approach the throne of grace with confidence (4:16)

How can I enter into the presence of God?

God is holy; I am unholy. God is love; I am self-centered. God is powerful; I am weak. How can the huge gulf between God and me be bridged?

This was a challenge for God too. On the one hand, God's love compels him to be among his people. On the other hand, he cannot abide mankind's chronic rebellion and self-centeredness.

Listen to his frustration: "Tell the Israelites, 'You are a stiff-necked people. If I were to go with you even for a moment, I might destroy you'" (Exodus 33:5). God became so exasperated with the rebellious children of Israel that he told Moses to go on alone. Moses must have felt something of God's pathos. God relented and went with them, but Moses knew the anguish of God's soul.

God devised a way to live with his covenant people, and it was a blood sacrifice that made it possible. God prescribed a mercy seat to cover the altar. There between two cherubim he would be present. Once a year, on the Day of Atonement, the designated high priest bore the blood of the national sacrifice. He stood for a moment before God and sprinkled the blood on the mercy seat.

God was foretelling the day when a more worthy blood would be spilled, the blood of his only begotten Son, Jesus. Then God would welcome sinners without passing judgment on them.

> *God in heaven, thank you*
> *for making a way for me to kneel in your presence.*
> *It is possible because of the atoning work of Jesus.*

Jesus at My Side

Let us then approach the throne of grace with confidence (4:16)

In the African cultures with which I am familiar, you dare not rush into the presence of an honored elder with insistent demands. Rather, the supplicant approaches the elder with humble decorum, sometimes touching his or her forehead to the earth.

It is with similar awe that I approach my heavenly Father. But God calms my fears as he reminds me that I stand before him in the name of his dear Son. Not only that, but Jesus is there at my side all the time. He stands with me as I praise, pray, and worship.

I hear the voice of my loving Father say, "Come near, for when I see you, I see my Son, Jesus, who covers you with his righteousness. Because of what your elder brother, Christ, has done, the store-houses of heaven are open to you. I will shower on you all the blessings of the atoning work of Christ. So draw near, dear one, and let me open the windows of heaven for you."

He continues, "My son, my daughter, do you have absolute and unquestioning faith in what Jesus has done and can do for you? Do you have full confidence in Jesus? If so, come near because I know much more than you and I am confident that all he has promised he is amply able to do."

> *God, with faith and boldness I enter,*
> *knowing without a doubt that I have worth*
> *because of the worthiness of Jesus.*
> *My Father, please supply all my needs*
> *through the grace of my Lord Jesus Christ.*

May 13

Jesus, My Atonement

The throne of grace (4:16)

For years I have pondered the tabernacle. Every time I do so, my mind and heart tarry longest at the amazing throne of grace. I am aware that the One who sits on it judges according to the law that rests under the seat, the immutable law of God. I know that I have transgressed the law.

I dread God's wrath, yet I need his blessings. As I wrestle with the pull and tug of this bewildering problem, I know that God cannot pronounce me innocent simply because he pities me. He cannot contradict himself. The law that is written on tables of permanent stone is stamped on everything in the universe. The law is a description of how the One who created the universe designed things. My rebellion against God is not a trivial flaw that can be overlooked and winked at, but a breach of the law on which all else rests.

It is against this backdrop that I see Jesus, God's own specially prepared Lamb, freely and willingly offering himself to take my sin upon himself and in some inexplicable way, suffer the consequences of my sin in his own body, crucified instead of me. My mind falters at this point, but my faith does not. Jesus entered the heavenly holy place where he applied his own blood to the throne of justice, making it a mercy seat. God can extend mercy because Jesus bore away my sin.

> *God, I bow in holy reverence as I see the mystery revealed.*
> *Look upon me as a thankful sinner,*
> *saved by your astounding grace.*

Jesus, the Master Timer

**So that we may receive mercy and find grace to help us in our time of need
(4:16)**

On a recent plane trip I asked my seatmate what he does for a living, as is my custom. He told me he is a jit consultant. "What," I asked "is 'jit'? Is it a new vehicle or a cleaning product?"

"No, no," he answered. "Jit means 'just in time.'" He explained that, to save money, some companies don't hold an inventory of parts, but instead have the parts delivered at the precise moment when they are needed to assemble a product. However, if for some reason an item does not arrive on time, the loss can be enormous. He said he was responsible for making sure all parties communicated perfectly and faithfully. "Communication is the key," he said.

I see that I must stay in communication with God at all times, through prayer, faith, and obedience. In that way, all heaven is mobilized to meet my need and the needs of all those who are disciples of Jesus.

Jesus has mercy and grace specifically prepared to be available to me in my "time of need." I need to remember that God had salvation perfectly prepared for me long before I needed it. Paul wrote, "You see, at just the right time, when we were still powerless, Christ died for the ungodly" (Romans 5:6). I rejoice in the phrase "just at the right time."

> *God, you are the Lord of time.*
> *You are never late in delivering any of your unwarranted*
> *but most-welcome graces.*

Jesus Is Merciful

Receive mercy and find grace (4:16)

There is a huge difference between receiving and finding. The most obvious is that one is passive while the other is active. Receiving mercy is passive. Finding grace is active.

The argument goes something like this: I sinned against God so he has the right to judge me. It is futile for me to even try to prove that it is not so. I deserve judgment and there is absolutely nothing that I can do to remove the sentence. My fate is in the hands of the Judge.

As I stand before the Judge, I hear him say, "The sentence I must give you is death. However, so that you may live and not die, I will take your sentence upon myself and die to its consequences. Then I can pardon you." That is precisely what happened when the Son of God/Son of man climbed Calvary's hill. My sentence was nailed to that cross for all to see. Jesus was crucified in a very public place. There my Judge took on himself and his body the consequences of my sinfulness. The wrath of God fell on my sin in Jesus.

That is why it is possible for the Judge of all to grant me mercy. Through Jesus, mercy is available. I need only to claim it and give my life to him. I do not find mercy, but mercy finds me. I am the glad object of God's work of redemption.

Thank you, God, for having mercy on me.
Jesus died for me on Calvary's cross.
Help me, Jesus, to keep that ever before my eyes.

Jesus Is Gracious

Receive mercy and find grace (4:16)

I "receive" mercy, but grace does not come like that. I must seek after and "find" grace. That means I must deliberately place my need before the Father, pray for grace to meet that need, then apply that grace where it is needed. Because of the atoning work of Jesus, I have every right to God's grace, but I must diligently seek it with all my heart, soul, and strength. That is humbling.

As a disciple of Christ, I meet one challenge after another. I know that God has sufficient grace to meet all my needs, but he expects me to plead for grace for each particular need. For me to be a candidate for his grace I must, as the hymn puts it, "trust and obey, for there is no other way."

As I face the challenge of aging, for example, I dare not simply drop everything, throw myself on the couch, and say, "Okay, God. My work is done. You take care of everything from here on in. I deserve a break. You bring grace to me!"

No, I must be an active participant in the walk of grace. That means that as I follow Christ, I will seek new grace for each new circumstance.

> *God, I am always and forever in need of the grace*
> *that flows from Calvary's tree.*
> *I anticipate grace. I live by it and am energized by it.*
> *I seek for grace, and by grace I find it and it is sweet.*
> *It is true, I receive mercy but I must seek grace.*
> *Lord, keep me finding grace!*

Jesus Knows People

**Every high priest is selected from among men and is appointed
to represent them in matters related to God (5:1)**

I stand amazed as I ponder the unthinkable—how God almighty compressed himself, so to speak, into the man Jesus. Jesus not only knows us through and through, somewhat like a doctor knows the patient, but he has himself experienced our infirmities in his own body. No religions dare make this claim about any of their prophets and leaders. Jesus is unique. The incarnation was a one-time event. Jesus was not just a prophet sent by God; he was God.

Why did Jesus become a person just like me? One reason was that he might fully sympathize with my frailty. But I know that sympathy, even Jesus' sympathy, cannot rescue me from my sinful condition. What help is pity if I am about to perish? I need to be saved, not just pitied or loved. I need eternal life, not sympathy.

This brings me to the point of today's verse. Jesus knows the "matters related to God," his Father. He knows what moves the heart of the Father. He knows the extent of God's justice and his love. He knows how God suffers and how much God desires to have fellowship with rebellious people.

> *Jesus, I rejoice because as my priest you represent*
> *the Father to me and you represent me to the Father.*
> *You are my worthy priest,*
> *and I rest in the effects of your atoning work.*
> *You know me and you know the Father.*
> *Through the Holy Spirit, remind me of this daily.*

Jesus Knows His Father

**Every high priest is selected from among men and is appointed
to represent them in matters related to God (5:1)**

Jesus, our high priest, knows God perfectly. This distinguishes him from Aaron, the first high priest. Aaron did not need to take a course on human weakness. He knew all about that. But he failed the course on knowing God when he joined the rebellious people in the fashioning of an Egyptian god to lead them. Aaron sympathized with the people so deeply that he joined them. He could see no way to save the people from their waywardness. He did not believe that God would do in the wilderness what he did in Egypt. So, in his unbelief he participated in fashioning an idol, the golden calf of Egypt.

Jesus is greater than Aaron. He knows us better than Aaron knew his people. He knew he had to die for us so the sins that separate us from God can be forgiven. He did this for us so we can enjoy the most precious thing, peace with God.

Jesus also knows what is in God's storehouse of mercy and grace, which he is eager to pour out to assist all those who call on him. Jesus knows his Father, he knows us, and he knows the power of his redeeming work. That makes him a high priest on whom we can rely with full confidence, forever.

I praise your name, Jesus.
Knowing the heart of God on the one hand
and my hopelessness on the other,
you satisfied in your atoning work both God and us.
That reconciling work was perfect.

Jesus, One of Us

He is able to deal gently with those who are ignorant and are going astray
(5:2)

It is no good sending an angel from heaven to represent man to God and God to man. What do angels know about human weakness? It takes a human being to understand fully the extent of human frailty.

As a missionary I tried my best to walk alongside the people I was called to serve. Those African cultures were so different from my own that I really had to work at it. Time and time again I thought I was beginning to understand their fears, hopes, hurts, and longings, only to discover that I could go only so far with them in their own world. I often stood baffled because I simply could not follow the logic they found meaningful. God never feels that way.

My heart leaps for joy when I think that God in the flesh, Jesus Christ, understands my condition, in my culture. He is all-knowing, not just because he is God, but because he became a person like me, first in the womb, then as an infant, as a boy, as a working man, as a prophet of God, as my Savior. I will never have a problem that is strange to Jesus. He was tempted on all levels, just as I am tempted. That embraces all cultures. Our Lord understands my African friend just as he understands me.

> *Lord Jesus, my exalted high priest,*
> *you are never confounded by my complexity,*
> *for you are just like me.*
> *You love me, you change me,*
> *and you present me to our heavenly Father.*
> *Joy unspeakable!*

Jesus, the Humble High Priest

Christ . . . did not take upon himself the glory of becoming a high priest
(5:5)

I come from a line of Mennonite clergymen. My maternal great-grandfather, Samuel Blough, served God and the church as a bishop. He strengthened the Mennonite churches in Northern Somerset County of Pennsylvania in the years after the Civil War.

My mother, his granddaughter, kept reminding us of his determination to serve God with all his heart. Her favorite story was about a terribly cold winter day when he arrived on horseback to preach at one of the churches. He was unable to dismount because, after the long ride in harsh conditions, he could barely move. They carefully removed him from his horse and took him inside, where they thawed him slowly at their stove. When he was able to move again he ministered the Word of God to them. According to my mother, his early death was brought on by his relentless determination to serve God. He knew the calling of God in his life.

I doubt that Bishop Blough ever hankered after a position of leadership in the church. In that culture it was no small matter to be called by God. They used the lot method then to choose their ministers and bishops, and it was a day to dread when the lot "fell" on a person. It was unseemly to want to lead the church. That was considered to be proud. Stories are told of intense and prolonged weeping as the "chosen one" felt the heavy hand of God calling him to a ministry.

Jesus, you knew what was ahead of you
when you determined to fulfill your calling.
Thank you for paying the price.

Jesus, the Humble Servant

Christ ... did not take upon himself the glory of becoming a high priest
(5:5)

I cannot vouch for what the called ones of old felt in their hearts, but the outward response was dramatic proof that they did not feel worthy to be chosen. The responsibility was a heavy weight on their shoulders, a dreaded task.

For Jesus, it was not a matter of feigning humility. He knew the suffering that lay before him. Unlike Jewish high priests, who served in a splendid temple, decked out in dazzling apparel, Jesus "did not take upon himself the glory of becoming a high priest." In fact, he laid aside his robe of privilege as God's Son and wore the robe of a lowly servant as the Son of man. The suffering he then endured had not one tinge of glory. It was humiliation, rejection, and that horrid death on a criminal's cross.

I see here the sign of a true high priest. He did not seek the glory of the office. He sought only to follow God. Jesus humbled himself so that he could glorify his Father.

Jesus did not live a life of privilege. He engaged Satan in fierce combat. He persisted in his calling in spite of mockery, shame, and rejection. That had not one shred of glory about it. First the crown of thorns, only then the scepter of glory.

Thank you, Jesus, for despising the shame
to become my high priest.

Jesus Prays Earnestly

He offered up prayers and petitions with loud cries and tears (5:7)

I know little of praying "with loud cries and tears." My praying is usually a very benign affair. I bring to God my thanksgiving, my faith, my love, and my devotion, then I remind him of the needs of others and my own needs as well. It is all done in a spirit of cautious reverence. Maybe at times Jesus prayed like that when he retreated to a quiet place to fellowship with his Father in heaven. He always came away refreshed, energized and full of faith.

So what about this reference to Jesus pleading with his Father with "loud cries and tears"? I believe it refers to that hour when Jesus reached his extremity. He left the upper room, knowing that in the next minutes he must decide whether or not to proceed as a "lamb to the slaughter." He took with him Peter, James, and John and retreated to what was probably a familiar place to him, the garden of Gethsemane, just east of Jerusalem. The disciples were astonished at the change that came over Jesus. Luke wrote, "And being in an agony he prayed more earnestly: and his sweat was as it were great drops of blood falling down to the ground" (Luke 22:44 KJV) Is this not praying "with loud cries and tears"? I hear only anguish of soul.

> *Lord Jesus, you were crushed in that valley of decision.*
> *Then I see that the agony of your spirit subsided*
> *   as you cried out to God,*
> *Not my will but thine be done.*
> *The loud cries and tears ceased.*

Jesus, My Intercessor

He offered up prayers and petitions with loud cries and tears (5:7)

The sorrow that overcame Jesus in the garden was something extraordinary. It was of a different nature than his sorrow earlier in the week when, as Jesus approached the city from the east, he was overcome with grief. Tears flowed down his cheeks. He wept over Jerusalem because that city established by God as his witness to the nations preferred to kill their prophets rather than repent. No city on earth enjoyed the favor of God more than Jerusalem. What Jesus saw moved him deeply. Tears flowed from his eyes.

I think I understand Jesus' sympathy and concern. But I can scarcely understand the sorrow of Gethsemane when Jesus faced the tragedy of the cross. There he faced the excruciating pain of dying to his self-will. He had to be willing to take on the sin not only of Jerusalem but of all mankind and to die of crucifixion on a Roman cross as God's Paschal Lamb. Who can plumb the depths of that sorrow? It taxed Jesus to the limit. In his extremity he confided with his three friends, Peter, James, and John, "My soul is overwhelmed with sorrow to the point of death" (Mark 14:34).

Too often, I forget what it cost to break the dominion of sin in my life. My peace with God was accomplished with loud cries and tears—not my own, but those of Jesus.

Jesus, my Savior, I thank you with all my soul, heart, and body
for those precious tears that mingled
with the "blood of the everlasting covenant."
Give me grace to tarry in the garden with you
so that I might know the demands of sacrificial love.

Jesus Abandons His Own Will

**He offered up prayers and petitions . . . to the one who could save him
from death, and he was heard because of his reverent submission (5:7)**

Some verses jangle the mind and heart. This is one. The writer tells of Jesus' agonizing prayers in the garden, marked by loud cries and tears. Never did a man pray so powerfully or so insistently. And this was no ordinary man; he was Jesus Christ, God's precious Son. And the hearer was God himself. Certainly that prayer would be heard and quickly answered. So when the writer of this letter says, "He was heard," we might conclude that God saved Jesus from death on the cross. But we all know that was not the case. Jesus died. Had he not died, there would be no atonement.

So what is the heart of this truth? Listen to Jesus pouring out his heart in the most earnest prayer that was ever prayed: "My Father, if it is possible, may this cup be taken from me" (Matthew 26:39). The Father had the power to take it away. He "could save him from death." Yet in his heart of hearts, Jesus knew that the Lamb of God must give up his life, that he must die. Agony indeed!

If I can be so bold, may I say it in my own words. Jesus pleaded to be spared from the death that awaited him. The Father heard his agonizing Son. He heard, and answered, "No, there is no other way!"

God often answers prayer with a simple, "No. There is no other way." Jesus' prayer was answered. The answer was no.

Lord, may I be willing to accept such an answer as "No. Trust me."

Jesus Reveals the Heart of God

**He offered up prayers and petitions ... to the one who could save him
from death, and he was heard because of his reverent submission (5:7)**

The Father knows our anguish. He hears our pleas. He understands precisely how we expect him to answer our prayers. No one understands us like our Father. His sympathy is perfect.

Nevertheless, our Father is not driven by sympathy. He knows what will be the best for us and best for his glory. God often surprises his children who are maturing in faith by not answering their prayers in any way like they want him to. Instead he does a mightier work by doing something marvelous through their submissive spirits.

When I graduated from Eastern Mennonite High School, we chose as our class motto, "Not my will but thine be done." Each graduate received a hand-painted picture on glass of Jesus praying in the garden with those words inscribed.

Little did I know how much I needed to ponder that verse as I too prayed earnestly many times, "Father, this is what I want. I have no doubt that you can do it exactly as I wish. Nevertheless I submit my will to yours. Do what is best for your glory." That prayer brings peace of heart and mind.

> *My God, I have discovered that you answer prayers*
> *in line with your perfect purposes.*
> *I am amazed that the answers are always*
> *for my ultimate good as well.*
> *What is good for you, my God, is ultimately good for me.*

Jesus, the Promised Red Heifer

**Once made perfect, he became the source of eternal salvation
for all who obey him (5:9)**

Under the old covenant (which always points to the new) people chose the best sacrificial animals they had. Their transgressions against God were so serious that nothing but the best would suffice. It would be unthinkable to give God the weak, injured, infirm, or old. That would trivialize sin. The more they recognized the gravity of sin, the more diligent they were to seek out and offer the very best they had—even though it meant depriving themselves of the benefits of having first-rate animals. Those they sacrificed to God.

God knows the frightening consequences of sin better than we do. Perfect redemption requires a perfect sacrifice.

Roy Hession of England, a beloved mentor of mine, described how the Jews must have longed for the day when a perfect red heifer would appear among their herds. The more perfect the heifer, some calculated, the more God must take notice and forgive sin. So each generation looked for the perfect red heifer, for if one could be produced, that would be the end of the sacrificial system.

As it was, no matter how diligent they were by controlling breeding and so on, they never managed to produce one red heifer that did not have a few black or white hairs here or there. Therefore, each year they offered an "almost perfect" sacrifice. They lived in hope that one day they could produce a heifer with 100 percent red hair. Their hopes were smashed as each year they failed to find one.

*Jesus Christ, in the fullness of time you appeared,
the perfect red heifer. That is the end of that!*

Jesus, the Perfect Sacrifice

**Once made perfect, he became the source of eternal salvation
for all who obey him (5:9)**

The Jews surveyed their herd, looking for the best yearling they had. When they identified that one, they removed it from the herd and delivered it up for a sacrifice. They offered their best.

Jesus was pronounced to be without spot and blameless. He was without sin. He was the long-anticipated red heifer, perfect in every way. So, in a sense, he was intrinsically perfect. But he was not the perfect sacrifice until he actually gave up his life in death on the cross.

That is the reason for the agony of the atonement. Jesus had obeyed his Father in everything. As Son of man, he was tempted just as we are, yet he did not sin. No blemish of disobedience could be found on him. That infuriated Satan. That is why he dangled every temptation before Christ, knowing that the moment Jesus would think or do anything contrary to the will of his Father in heaven, the sacrifice would be flawed.

All the furies of hell turned on Jesus as he faced the cross. Satan turned the screws tighter and tighter as Jesus came closer and closer to that moment when he, the righteous Son of God, would become sin for us. That is why we hear loud cries and the soft drip of hot tears breaking the silence of Gethsemane's night.

> *Jesus, although you were God's Son,*
> > *you learned obedience by the things that you suffered.*
> *You gave your life freely in love.*
> *That finished the perfecting work.*

Jesus Helps Me to Obey

He became the source of eternal salvation for all who obey him (5:9)

Because Jesus obeyed, I am saved. I owe a huge love debt to Jesus. It would be brutish of me to turn my back on him, thanking him for saving my soul, then going on my merry, self-centered way, refusing to do what he asks me to do. That is not his way!

I need to be reminded of this central historical and spiritual fact: my soul is eternally secure in Christ because he obeyed his Father, even in the most strenuous circumstances. I suppose we could say that Jesus "earned" our salvation by his obedience, but I believe it goes much deeper than that.

Jesus guarded his intimate relationship with his Father. Both Father and Son knew that any rebelliousness on the part of Jesus would shatter that unity. The Father and the Son, and the Spirit were one before the universe was formed. Jesus did not obey so that he could qualify to be God's Son; he was God's Son and as such he wished to obey.

I believe it should be that way with me. By the miracle-working power of his atoning sacrifice, Jesus enters my life and abides there. He and his Father are one, therefore he knows the voice of his Father, but I, on my own, do not. Christ in me always responds to his Father in love and obedience. That is my hope and joy.

As a hymn puts it, "My hope is built on nothing less than Jesus' blood and righteousness."

> *My Jesus, you are the perfect sacrifice,*
> *for you were perfected through being offered entirely to God.*
> *That divine perfection is my hope and security.*

Jesus, Our Eternal Salvation

He became the source of eternal salvation for all who obey him (5:9)

Does this mean I am saved by my obedience to Jesus? Horrors. That was the great heresy of the Jews. I cannot earn salvation by obedience any more than they could. Yet I cannot leave obedience out of the equation. It is tied in some way to my eternal salvation.

The answer is to be found in the mystery of what the apostle Paul called "Christ in me." He wrote, "For it is God who works in you to will and to act according to his good purpose" (Philippians 2:13).

Jesus in me is both my will to obey and the power to obey. What I am coming to realize is that I cannot even want to do what God wishes unless he puts into my heart the desire to want to. My rebellious ego hates the idea of submitting to anyone but myself. That is what I inherited in my "sin DNA." It is a bondage that can be broken only by inviting Jesus into my life and abdicating the throne so he can reign. He is eager to obey his Father in me.

At times I find that I have a bad attitude. It is easy for me to either deny it or make excuses for it. I am not willing to own it and go to Jesus with it. That is when I need help. I am finding that, as I bring my unwillingness to Jesus, he becomes my willingness. That is a special grace for which I will be eternally thankful.

> *Praise your name, my Jesus,*
> *for being willing to reside in me.*
> *You are my willingness to obey the Father*
> *and the power to put that obedience into action.*

May 30

Jesus, Always Preparing for Harvest

**[Jesus] was designated by God to be high priest
in the order of Melchizedek (5:10)**

Melchizedek appeared on the scene after Abraham was victorious in battle. When Abraham was returning home victorious, he met this person who figures prominently in Hebrews. "Then Melchizedek king of Salem brought out bread and wine. He was priest of God Most High, and he blessed Abram, saying, 'Blessed be Abram by God Most High, Creator of heaven and earth. And blessed be God Most High, who delivered your enemies into your hand.' Then Abram gave him a tenth of everything" (Genesis 14:18-20).

I am surprised that the author of this letter, who is writing to the Jews, made reference to a non-Jew who served as a priest of Yahweh six hundred years before Aaron, the first Jewish priest. What makes this man so important? We will try to figure that out as we go.

As a missionary I often wondered how the grace of God works. I lived among people who did not have the witness of the gospel until two or three generations ago, some of them only in this generation. Does that mean God neglected them? I think not. I believe that God is not without a witness in any culture in the world. Nature itself is a strong witness of the grace of God. In addition, God has placed people in all cultures who have some idea of his existence, like Melchizedek. I call this "preparatory grace," and it is marvelous. There are men and women like Melchizedek in every culture, eager to know the love of God in Christ Jesus. When they see Jesus, they embrace him totally.

*Lord, thank you for bringing this to my attention
as I ministered in your name in Africa.
You prepared the soil. I enjoyed the harvest.*

150

Jesus, Our Melchizedek

**[Jesus] was designated by God to be high priest
in the order of Melchizedek (5:10)**

I see the old Jewish cocoon splitting, ever so slowly. Out of Israel will come, in full glory, like a spring butterfly, the great high priest, Jesus Christ of Nazareth, my Savior, my Lord, and my priest. He will joyfully break open all the boxes that limit the grace of God. Jesus is not like Caiaphas, who was high priest at the time of Christ, or even like Aaron, but like Melchizedek.

As we ponder the verse again, we see it was God himself who called and appointed Melchizedek. Abraham did not do that. When it came to Aaron's calling, God appointed him, but through Moses, who had a hand in installing Aaron. Not so with Melchizedek. He was "designated" by God himself. I understand that the Hebrew word used in this instance means "acknowledged." He was acknowledged by God to be high priest because he was high priest by character. His calling simply affirmed and acknowledged what he already was.

My spirit rejoices when I muse over the wonder of Jesus' favor with his Father. He was God's Son, to be sure. That gave him privilege. Yet he was obedient in suffering even unto death. His sonship and his self-giving as God's Paschal Lamb reflected his character. It was not something that he did that made him Son and Lamb, but what he was. He was all that before the foundation of the world.

*Teach me, dear Jesus, to rejoice, first of all, for who you are,
then for being willing to go through everything you did
to become my high priest.
I will follow you in life and through eternity. Amen.*

Jesus, Solid Food

**But solid food is for the mature, who by constant use
have trained themselves to distinguish good from evil (5:14)**

Appetizers and desserts tantalize the palate, but they are meant to accompany the main meal, not to replace it. Our children must have been exasperated by our dictum, "No dessert until you eat your meal."

So it is in my life with Christ. In my immaturity I crave dessert all the time. I have noticed that God often caters to our need for the spectacular in our early walk with Jesus. As he discerns that we are able to trust him more completely, he then provides us with solid food that gives solid disciples solid resolve. God knows that I need more than the excitement of the moment to deal with the perils of life that will be my lot.

Exhilarating past experiences will not carry the day in the midst of overwhelming challenges. I need to have the solid substance of the source of all grace, the atoning work of Jesus. That is solid food.

But I do enjoy the foods of ecstasy as well. Jesus sets before me a "full board," because I need all the spiritual nutrients I can get to live a life of victory. I need the food of tears and the food of laughter and joy. I find the total meal to be Jesus, who lived life here on earth to the full.

The writer then surprises me with the way he connects eating only sweets with living holy lives. He implies that by living on fluff we lose our ability to discern good from evil. Haven't I seen that? I tend to want spiritual experiences instead of righteousness.

Jesus, you are the master of my table.
Provide me with just the right balance
of solid food and exhilarating experiences
that I might know what is good and what is evil.

Jesus, the Foundation

**Therefore let us leave the elementary teachings about Christ
and go on to maturity, not laying again the foundation (6:1)**

I must confess that I have been perplexed by this verse. Earlier on, I took it to mean that I should abandon "the foundations" and mount to higher levels of holiness. Upon reflection, I realize that is not what is meant at all, because the grace to repent, for example, is a constant grace.

To "leave" must surely mean to leave them as they are, as foundational. We might say, to leave them in their God-given place and build on them.

A few months ago I had the joy of helping my son-in-law build an addition onto their house. The contractor, Larry, went to great lengths to make absolutely certain that the foundational walls were set perfectly, because the line of the foundation would determine the line of everything that was to be built above. Each corner of the foundation would predict a corner in the completed building.

I realized again how important it is to get the foundation right. It will be almost impossible to go back and correct a foundation error after the building is underway. Paul knew this, and he wrote, "For no one can lay any foundation other than the one already laid, which is Jesus Christ" (1 Corinthians 3:11). We adjust that foundation ever so slightly and we inevitably skew everything that is built on it.

> Lord Jesus, settle my heart in the knowledge
> that you are my foundation.
> Everything that will be built on you will reflect your character.
> May the Holy Spirit help me never to try
> to tamper with my sure foundation, Jesus.

Jesus, the Sure Foundation

**Therefore let us leave the elementary teachings about Christ
and go on to maturity, not laying again the foundation (6:1)**

Having laid the foundation of biblical, Christ-centered theology, resist the temptation to go back and make alterations.

I can illustrate this from my own experience. As I matured in my understanding of the Bible, I began to question the reality of miracles. I was well schooled in the rational, scientific method. So I clipped out, so to speak, the biblical passages that referred to what I considered far-out miracles. I found that I could still be a Christian and do that.

My nicely built house of cards collapsed in Tanzania. The people there, even nonbelievers, had no problem at all with the supernatural. Their whole worldview was built on the idea that spiritual powers can and do intervene in natural events. How I came to believe in miracles once again is a long but exciting story.

I learned that the great doctrines of the Bible are firmly rooted in the miraculous. Why should I begin to doubt that? This is but one illustration of how important it is to build with authentic continuity on the person of Jesus Christ as revealed in the Scriptures. In all things, consider Jesus.

Lord, you are the sure foundation.
May I build according to the dimensions and lines
of that perfect foundation.

Jesus Lives with the Repentant

**Not laying again the foundation of repentance from acts that lead to death
(6:1)**

Build on the foundation stone of repentance.

I do not think I will ever get used to repenting, because it is such a pain. I prefer to close my eyes at night, thinking of the stream of blessings that visited me that day rather than realizing that I should repent of harboring a critical spirit or some harsh word or unloving deed.

Repentance is painful because it deflates the proud ego. In a way, repentance is dying a little, dying to self. There are times when it is just easier to sweep the dirt under the carpet than to get it out into the open and actually sweep it up under Christ's cross.

Repentance is not something that I do easily, but having admitted that, I know in my heart of hearts that nothing opens the floodgates of grace like acknowledging my sinful attitude and fleeing to the Lamb of God for cleansing. That is an act that leads to life. I know that to be gospel truth!

Isaiah reminds us, "This is what the high and lofty One says . . . 'I live in a high and holy place, but also with him who is contrite and lowly in spirit, to revive the spirit of the lowly and to revive the heart of the contrite'" (Isaiah 57:15).

I know that intellectually, but that does not make it one bit easier to do. I much prefer to be right than to be penitent.

> *Help me, Lord, to quickly acknowledge when I harbor*
> *an attitude that is not consistent with your character.*
> *Push me up to the cross, where I know cleansing*
> *for that infraction is available.*

Jesus Leads to Life

Not laying again the foundation of repentance from acts that lead to death
(6:1)

Jesus is the life. He knows that hard hearts slowly shrivel up. This foundation stone is as essential as it is demanding. I see fellow believers get into all kinds of difficulty because they cling to their rights.

I recall counseling a missionary who got himself into boiling hot water by always insisting he was right. I must admit that often he *was* right. He may have been right, but his attitude was dead wrong. "Why," he asked, "should I ask for forgiveness if I was right?" He had a point. As I thought of it, it is not a matter of being right, but of having the right spirit. I reminded him that a car without a reverse gear would ultimately end in big trouble. The reverse gear is there for a purpose.

Like my friend, my problem is my attitude. I get critical about the smallest things. I get exasperated and put off when things do not go my way. I also convince myself that I have certain rights that I must protect. Like a porcupine, I spread my spines when people erode my time and energy. "Let me alone. I am retired."

Most believers manage to avoid committing grave sins like murder, adultery, theft, or lying, while tolerating attitudes that must surely make the Lord weep. What is so bad about bad attitudes? Hard hearts lead to spiritual death. Repentant hearts lead to life.

I am about to make an admission. I find it easier to write these nice words and tell others to repent than to bow my own stiff neck.

Lord, have mercy!

Jesus Depended Entirely on his Father

Not laying again the foundation of . . . faith in God (6:1-2)

Certainly no believer would even consider for a moment abandoning faith in God, another of the foundation stones. That block supports the entire building. It could well be that some Hebrew believers were taking things into their own hands in an effort to earn favor with God, in which case they would place trust in themselves, not in God.

Is this not the plague of many modern churches? Instead of hearing about trusting God for everything, believers are encouraged to pursue self-actualization. Modernists tell us that mankind has come of age, which means that we can no longer blame everything on God, but must take personal control of our lives. At least that is better than to say, "Satan made me do it."

Some critics of modern Christianity describe churches as self-help clubs. The end result of this rampant individualism is the abandonment of faith in God. We find ourselves conformed to this world, which has no place for God in its man-centered worldview.

Now and again I face a steep mountain in my life. Before I know it I am asking, "Must I ask the Lord to help me or can I climb this one in my own strength?" The underlying premise is that I should call on God only when I am stymied. I am trying to have faith in God at every step, in every venture.

My God, you are all-knowing, all-wise, ever-loving,
all the time. Renew my faith in you today.

Jesus Knows Many Baptisms

Not laying again the foundation of ... faith in God, instructions about baptisms (6:1-2)

Is it possible to build a Christian life on the foundation, "God cannot be trusted"? Perish the thought! Faith in God is foundational.

The second phrase is a bit harder to get hold of—"instructions about baptisms." Evidently the early Christians kept debating some aspects of the biblical teaching on baptism. Maybe it had to do with the mode of baptism, a bone of contention even today.

Is the mode all that important? Why not just say that the real baptism is the washing of the blood of Christ? It is essentially a spiritual thing. We all know that all believers must be baptized in the "soul-cleansing blood of the Lamb," as a hymn puts it. Who can contest the validity of that? So why do we complicate it by arguing about the visible mode of baptism?

I think this is the meaning of the passage. Or it could be, as a friend of mine has suggested, that "baptisms" continue throughout life. He noted that Jesus had many baptisms in addition to that in the Jordan River. Jesus experienced the baptism of fire, the baptism of suffering, the baptism of ecstasy, and so on. If that is the meaning, it is an encouragement to be open to all divinely sent baptisms.

Lord, I affirm my absolute trust in you and praise you
for the gracious gift of the bath of baptism
and the daily washings.
You have the right to baptize believers in any way you wish.

June 8

Jesus Blesses with a Touch

Not laying again the foundation of . . . the laying on of hands (6:1-2)

There is a debate going on now about what happens when the church "lays hands on" people. I wonder about it too.

I was familiar with the official laying on of hands for ordinations, such as when the elders of the church laid hands on Anna Ruth and me in the summer of 1953 for missionary service in East Africa. It was meaningful, at the time, but nothing dramatic happened. I did not experience any new gifting for the task, at least that I can recall. I did not expect any. The gift we received there was the gift of encouragement.

The second time was in 1964, when the Tanzania Mennonite Church called me to serve as their bishop. It was gratifying to know that the church had confidence in me to do a task that I found daunting. Both of those experiences strengthened my faith and encouraged me. In both instances the church could have simply sent me a letter of appointment. But I am glad that is not the way it works, because the laying on of hands is done for the whole group, in fellowship.

I do admit that I experienced many giftings. How much of that do I owe to the laying on of hands by the church? Good question. I believe I have some gifts that are almost innate, like teaching and peacemaking and encouragement. But as a missionary I was called upon to do things for which I had no preparation, like healing the sick, administering large groups of people, leading people in worship, and so forth. I have learned that the giftings are there for what God has called me to do.

Lord, I believe that the human touch lends credence to the act.
As we bless one another with a touch, an embrace, or a handshake
in your wonderful name, we are building on the foundation
of "the laying on of hands."

Jesus, Our Brother in Fellowship

Not laying again the foundation of ... the laying on of hands (6:1-2)

Evidently the early church expected much more from the laying on of hands than I did.

In 2 Timothy 1:6, Paul wrote, "Fan into flame the gift of God, which is in you through the laying on of my hands." Paul did not describe the "gift of God" that he was writing about. Maybe he was speaking in general terms. Perhaps it was something specific. He and Timothy obviously knew, and that is what mattered.

I think of many instances when human touch has a divine effect, from the laying on of hands at a commissioning to the ordinary, common handshake. I believe that the writer refers to all genuine fellowship. Through the body, the Lord Jesus builds us up. Everyone needs that continual touch of fellowship.

What actually happens or what should happen spiritually when we touch a brother or sister in the name of Jesus is open to discussion. But one thing is absolutely certain: to be on a firm foundation, we need the embrace of the fellowship of God's people and we need to reach out in love to all who need the human touch as a token of God's love. And we should expect something good to happen when hands are laid on us for specific tasks.

We should open ourselves to be touched and be brave enough to bless others with a human touch. Greetings vary around the world. In Tanzania, a great hug will do. In Ethiopia, three kisses!

Lord Jesus, thank you for touching me.
You have done it in the Spirit and you have done it
by the human touch of divine love.
Now, by your grace, enable me to bless others
with a touch of your refreshing grace.

Jesus, the Resurrection

Not laying again the foundation of ... the resurrection of the dead (6:1-2)

Some commentators interpret this reference as the writer asking the Jews to leave behind their traditional interpretation of the resurrection and embrace the Christian one. At the time of Christ the Jews did not have a very clear doctrine of the resurrection. The prevailing point of view, encouraged by the Sadducees, was that there will be no resurrection and that it is simply a metaphor for hope. The Pharisees held to resurrection of the dead. It is undeniable that the Old Testament left this subject quite open.

I can imagine early Jewish believers discussing the nature of the gospel's teaching on the resurrection. Some may have even questioned the whole idea. Greek philosophy had no place for bodily resurrection. At the time of Christ, Philo of Alexander attempted to make Judaism palatable to Greeks by spiritualizing the concept of resurrection, knowing that the Greeks could not conceive of the "evil" body being raised to eternal life.

Our text places the resurrection of the dead as one of the foundation stones. It is not to be spiritualized or deleted. Jesus rose from the dead. He did not leave his physical body on earth. His physical body was transformed. So will it be with all who die in Christ. They will be raised with him. He is the first fruit.

> Lord Jesus, even though I cannot visualize
> how the bodily resurrection will occur,
> I believe it will happen,
> and I am satisfied to leave it at that.
> I want that foundation stone to remain.
> When it happens, I will rejoice,
> for then I will see you as you are
> and will enter fully into your joy.

Jesus, the Life

**Not laying again the foundation of . . . the resurrection of the dead,
and eternal judgment (6:1-2)**

Were we to consider the resurrection a mere metaphor for the eternal nature of the soul, as some do, we'd miss the point entirely.

Jesus keeps us as his beloved "saved ones" by his atoning power. He will do likewise when we pass from this life to the next. I gladly place my life and my death in the hands of my marvelous Lord Jesus, who was raised from the dead and appeared bodily before he ascended to the Father.

The final doctrine of the six foundation stones is eternal judgment. I have no idea what the Hebrews' discussion was about on this point, but I can well imagine some insisting that if we have died with unforgiven sin, we will enter a place of temporary punishment for those sins, after which we will join the celestial host. It could have been some other disagreement about the final judgment. Maybe some disputed the meaning of the word *eternal,* as is the case these days. Is hell forever, or is it for a while only?

Some disagreement is expected where there is no clear revelation, I suppose. Be that as it may, the foundation stone that remains for all believers is that sin must be judged and in Christ sinners find forgiveness. Sin that is placed upon Christ, God's lamb, has been judged already. The final judgment holds no dread for those who know the daily cleansing of the blood of Christ. As I live in Christ, so I die in him, pleading nothing but the blood of God's Lamb, which covers me completely.

> *Jesus, I believe that eternal life is mine*
> *as a gift of your marvelous grace.*
> *May I rest eternally on the assurance of your full salvation,*
> *which is mine by faith.*

Jesus Keeps Me from Falling Away

**It is impossible for those who have once been enlightened . . . if they fall
away, to be brought back to repentance (6:4, 6)**

This little paragraph has been a battleground on which theologians have fought for ages. Some insist that once a person is saved, there is no way that person can spurn grace and return to the world, thereby losing salvation. Others, emphasizing freedom of will, contend that a person who once knew the Lord can indeed fall away.

My short summary of the matter is that in Jesus I am eternally secure, yet I have it within me to disobey the very Jesus who saves me. Jesus left no doubt on this point: "If anyone loves me, he will obey my teaching" (John 14:23). He did not give us a "should" but a "will."

As I understand it, if I love Jesus I will do what he wishes, for it is a relationship of love. How can I, with any integrity, flout the character of the One I dearly love and by whom I am acceptable to the Father?

As I muse over this Scripture, I believe that the writer is declaring that if I maintain my relationship with Jesus Christ I do not "fall away," because my stubborn self-will is brought under subjection.

Paul asserts that when a person is born anew, sin ceases to have dominion over the believer (see Romans 6:14). It is possible not to sin! If, to our horror, we do sin, we have an advocate with the Father, Jesus. He casts all sin that is brought to him in repentant faith into the depths of the sea.

> *My Lord Jesus, may I never wander away from you,*
> *not for a moment.*
> *And please, as the Holy Spirit puts his finger on anything in my life*
> *that creates distance between us,*
> *give me a humble, contrite heart that is quick to repent,*
> *thus renewing our fellowship once again.*

Jesus Desires Integrity

It is impossible for those who have once been enlightened . . .
if they fall away, to be brought back to repentance (6:4, 6)

My mind goes back to East Africa, where I learned many new lessons about walking with Jesus. It was a time of extraordinary Holy Spirit activity. Thousands experienced forgiveness of sins and the life-changing power of Jesus Christ. It was a moving thing to see them coming to Christ.

I have also seen many "fall away." Who am I to judge whether they were or were not truly converted? Some who press the doctrine of predestination might insist that those who fall away were never born again in the first place.

I do not know enough about divine grace to figure that out. All I can say is that I have seen men and women fall away. The major reason was that at some point those who fell away refused to be broken and insisted that their way was right, even though their attitudes were contrary to that of Jesus.

Some threw up their hands when their prayers were not answered. Some allowed the enemy access into their lives by consulting medicine men and women who promised healing in the name of the dead. Others fell into the bondage of legalism. Still others refused to take the way of the cross because they feared that Jesus would somehow do them harm by destroying their freedom or by taking away some privilege they enjoyed.

Forbid, Lord, that I should stand in judgment of any individual.
You are the judge and you judge
according to your standards of truth and grace.
My concern is that I not be among those who fall away,
but among those who cling to you to the end.

Jesus, Crucified Again When I Disobey

**To their loss they are crucifying the Son of God all over again
and subjecting him to public disgrace (6:6)**

This verse, as the old hymn goes, "causes me to tremble, tremble, tremble." When I disobey the Lord and go my own way in anything, am I really causing Jesus pain similar to the pain of being crucified? That is a sobering thought. How could I dare harm the One who died to reconcile me to God? Just the thought is abhorrent, but even more awful is the realization that I am guilty of doing this more often than I know.

Not so long ago I had a new vocation, looking after my dear wife, Anna Ruth, as she recovered from two total hip replacements. I tried to be aware of everything that caused her pain and then tried to do something about it. I did not dream of inflicting any additional pain on her. She had enough already!

When I transfer that idea onto my relationship with Jesus, I am indeed humbled—and condemned. Jesus already bears the wounds in his hands, his head, his feet, and his side. Yet my disobedience drives another dart of pain into him. I need to think about that.

And does my vacillating walk with God bring disgrace on Christ? Is my inconstancy shouting a message to all that Jesus is somehow inadequate? If so, it must pain him terribly.

Jesus, my Lord and Savior,
I would not willingly inflict any more pain on you
nor would I disgrace you by doubting your grace.

Jesus Desires Integrity

**To their loss they are crucifying the Son of God all over again
and subjecting him to public disgrace (6:6)**

Either Jesus satisfies or he does not. When I seek my own righteousness or take my own way, I am announcing that he is not able for this particular problem. I might go on preaching that Jesus is able, yet in my heart of hearts I doubt it. That brings disgrace on him.

Imagine me saying about an issue that I am facing in my life, "I am able for this; Jesus is not." What blasphemy! But that is exactly what the Holy Spirit is clarifying in this Scripture. It is the height of hypocrisy to claim that Christ is all-sufficient and then turn around and take charge of our lives as we did before we knew the Lord at all.

Hebrews is known as the book of warnings. Every chapter seems to carry a warning. This can put us off, but that is not the intention of the Holy Spirit, who breathed into these Scriptures. The warnings are not intended to cause us to despair and throw up our hands in defeat but to alert us to the dangers so we can mend our ways and follow Christ more diligently. The purpose of each gracious warning is to settle us more firmly on Jesus Christ, finding in him, and in him alone, all that our souls long for and require.

> *Lord Jesus, forbid that I should stray from you but for a second,*
> *lest I wound you anew or hold you up to disgrace as a liar,*
> *causing others to doubt your Word.*
> *Cover me daily with the canopy of your atoning grace.*

Jesus Gives Natural Blessings to All

Land that drinks in rain ... land that produces thorns (6:7-8)

We have here two different responses to the goodness of God. One is commendable; the other is not.

The work of the Holy Spirit is to give us a hunger and thirst for the goodness of the Word of God and to get us excited about the power of Jesus to do marvelous things. It is up to us to either drink in the rain to produce a good crop or use the blessing of the rain to produce something harmful, like thorns.

I see Jesus approaching Jerusalem on Palm Sunday. Laid out before him was the city, dominated by the magnificent newly built temple. A tourist would have been awestruck by the glorious sight. But Jesus was not a tourist; he was the Lord of God's harvest.

When Jesus saw that city, the waters gushed from his breaking heart. Almost two thousand years of history were distilled into those tears. The reason for them? Jerusalem received the rains and produced not fruit, but thorns.

Rain is the universal blessing. It falls on all soil. God does not discriminate between the deserving and the undeserving when he pours out his grace. As noted in the opening verses of this chapter, the Holy Spirit is active in both those who respond to God and those who do not. He never gives up. People do that.

> *Our Father in heaven, thank you for your daily blessings.*
> *Give me the grace to share those blessings*
> *so that your name is glorified.*

Jesus, Our Thirst

Land that drinks in rain . . . land that produces thorns (6:7-8)

No people on the face of the earth were ever blessed as the children of Abraham and Sarah were blessed. God promised to bless them so that they could bless all peoples. Hear his words: "I will surely bless you and make your descendants as numerous as the stars in the sky and as the sand on the seashore. . . . And through your offspring all nations on earth will be blessed, because you have obeyed me" (Genesis 22:17-18).

God did his part. He sent the former and the latter rains, withholding nothing from the people with whom he made covenant. Why, then, had Jerusalem become a field that could produce nothing but injustice, egoism, and legalism, and then slay their own promised Messiah, Jesus Christ? In that lies the mystery. The most blessed should produce the best fruit.

By birth, I am an American. Who can question the obvious blessings poured out on this nation and our sister nations in the west? I believe that God prospered us to bless others. This prosperity enabled the Christians in our nations to engage in missions for a century and a half, increasing the percentage of world Christianity from 8 percent in 1800 to 33 percent in 1950. Will the believers in our land continue to produce such delightful fruit?

> *Lord Jesus, as I peer into the future, I pray that your followers*
> *will hold fast to their first love*
> *and continue to produce fruit that lasts to eternity.*
> *May our response to your rain of blessing be that of a farmer*
> *whose great delight is to produce crops to bless others.*

Jesus, Better Than Anything Carnal

Dear friends, we are confident of better things in your case (6:9)

I squirm a bit, more than a bit to tell the truth, when I hear these stern warnings. How is it with me? Am I carnal, seeking after things that are selfish, or am I maturing spiritually? It is painful even to ask the question, but the Holy Spirit knows how necessary it is, because it is so easy to slip into a carnal frame of mind.

So, after my trembling ceases I consider once again Jesus, the author and finisher of my faith, and I go on. I reconfirm my unshakeable faith in all that flows from the atoning work of Jesus, not doubting for a moment that he is able to fulfill in me all he promised he will do. Let the chastening do its work.

How comforting, then, are the words of today's verse? The writer gives the reason for that confidence. He commends his dear friends, because they are diligent about working for the Lord and are helping the brothers and sisters in the faith. Their good works flow from their walk with Jesus.

So works do matter! They show where one's faith is anchored. Good works are a sign that points directly to Jesus Christ.

God is not overly impressed with my sentiments of love and gratitude. He expects fruit. God is pleased when I consent to a list of biblical doctrines, but what truly pleases him is when he sees actual, solid fruit.

> *My Lord, put a song of thanksgiving in my soul,*
> *a smile of contentment on my face,*
> *but above all, put fruit on my vine!*
> *I want to bear fruit for you that will last to all eternity.*

Jesus, Better Things

Dear friends, we are confident of better things in your case
—things that accompany salvation (6:9)

My wife has a good definition of belief. "If you calmly say, 'I believe my house is on fire,' and sit there idly doing nothing about it, it might be belief but it is surely belief without works."

Applying that to today's passage, if I believe that people need Jesus in order to know God's salvation but do nothing about it, what good is belief? Jesus describes this as nothing more than noise—clanging cymbals.

Embedded in the good news is the truth that will reappear time and again in this letter to the Hebrews: better things. Someone has called the book of Hebrews "the book of better things." The Holy Spirit takes us from where we are to a much deeper or higher level of faith, to better things. The Lord is always introducing us to better things as we walk in fellowship with him and with one another.

My heart is comforted when I hear the Lord speak of better things. A true lover of Jesus lives with the hope of better things every day. Outside of Christ, the storm clouds gather, and life is ominous. But in Christ every challenge is the doorway to better things. The best thing is Jesus, of course.

Lord, I long for better things.
I live on the tiptoe of anticipation.
Never, ever, dull this hunger.
As I enjoy better things, may I also get better.

Jesus, My Endurance

**We want each of you to show this same diligence to the very end, in order
to make your hope sure (6:11)**

Christian maturity requires a high level of diligence. That is hard to sustain as I become chronologically enhanced! I am now in what our culture calls retirement. Who am I now? I worked in a structured program for many years. I was diligent to please those for whom I worked. Without realizing it, I was buoyed up by human expectation. I see that very clearly now as I reorganize my life.

Paul got it right when he confided, "I want to know Christ and the power of his resurrection and the fellowship of sharing in his sufferings, becoming like him in his death" (Philippians 3:10). It is helpful to remember that Paul wrote this as a prisoner in Rome. For years he moved about among the churches encouraging and teaching them. For that he needed the power of Christ's resurrection because it was a demanding life. But in prison? Inactive? For those challenges he needed the power even more! I am beginning to understand that. His diligence was the by-product of the most meaningful relationship he had, his life in Christ, and did not flag as a prisoner in Rome.

I must be diligent in living moment by moment in the reality of Jesus in my life. My song in eternity will be, "Worthy is the Lamb who was slain." Why should I not pour out my soul now in gratitude and praise for him and go on living with "diligence to the very end"?

> *Jesus, my endurance, all I need do if my diligence flags*
> *is place myself in that heavenly choir*
> *and sing the song of Zion together with all the redeemed,*
> *of all ages, all races, all peoples, and all tongues.*
> *My song on earth is the song of heaven. Jesus, you are worthy!*
> *Then I can go on.*

Jesus, My Hero

**Imitate those who through faith and patience inherit
what has been promised (6:12)**

It sounds a bit strange to say, "Jesus is my hero." But it is the truth. I place my entire hope, my life, on him. I cannot imagine life without Jesus. He is the foundation on which I build, the person who is absolutely unique in time or eternity. Jesus has become a vital part of who I am. My destiny is enmeshed with him in such a way that but for him in my life, I am nothing.

My hero, Jesus, has no blemish, no fault. Every word he spoke is true. Every thought he had was in accordance with his Father in heaven. He is the way, the truth, and the life. No one can ever prove him wrong. He is my hero with a capital H.

As today's passage says, I should imitate those who have made God their hero. Their complete confidence in God, the Father of our hero, Jesus Christ, carried them through wind and storm. Their faith in God enabled them to patiently move on with God, no matter what. They received the promised inheritance, not because they earned it, but "through faith and patience."

Later in this letter we will see a parade of saints who made God their hero under the old covenant. Their lives were transformed as they followed him.

Jesus, you are worthy to be my hero.
My greatest joy in life and in eternity is to exalt your name.

Jesus Forgives Our Impatience

After waiting patiently, Abraham received what was promised (6:15)

This sentence jars me like a flashing neon sign. Abraham waited? I thought of him as impatient. If he had been patient and waited, there would have been no Ishmael. If there had been no Ishmael, there would have been no Muhammad and no Islam. These are the consequences of Abraham's impatience. All Hebrews who read this letter knew all about Abraham's impatience. Yet it is not mentioned.

It could be that Abraham actually thought that Ishmael was the son of promise. It appears so, because Abraham, then an old man, was circumcised at the same time as Ishmael, who was thirteen years old. In hindsight we know that Isaac, born about a year after Ishmael was circumcised, was the promised heir, son of Sarah.

Who am I to point my finger at Abraham? How many "Ishmaels" have I fathered in my own life? Only time will tell. I too am impatient. I tend to run ahead and hope that the Lord will catch up! There are times when God is too slow for me.

I see clearly that impatience is a terrible sin because it shows that I do not believe God. An African proverb says, "God needs help." *(Mungu husaidiwa.)* Wrong! God does not need help. Be patient.

Jesus, forgive me for my impatience.
I choose to believe and wait patiently on the Lord. Always.

Jesus Walks in a Stride with His Father

After waiting patiently, Abraham received what was promised (6:15)

How many messes has the Lord had to straighten up because I rushed ahead? No doubt many. Praise him for his marvelous grace. It puts right many things that I did wrong because I moved before he prompted me to move and hesitated when he clearly wanted me to move.

When Sarah, Abraham's beloved wife, gave birth to Isaac, a healthy baby boy, Abraham must have had two sets of emotions as he held him in his arms. One was regret that he had not simply said no when Sarah, his wife, suggested that he have a child by Hagar, the Egyptian handmaiden. Ishmael was born of impatience. Perhaps Abraham thought that God would make it all right in the end.

The other emotion was the pure joy of holding God's special miracle, little Isaac, in his arms. Who ever heard of a woman of about a hundred years producing a son? This was nothing other than the grace of God at work. Isaac was truly the child of promise, the child of patience.

In my own life, waiting patiently for what God promised produced the best fruit. What I did because I was unwilling to wait for God's leading has produced a mixture of fruits, some noxious. Impatience produces Ishmaels, patience and trust produce Isaacs, sons of promise.

> *Lord, forbid that I should run ahead of you.*
> *Likewise stir me up when you do want me to move forward.*

Cleave to Jesus

We who have fled ... take hold of the hope offered to us (6:18)

In Genesis 2:24, it is written that a man will leave his mother and cleave to his wife. Unless he leaves his mother, he cannot fully cleave to his wife. He has to decide, is it Mom or wife?

The first step is to leave the warmth and protection of Mother. This is not pleasant, because there is always the risk that his wife will be a poor substitute for Mom. Then what? It also works the other way around, the wife may have a profound relationship with her father. Will the new husband be the kind of man that she came to expect, knowing her own father? In a way, she must also leave him. That can be painful.

The second challenge is no less daunting, to cleave to your wife or husband. That implies considerable risk. However, leaving Mom and Dad and cleaving to the new spouse must both be done decisively and well. Every successful marriage hinges on how well.

That is exactly how it is in the Calvary way. The journey begins as the pilgrim bids farewell to this world. In his memorable tale *The Pilgrim's Progress*, John Bunyan has Christian fleeing from this world. Christian's friends try to dissuade him from such a reckless course, but he is a determined pilgrim, so he pays no heed. He must flee. That is just the beginning of the story. He then bonds with his Lord to aid him to attain his goal.

The book of Hebrews emphasizes the critical importance of fleeing from this world. But that is only the beginning. There is not much to be gained if one is freed from bondage, only to die in the wilderness. The argument in Hebrews is that we leave the place of slavery in order to enter into a place of rest and freedom.

My Jesus, the Holy Spirit drives home the fact
that to be your faithful follower I must flee this world
and cleave to you.

June 25

Hold on to Jesus, Our Hope

We who have fled . . . take hold of the hope offered to us (6:18)

Jesus startles us with statements such as, "If anyone comes to me and does not hate his father and mother . . . he cannot be my disciple" (Luke 14:26). We recall that Peter, James, John, and Andrew left their nets and clung to Jesus. All disciples flee something in order to cleave to Jesus.

This idea is embedded in Christian baptism. The believer must die to this world, to be drowned to it, so to speak, and then arise to newness of life.

As a missionary, I baptized hundreds of people. I remember baptizing 130 or so in one day. I wonder how many of them truly cut their cords with this world. I was fully aware that some might "add" Christianity to existing beliefs, even though each had been through a rigorous catechism.

Some may shuttle back and forth between the world of ancestral spirits and the world of the gospel of Jesus Christ. Some people falter as they face the decision to abandon all hope in ancestral spirits and depend entirely on the power of Christ. That can continue for only so long. Ultimately a choice must be made. Thankfully, many do believe in Jesus so much that they put their entire trust in him, no matter what the consequences. Would that all who begin the journey with Jesus do that.

> *I find it to be true, Lord Jesus, that things of the old life*
> *tend to cling to me even though I am saved, sanctified,*
> *and filled with the Holy Spirit.*
> *No matter what, I have fled this world and am still fleeing.*
> *Help me to flee all the way to glory.*

Jesus, Our Secure Hope

We have this hope as an anchor for the soul, firm and secure (6:19)

Anna Ruth and I were excited when we first saw the Queen Mary at the New York dock in 1953. She was to be our home for a week, the first leg of our journey to Tanzania.

I had never seen a vessel like it. I recall vividly the huge anchor snuggled up tight against the bow of the ship. It had to be mammoth to anchor such an immense ship in severe storms. Good ships have good anchors.

Our African home was on the shores of Lake Victoria. Boats lined the lakeshore. Each fishing boat, no matter how simple or elaborate, had an anchor as standard equipment.

It is not beyond imagination to envision a fishing boat without an anchor. Anchors are expensive, so a boat owner may be tempted to do without. But that would be foolish. Anchors are required to keep a ship safe.

My soul is a ship on a turbulent sea. Without a trustworthy anchor, it is in peril. Before I knew Jesus as my personal Savior, Lord, and friend, I had no anchor. I was at the mercy of the storms of life. That is perilous.

That all changed when Jesus became my anchor. My heart rejoices every time I think of that remarkable turn of events. I had no hope. In a moment, I had hope. It was as simple as that. I was adrift, then I had an anchor.

> *Lord, I wish I could say that I always trusted you*
> *as my one and only anchor,*
> *but I can say that you have served*
> *as a trustworthy anchor through violent storms.*

June 27

Jesus, Our Anchor

We have this hope as an anchor for the soul, firm and secure (6:19)

The idea here is that we have a hope that drives us forward. It is not hoping in something fanciful. It is hope based on reality. That reality is that Jesus Christ entered the Most Holy Place by the merits of his own blood and that he is there now beckoning me to come in with him to enjoy fellowship with the Father.

He broke all the walls that separate us from God, the final one being that thick curtain that blocked entrance into the presence of almighty God. As he gave his life as the Paschal Lamb, that veil was rent, top to bottom. He entered in first by his own blood. That blood answered all the demands of divine justice and love. Jesus of Nazareth, Son of man and Son of God, pleased the Father entirely. The Father and all of heaven broke into song, "He is worthy." Jesus is the answer to heaven's prayers.

Having entered in, Jesus now grabs my anchor and places it firmly in the mercy seat, the very throne of God. As a brother once said, "I am anchored up." My anchor is in the most wonderful place in the heavenlies, where God reaches out to sinners. It is the place of the Shekinah glory of God. I am anchored in the mercy seat of God almighty.

Jesus Christ, you are my soul's anchor, firm and secure.
You fastened my anchor eternally
*   to the mercy seat in heaven itself.*
I know that my anchor holds because it is secured
*   by your sure atoning work.*
That seat of mercy is the place of my security.
Eventually my soul will rest eternally where I am now anchored.

June 28

Jesus Secures My Anchor

[The anchor] enters the inner sanctuary behind the curtain, where Jesus, who went before us, has entered on our behalf (6:19-20)

It hardly seems possible that Jesus did this for me. But he did. He secured my anchor to a rock that can never be moved, the throne of almighty God. He did it at phenomenal cost, the life of his only begotten Son.

As we have noted many times, Jesus' atoning blood met all the demands of divine justice and divine love. As to justice, Jesus bore all sin and evil in his own body on that tree. The wrath of God fell on my sin in Jesus and was there judged with exacting justice. The demands of divine justice were met. As for the demands of love, what greater love is there than to lay down your life for rebellious sinners, even before they've asked?

With the door flung widely open, Jesus entered in, carrying my anchor in his own wounded hand and lovingly lodging it in the throne of God almighty. Glory to his name! Every moment of every day I find profound comfort in knowing that the ship of my life is not drifting on troubled seas. My anchor is cast forever.

I am inevitably drawn to the place of my anchor. A strong cable binds me to that seat of mercy where the benefits of the atoning work of Jesus are lavished on those in need.

> *Jesus, every day I inch a bit closer to that dwelling place of God.*
> *The winch of faith is working. I know my destiny.*
> *My anchor is secure.*
> *I will someday be where my anchor is already,*
>   *gripping tightly God's saving grace.*

Jesus, On My Behalf

Jesus, who went before us, has entered on our behalf (6:20)

There comes a moment in the life of every believer when the overwhelming realization strikes, like a bolt of lightening. "It was for me!" He did it "on our behalf."

Indeed it was a moment of profound joy when Jesus, God's precious Lamb, broke open the veil with the power of his own blood. It was a day of triumph for Jesus. He had overcome Satan by his steadfast love for the Father and his willingness to take on himself the sins of the world, nailing them to his cross. He triumphed over death and hell. As he stood outside that empty tomb on Easter morning he overflowed with joy. It was done!

It was a moment of triumph for the Father also. He risked all when he sent his only begotten Son. Were Jesus to fail, all hope of eternal life would vanish. The joy of the Father was great when he witnessed the steadfast faith and trust of his Son, Jesus, as he set his face as a flint to defeat Satan by offering his own sinless life on the cross. The Father looked on Jesus and was satisfied.

That which satisfied the Father and Son certainly satisfied the Holy Spirit. He had invested all in Jesus, from the moment he descended on Jesus, as a dove at his baptism, to the moment of triumph when Jesus disarmed Satan on the cross. The Holy Spirit rejoiced and was satisfied.

So it is with me. Jesus satisfies me completely. Can I do less for him?

Praise the triune God, Father, Son, and Holy Spirit,
for doing all this for me—on my behalf.

Jesus Entered for Me

Jesus, who went before us, has entered on our behalf (6:20)

Heaven's drama was heightened and accentuated as the chorus swelled, "Worthy is the Lamb!" My imagination is caught up in this marvel of marvels, the triumph of love over hate, of light over darkness, of life over death, of grace over despair, and of faith over unbelief. There is drama enough here to set my heart to praising forever and ever.

As the joy reaches a crescendo, I find myself undone, broken, and humbled beyond words. When they set off fireworks, they save one huge bang for last. The huge bang here is that it was all for me! He did it all on my behalf because I could do nothing at all. I was doomed. "For me" echoes through the canyons of my being.

Slowly the reality of it all floods the mind, the heart, and even the body. It dawns on me that were I the only sinner on earth, this is what would have had to happen to redeem me from destruction. Furthermore, the love of God would have compelled him to do it all just for me. Grace beyond words.

It is through tears of thanksgiving that I see Jesus going through the agony of the cross, splitting the veil top to bottom, and then ascending to the Father in heaven, there to intercede for me. He did it all on my behalf. Wonder of wonders!

Shall I ever comprehend this kind of love? It is too great for me. I simply accept it and rest in the hope that it stirs in my heart.

Thank you, Jesus. It was for me!

Jesus Loves the World

He has become a high priest forever, in the order of Melchizedek (6:20)

Melchizedek keeps popping up. As noted earlier, he was not a Jew. In fact, he was a priest of God among the Canaanites when Abraham arrived there. He was not even included in the covenant God made with Abraham. Melchizedek had no hereditary right at all to be God's priest nor was he among the Jewish "chosen ones."

Furthermore, Abraham recognized that this non-Jewish priest served the same Yahweh that he served. Even more startling, Abraham considered Melchizedek to be an authentic priest of God.

Jewish scholars, especially the more conservative ones, have wrestled with this issue time and time again. They know that the Jews have a unique relationship with God because they believe that it is only with them that God made the covenant. They take this a step further and presume that people have to become Jews to fully please God.

But Melchizedek walked with God and he was not a Jew. Jewish scholars still haven't settled the riddle. For me, it shows that God's love and justice are at work in the most obscure of places. This is a mystery, known only by God himself. What I know is what has been revealed: that God wants every person to know Jesus.

> *Lord Jesus, you are in the order of Melchizedek.*
> *You are above culture, above race, above religion,*
> > *above language and history, which makes you available to all.*
> *You invite all to come to you, just as they are.*
> *You are eminently available.*

Jesus, Ever-Living, Ever-Serving High Priest

He has become a high priest forever, in the order of Melchizedek (6:20)

Melchizedek's authority did not depend on human appointment nor was it a position in an institution. He was a priest of God because he walked with God.

This letter was written to the Jews, God's chosen people. I can see eyebrows raised as they grasped what the Holy Spirit is saying. Melchizedek, a Canaanite, blessed Abraham. If this was true, it would upset almost everything. The thought was so outlandish and threatening that the best thing to do was to slam the door on such nonsense. Many did just that.

The point that the Holy Spirit is making is that Jesus of Nazareth was appointed to be God's high priest while Caiaphas reigned. Not to succeed Caiaphas, but to replace Caiaphas, and all other priests, for that matter.

Caiaphas was a Levite; Jesus was Judean. Caiaphas had the right to be the high priest. The Jews had appointed him. They had not appointed Jesus to any office. Jesus is an imposter, they asserted.

Jesus is the great high priest of God because that is what he is. He needs no human appointment to that role. He was appointed to his high priestly work in the counsels of heaven. We have seen how he was made perfect through the suffering of the cross, where he died to take away our sin, a work that was itself the most profound high priestly work. This qualifies him to be my high priest and yours.

Lord Jesus, you are my high priest forever.

Jesus, According to the Law

He has become a high priest forever, in the order of Melchizedek (6:20)

I love the scene in Revelation 1 where John saw someone moving among the candles. It was Jesus, the great high priest, on duty day and night, year after year.

Under the old covenant, every year the Jews chose one of the priests to be the high priest for that year. His task was awesome—to present to God the blood of the national sacrifice. The nation chose the most perfect bullock and the most perfect goat from among all the herds of Israel. They prepared and slaughtered the animals precisely as the law prescribed. The high priest transferred the sins Israel committed that year onto the sacrificial animal. All had to be done with great attention to detail, for God cannot accept a sacrifice given in disobedience.

On the Day of Atonement, the high priest lifted the heavy curtain to enter the Most Holy Place where God dwelt in Shekinah glory. He first presented the blood of his personal sacrificial animal, then the blood of the national sacrifice, on which were transferred the sins of all of the people. The high priest felt a blend of hope and fear—hope that God would accept the sacrifice and fear that God might reject the sacrifice as insufficient. If God rejected it a wail of despair would be heard all over the land.

Jesus, our high priest, you prepared the sacrifice just right,
*   in every detail.*
In fact, you are both high priest and sacrifice.
When you entered the presence of your Father,
*   you were received with choruses of grand amens.*
My sins were on those wounded shoulders.
Praise be to God. Amen.

Jesus, Always on Priestly Duty

He has become a high priest forever (6:20)

Forever. As the high priest emerged unharmed from the meeting with God, a great national hallelujah rose from Zion, the holy hill. In one amazing moment, all the sins that Israel transferred to the Paschal sacrifice were blotted out, gone forever.

The primary work of the high priest was to ensure that the proper sacrifice was chosen, that all of the rituals were carefully followed regarding its preparation to be an acceptable sacrifice, and that it was presented in just the right manner before the throne of almighty God. So, as the priest exited the Most Holy Place alive, it was proof that he had done his work well and that God was pleased with the sacrifice offered.

That was reason for celebration and thanksgiving, for God had once again restrained his judgment against sin. My African friends would have called that a "hallelujah time."

But the Israelites' joy of sins forgiven must have been mixed with the sobering thought that the reservoir of personal and national sin would surely be filled all over again, waiting until the sacrifice of next year. This brings us to the point of the phrase "a high priest forever"—one of the most glorious pronouncements ever boomed from heaven.

> *Jesus, because you gave yourself to atone for my sins*
> *and the sins of all who would believe,*
> *your cleansing, energizing blood*
> *is always available to restore my soul.*
> *Every day is a precious day of atonement.*
> *Praise your name forever.*

Jesus, King of Peace

This Melchizedek was king of Salem (7:1)

The writer devotes an entire chapter, one of thirteen, to the ways in which the priesthood of Jesus resembles that of Melchizedek. If it was important to the author, we should pay careful attention. For most of us this is new territory, so we will walk through it carefully.

The first thing that impresses me is that I thought the writer would have likened Jesus to Aaron, Israel's famed high priest. Instead he said Jesus is like the rather obscure Melchizedek, who is mentioned but a few times in the Bible.

Second, priests of Israel could never be kings. It must have struck Hebrew readers as an oxymoron to be told that Melchizedek was both a priest and a king.

Third, Melchizedek did not rule over a nation as such, but he ruled over an idea, a virtue called peace. Melchizedek had no army as far as we know. His kingdom was Salem—peace. He was not a warrior king. He was a completely different kind of king than we usually think of. He was but a bystander when Abraham liberated his brother Lot from the clutches of Sidon.

I have read history all my life. Human history is a sad series of stories of kings of war, not kings of peace. It comes as a marvelous, refreshing thought that there was a king named Melchizedek who was a king of peace, but even more precious to know that Jesus Christ, my Lord and Savior, is the true king of peace.

Jesus, you defy all themes of human history.
You came among us to introduce an entirely new concept,
a kingdom of peace, ruled by the Prince of Peace.
I delight in being a citizen of that kingdom.

Jesus, Priest of Almighty God

Melchizedek ... priest of God Most High (7:1)

Great as he was, Abraham was not a priest. He never thought of himself as one. He was a patriarch, a king, so to speak. He was called to establish a nation under the leadership of God, to bless all nations. That was an awesome call.

Similarly Melchizedek was a king, the king of peace. Abraham obviously respected Melchizedek as king but what really impressed him was Melchizedek's walk with "the Most High God." That is why he offered Melchizedek a tenth of the plunder that he had taken from Sidon. He had no military reason to do so.

In my cultural studies, I find priests throughout history. The world has never lacked priests. There are always people around who claim to be able to link the living with the departed spirits.

Melchizedek was not one of those priests who served local or tribal gods. Abraham discerned that Melchizedek was not a priest of a national god or a fertility god, or a god of war. He was "priest of God Most High," Yahweh, the very God who appeared to Abraham. As far as we know, Abraham did not meet anyone else who worshipped and served Yahweh like this man, Melchizedek. This priest resembles Jesus.

Blessed Holy Spirit, thank you for opening the eyes of Abraham
to recognize that this stranger served the same Yahweh he did.
Likewise open my eyes to recognize those who love Jesus dearly.

Jesus, High Priest for All Nations

Melchizedek ... priest of God Most High (7:1)

Even today, the Holy Spirit is at work bringing sincere seekers at least some knowledge of the light of God. The apostle Paul concluded that "since the creation of the world God's invisible qualities—his eternal power and divine nature—have been clearly seen, being understood from what has been made" (Romans 1:20). God is not without a witness in any culture of the world. Having stated that truth, Paul maintained that salvation is only through Christ because he alone atoned for our sins. Paul believed that the knowledge of God is universal but saving grace is only in Jesus Christ.

I recall sitting as a student in a college Bible class when someone asked the teacher, "What about godly people who have never heard of Christ?" The teacher responded, "If anyone genuinely seeks God, the Holy Spirit will enlighten that person." Like Melchizedek?

Some adventurous Christian theologians now and again suggest that, in addition to Jesus, great prophets of God, such as Muhammad or the Dalai Lama, have arisen in other religions. Jesus, they claim, is just one of God's prophets. I doubt that Jesus, our Melchizedek, would be very happy with that point of view. Since Jesus was crucified and rose from the dead as our Savior and Lord some people have doubted the uniqueness of his incarnation and his sacrificial death. Many hammers have been spent on that anvil.

> *Lord Jesus, you are not just another prophet of God.*
> *You are God's Paschal Lamb, the one and only.*
> *You alone made atonement for sin.*

Jesus, Son of Man

**Without father or mother, without genealogy, without beginning of days or
end of life, like the Son of God (7:3)**

Melchizedek is a shadowy figure in the Bible. He appeared out of nowhere, yet Abraham acknowledged him as greater than he himself. Who taught him about Yahweh? Who were his father and mother? What motivated him? If he was greater than Abraham, about whom we know much, why do we know so little about him? The Holy Spirit lets those questions go unanswered. The focus is on Jesus.

We know much about Jesus, including his ancestry. He had a mother, the virgin Mary. She was probably of the tribe of Judah, even though her genealogy does not appear in the Bible. The Jews did not trace bloodlines through women, but she was a true daughter in Israel.

Joseph was Jesus' presumed father. Matthew, writing for Jewish readers, traced Joseph's ancestors as far back as Abraham, the father of the Jewish nation. Luke, writing for Gentile readers, traced Joseph's ancestry right back to Adam, the first man.

In both cases, the Bible acknowledged that Jesus was indeed the Son of man. He had a mother, a father, a nationality, a birth, a death, and an entire biography that we know about. In this regard, Jesus is not like Melchizedek. He is like us.

Jesus, you are indeed like me, a son of man—the Son of man.

July 9

Jesus, Son of God

**Without father or mother, without genealogy, without beginning of days
or end of life, like the Son of God (7:3)**

Jesus is the Son of God and the Son of man. I must always keep in mind his dual nature. The apostle John wrote, "The Word became flesh and lived for a while among us" (John 1:14). That is the incarnation in its essence.

It is here that I stand before a mystery: God became a person. My mind cannot embrace this truth. No matter what logic I use, my rationality tells me that the Creator can never become a creature. No logic that I am aware of would support such an argument. Yet the entire gospel of salvation by grace rests on this astonishing assertion. If the Son of God is not the Son of man, I remain in my sins.

As I ponder the tragedy of the cross, I see Jesus taking my sin upon himself as the Son of man who is one of us, our true representative. Yet at the same time I see him as the Son of God who has the authority to forgive my sin and to grant me life eternal.

> *Jesus, my Lord and Savior, when I examine your spilled blood,*
> *   it is a blend of the Son of man and the Son of God.*
> *My heart knows it is true, and my mind recognizes a logic of divine,*
> *   eternal, compelling love.*
> *I believe. As the blind man said, "Now I can see!"*
> *I see not because I have solved the mystery by logic*
> *   but because my heart responds to a logic*
> *   that I can embrace only when I believe.*
> *If that is a conundrum, so be it.*
> *I believe, my Lord, with heart and head.*

Christ in Glory

Like the Son of God he remains a priest forever (7:3)

Our writer switches comparisons here. Having argued that Jesus is like Melchizedek, he lifts up Jesus and ponders how Melchizedek is like him. Jesus is the standard, the substance of which Melchizedek is but a sign. Melchizedek has value only as he is like Jesus.

As Son of God, Christ has no affiliation with anything human. That is, he is coexistent with the Father. The Father did not "have" Christ as a human father begets a son. God is a triune God. He was never anything else nor will he ever be anything else. God is Father, Son, and Holy Spirit. That statement is easy to write, but it is difficult to believe and even more difficult to explain.

It is not unexpected that we should try to put labels on Jesus. I recently ministered in an area where I did not know many people. So as I shook hands, I asked, "What is your name?" "What is your work?" I had to find some way to put labels on people so I could remember them.

That does not work with Jesus. Many tried that and stumbled, such as those who labeled him as the son of nondescript parents, Joseph and Mary, common peasants. Some scorned him because he came from Nazareth. They thought nothing good could come out of that place. He is a Jew, a Galilean. But Jesus is much larger than human affiliation or any office he holds. He is as God is.

Jesus, I want to know you.
You are Son of man, so it is interesting to know your heritage,
but you are the promised Messiah, the Son of God.
I need to know more.

Jesus, the Founder of a New Kingdom

Like the Son of God he remains a priest forever (7:3)

This brings us to the point: Jesus Christ remains a priest forever because he is the Son of God. He had his identity from the foundation of the world—a spiritual identity.

One thing is abundantly clear. He was the Lamb of God before the foundation of the world. Likewise he was and is God's Son. He is a priest forever. He was not appointed to be priest; he is the priest who mediates between God and mankind. These thoughts lift us to a new plane entirely.

My human questions about who Jesus is cannot possibly help me to label him as Son of God. In my imagination, I ask Jesus, "Are you Joseph's son?" His reply, "My Father is in heaven, hallowed be his name." "What do you do, Jesus?" "I do the will of my heavenly Father." "What is your name?" "Prince of Peace, mighty Counselor, Savior, Lord, King of kings. . . ."

Do you not agree with me that Jesus Christ is absolutely unique? No one was ever Son of man and Son of God. My mind goes back to our previous meditations. Both Matthew and Luke opened their gospels with Jesus' human genealogy. They closed their gospels with no reference to that family tree at all, but with the door wide open to everyone on the face of the earth to come to Jesus for full salvation and eternal life. The atonement removes all privilege.

> *Jesus, that is the way it is for all of us.*
> *We usually come to know you first as the Son of man,*
> *then we discover to our amazement*
> *that you are none other than the Son of almighty God.*

Jesus, Sinless Priest

If perfection could have been attained through the Levitical priesthood, . . .
why was there still need for another priest? (7:11)

The writer declared that Aaron's priesthood could make no one perfect. This flew in the face of deeply held Jewish belief. Was not the Aaronic priesthood established by God himself, as described in the book of Leviticus? That system served the Jews remarkably well for many centuries. What was wrong with it?

Something must have been wrong, because the Bible itself noted as early as Genesis 14 that, by offering Melchizedek the tithe, Abraham was acknowledging Melchizedek's spiritual equality if not his superiority.

King David had a word of prophecy: "The LORD has sworn and will not change his mind: 'You are a priest forever in the order of Melchizedek'" (Psalm 110:4). This was written while the Aaronic priesthood was in full swing.

The reason the Levitical sacrifices could not make perfect is that "it is impossible for the blood of bulls and goats to take away sins" (Hebrews 10:4). We might say that the priesthood provided a perfect function, but it could not offer perfection. It was impossible for imperfect priests to promise perfection. The promise was that a better priest would replace the flawed priesthood of the Levites, one who would not need to offer a sacrifice for his own sin.

> *Jesus, you are undoubtedly the better priest.*
> *Only you who are perfected can offer perfection.*
> *Not only that, but the sacrifice you offer is the sacrifice of yourself,*
> *the only sacrifice that can give us peace with God.*
> *I embrace you as my better priest.*

July 13

Jesus, Our Perfection

If perfection could have been attained through the Levitical priesthood,...
why was there still need for another priest? (7:11)

Even before the Levitical priesthood was established, God promised a better way in the order of Melchizedek. Jewish scholars were aware of this, but they refused to believe it. Was it because they found it difficult to believe that sinful people could ever have fellowship with the Holy God?

The perfection offered in Jesus Christ is a perfect relationship with God. Granted, true saints are acutely aware of their many imperfections. Therefore they repent of those shortcomings and glory in the forgiving power of Jesus Christ, God's precious Lamb. But they know that all hindrances from God's side have been removed by the atoning work of Jesus. We are urged to risk it all in the blood of Christ and enter the presence of God of heaven and earth.

I am aware of the temptation to look for other ways to obtain perfection. I have friends outside of Christ who are seeking fulfillment by pursuing knowledge or the arts or religion or some other worldly pursuit. Our culture promises a hundred ways for self-actualization, from lofty philosophical speculation to undisciplined hedonism.

I need to hear the truth once again. If perfection can be found in any other way, Jesus Christ is irrelevant. He cried out, "If there is some other way. . . ." He knew there was no other way. He tread the only way, alone.

> *Thank you, Jesus, for dying for me and rising from the dead*
> *to intercede for me forever.*
> *No other can do that.*

Jesus, the New Law

When there is a change of the priesthood, there must also be a change of the law (7:12)

The Jews contended that there was nothing at all wrong with the Levitical priesthood system. Because it was God who instituted this arrangement, albeit through Moses and Aaron, they rightfully felt it was the very best way for people to satisfy God. As far as the Jewish mind was concerned, the Levitical priesthood and the blood sacrifices would never be superseded by anything. The Jewish cultural and religious life was built on those two foundation stones.

I can almost hear them insisting that the Levitical priesthood and animal sacrifices are God's best answer. The letter to the Hebrews challenged that belief. For the vast majority of the Jews, the gospel was pure heresy. They could not imagine any other way to fulfill the Law of Moses. Temple sacrifices and temple worship formed the core of their identity.

I wonder if they would have changed their minds if they could have foreseen the destruction of the temple about twenty years after this letter was written. The Levitical ritual and the slaying of sacrificial animals ceased in AD 70. Jesus knew and predicted that it would happen. So even before the sacrificial system came to an end, God had in place something much better, the new covenant, based on the eternal sacrifice and the eternal high priest, Jesus Christ.

Thank you, Jesus, for revealing this to me and to all who love you.

Jesus, Master of Time

**When there is a change of the priesthood, there must also be
a change of the law (7:12)**

I have been thinking about the wisdom of God's timing in my life.

Unknown to me, but known to God, my wife would need total hip replacements. The house we lived in for almost thirty years had all kinds of stairs and steps. Through a series of events, we sold it and bought another, not because we foresaw the surgeries but because we wanted to be near our daughter and son-in-law. The new house was just perfect for my wife's needs. We did not foresee that, but the Lord did.

I see this same thing happening in the letter to the Hebrews. It was written about AD 60. Jesus foresaw the destruction of the temple in AD 70. It was part of God's gracious plan. He made a way in Jesus Christ for all those who trusted in the old, imperfect sacrificial system to move into the new, where Jesus Christ is the perfect sacrifice whose priesthood is perfect and eternal. Those who did so, such as Saul of Tarsus, could not contain their praise and thanksgiving for God's marvelous provision.

I ache for the Jews who turned their backs on Jesus. They redoubled their efforts to make sure nothing would interfere with the steady flow of animal sacrifices for thirty-five years after Jesus rose from the dead. It was all futility, for the final sacrifice had already been offered.

> *God, you knew that the day was hastening*
> *when the Jewish high priest*
> *would slay the last animal on the altar.*
> *While that flawed era was closing,*
> *you sent Jesus to establish the new covenant.*

Jesus, My New Law

When there is a change of the priesthood, there must also be a change of the law (7:12)

When a person embraces Jesus Christ as his or her priest, it follows that the laws governing all of life change. I see this clear as crystal. It happens in my own life. When I depend completely on Jesus, trusting him to do his good work before God, I find myself acting like him. I become more like the person to whom I entrust my life.

The Old Testament prophets kept warning the Jews that they would become like the idols they worshipped. People become like their gods because they fashion those gods for themselves, hoping to receive power from them. Then they spend the rest of their lives acting out what they believe those inert idols want.

The idol we worship determines how we act. Commercials and other advertisements confirm this. If you worship a god of thinness, then you have to attain thinness. Or if you worship a god of success, you have to pay the price to obtain it.

That is what the Holy Spirit is driving home in this verse. If I trust Jesus with my whole heart to save, sustain, empower, and intercede for me, a new law dominates my life. I begin to act like Jesus.

> *Jesus, you said it so clearly.*
> *You expect those who love you to do what you command.*
> *You become their new law.*
> *I know how very important it is to me*
> *to keep you clearly in view at all times*
> *so that I might not lose my way and follow strange laws.*

The Rule of Christ

**When there is a change of the priesthood, there must also be
a change of the law (7:12)**

Jesus must invade a life in order to establish his new law. What good is it to try to obey his teachings if he has not already overpowered me? Some people seem to think that the reason Jesus came was to bring us a higher ethic than any other religious leader. He did bring the highest ethics, indeed. But that is not what the gospel of Jesus Christ is about.

I cannot live out the rule of Christ without the indwelling presence of Jesus in my life. If my natural disposition could attain to the high ethic of Jesus, then why did God pay the unbelievably high cost of the atonement?

Oswald Chambers had it right: "I must know Jesus Christ as Savior before his teaching has any meaning for me other than that of an ideal which leads to despair." Jesus did not intend that any human being could attain to the ethic he taught without the indwelling power of Christ.

When I try to obey the commandments of Jesus without first knowing the power of Jesus' indwelling presence by faith in my heart, I fail miserably. As Jonah said, "Those who cling to worthless idols forfeit the grace that could be theirs" (Jonah 2:8).

Thank you, Holy Spirit, for pointing out to me
when I fail to obey the clear word of Jesus Christ.
I refuse all idols. I will obey none other than Jesus.

Jesus, Delightfully Unpredictable

**One who has become a priest, not on the basis of a regulation as to his
ancestry but on the basis of the power of an indestructible life (7:16)**

Not ancestry but power. Again we are reminded that Jesus was not of the priestly tribe, the Levites.
How then could he be the high priest? It was quite simple. Jesus was priest because he is priest. It has
nothing at all to do with human appointment.

The writer reminded the Jews that imbedded in their revered Scripture was the promise that another
sort of priest would arise who would be like Abraham's friend, Melchizedek, a non-Jew, a priest of the
God Most High. It was God who made Melchizedek a priest, not religious authorities. What makes
Jesus absolutely and eternally unique is that he did not become the great high priest. It was by God's
appointment. Jesus was chosen by God. He was always high priest.

The Holy Spirit surprises us even today and sends messengers of hope for his own purposes. I
have seen powerful leaders arise who were chosen by no one. They just appeared. I recall the story of a
person in Tanzania who felt called to fast and pray on a mountain. While there the Lord told him to go
and minister in his name. After coming down from the mountain, he was astonished that Jesus used
him to preach, heal, and cast out demons. This presented a problem to the church leaders. They had not
given the Lord the authority to call and empower that person. I leave to the reader's holy imagination
what happened.

My heavenly Father, you are the consummate surpriser.
Keep my eyes and my heart open to your many surprises of grace.

Jesus, Our Better Hope

A better hope is introduced, by which we draw near to God (7:19)

I try to imagine that I am a Jew receiving this letter. My hope rests on the law given to Moses at Sinai. As a Jew, I recount how diligent I have been in obeying the law and how obedient I have been in providing all of the prescribed sacrifices and offerings. The law and the Aaronic priesthood shine with the brilliance of the noonday sun. The law is glorious beyond measure. Was it not delivered by angels? As a Jew, I am convinced that the law is strong and effective. My ancestors believed that and placed all their hope on the law and the sacrifices.

A better hope? Imagine the consternation of the Jews when they hear that the glorious law and sacrifices are weak and useless. Heresy! Humans might fail, but the law is strong. There is nothing wrong with the law! Oh, yes, there is, the writer of Hebrews insists, because it cannot bring a sinner into fellowship with God. True worship is fellowship with God. The law was not designed to do that.

The law and the sacrifices can never usher a supplicant sinner into the presence of almighty God. Jesus can. His life, his sacrificial death, and his resurrection opened the door wide for any person anywhere at any time to be reconciled to God and to people. That is good news with an eternal promise.

Jesus, you are the blessed "better hope."
You fling open the door to the presence of our heavenly Father.
For a believer, that is gold in the bank.
It is for now, it is for all, and it is for eternity.
Lord Jesus, you are the way to fellowship with almighty God.

Jesus, God's Oath

The Lord has sworn and will not change his mind:
"You are a priest forever" (7:21)

In all of Scripture, God swears sparingly. He did so when he made the original covenant with Abraham and the Jewish people and again at Sinai when the law was established. Those oaths marked the two high points in the life of the Jewish people.

In the third instance, God swore he would provide a priest like Melchizedek who would be a perfect priest forever. The Hebrew writer can barely contain his enthusiasm at this point.

God swore. When a person swears, he or she appeals to the authority of a mighty power. So by whom does the almighty God swear? He swears by himself. There is no higher power. This oath of God, appealing to his own eternal power and wisdom, was taken to assert absolutely that he would provide a priest whose priesthood would know no end. Jesus Christ is that promised Messiah.

With the oath comes a guarantee. I am profoundly moved by the fact that whoever wrote this letter based all hope on Jesus Christ, a hope that is as firm and sure as the nature of God.

> *Lord, may my vision of Jesus so fill my life*
> *that there is simply no place for competing loyalties.*
> *He is my all in all, my one and only.*

Jesus, My Complete Salvation

**Therefore he is able to save completely those who come to God
through him (7:25)**

How is the idea of completeness used here? Is it like talking about a house that was once only a blueprint but is now a finished house? I do not think so.

The writer uses *completely* to say that my salvation is complete because Jesus Christ in whom I live is complete. He is the perfect sacrifice. He is the perfect high priest. He is the perfect Savior. He is the perfect Son of man. He is the perfect Son of God. He is the perfect teacher. He is the perfect prophet-king. He is perfect in every regard. When I am in him and he is in me, I partake of his perfection and completeness. As long as I remain in him and as long as his Word remains in me, I am, before God, completely saved.

But I may, and often do, find flaws and sin and inadequacies in myself. I am a long way from that goal of perfection. I am not yet the completed product that my designer has so carefully planned. Nevertheless, at this very moment, I am complete because of Jesus. I am complete in him. Outside of him I am a sitting duck for Satan's powerful shotguns. But in him I am as safe as safe can be.

> *Jesus, you know very well how frail and helpless I am*
> *apart from you.*
> *That is why you prepared a place of complete safety for me*
> *in your wounded side.*
> *As a branch, I am grafted into you,*
> *the vine, safe and secure as long as I remain there.*

Jesus, My Completeness

**Therefore he is able to save completely those who come to God through
him (7:25)**

In his letter to the Colossians, Paul saw it all so clearly: "In Christ all the fullness of the Deity lives in bodily form, and you have been given fullness in Christ" (2:9-10).

Some versions use the word *complete* to describe this. I like the idea of fullness because it speaks of "full" in the sense that there is no room for anything else. If a bucket is full of water, it can hold no additional water. The water will simply spill over.

So completeness speaks of Jesus filling our lives to the brim. If he fills my life, there is no room for more. He is completely able to meet my every need.

That is why I can confidently say that Jesus is saving me completely right now, because his fullness is filling my emptiness as I yield to him and obey his commands, mindful always of the promptings of the Holy Spirit as I walk with brothers and sisters in the body of Christ.

> *Thank you, Jesus, for emptying yourself on Calvary's cruel tree,*
> *breaking before the will of your Father, and in so doing,*
> *dying for my sin.*
> *Having emptied yourself, God poured into you all the fullness of Deity.*
> *That, O Lord, is the way for me: dying to sin and self*
> *and receiving as a marvelous gift the fullness of Jesus Christ,*
> *in whom is fullness indeed.*

July 23

Jesus, My Constant Intercessor

He always lives to intercede for them (7:25)

A lot is tied up in the words "He always lives" and even more in the words "to intercede."

It is not only that Jesus exists yesterday, today, and tomorrow, but that he is doing what he does all the time, day and night, summer and winter, near and far, with great varieties of people, without tiring.

The arresting reality, however, is that he always lives to intercede *for me*. It does not surprise me that God cares for his universe. He is an expansive God with enormous responsibilities. He has a lot to oversee. As I gaze into the sky I realize that our galaxy contains a trillion suns and there are a billion galaxies out there. I am awed by the immensity of it all. I am also awed by its order and its constant flux. Even now, stars are forming while others die in dramatic sequences of cosmic power. When I ponder these matters, I realize how puny I am, an atom on a speck. I am driven to admit that I do not really matter.

Then I read this verse. The co-Creator of it all, Jesus Christ, God's beloved Son, "always lives to intercede for" me. I am important to Jesus, so important that he spends all his time praying for me. Can it be?

> *My Lord Jesus, if I ever doubt my worth,*
> *I only need to see you there in the presence of your loving Father,*
> *interceding for me by name.*
> *Thank you, Jesus, for spending all your time thinking about me.*

Jesus, My Faithful Intercessor

He always lives to intercede for them (7:25)

Within the past year the Lord has worked in a most remarkable way to bring many things together at just the right time for our family.

When I am tempted to believe that I am clever, I need only muse on the wisdom of my Lord. I have not one shred of doubt that Jesus lives to make intercession for me. How else could I explain one inexplicable thing after another?

Jesus amazes me. As a human being, I divide the large from the small, the significant from the insignificant, the cosmic from the particular, the important from the unimportant. The Lord does not view reality like that at all. Or if he does, he does not work on the same assumptions that I do.

Biblical writers probed only so far, then stopped as they realized that the ways of God are past finding out. Every sensitive heart pauses at this point, in holy humility. I confess I only know in part and see in part. But one thing I do know: Jesus is alive and his vocation, day and night, is to present me with all my needs before his Father. I cannot explain it, for the only explanation for grace is God's eternal love, and that is an ocean of truth, far surpassing my powers of comprehension.

> *Lord Jesus, I know that you died to defeat Satan,*
> *to set the prisoners free,*
> *to put all mankind on equal footing for salvation.*
> *I revel in those huge themes.*
> *I praise your name because I at last begin to understand*
> *a bit of what happened when you gave your life*
> *to set all sinners like me free.*
> *But what really staggers me is the thought that right now,*
> *at this very moment, you are telling your Father,*
> *"Don loves you. I know that for sure." Can it be? It is.*
> *Praise you, Jesus, forever.*

Jesus, Unlike Aaron

**Such a high priest meets our need—one who is holy, blameless, pure,
set apart from sinners, exalted above the heavens (7:26)**

Ironically, Israel's first high priest, Aaron, is known for his flaws, the most notable of which was his willingness to help the rebellious Jews to fashion an Egyptian god. That was the darkest day on the journey.

I wonder where Aaron was as the hearts of the people eagerly embraced an Egyptian god? Did he join the rebellious throng, also throwing off all restraint as the gold calf was unveiled and glistened with splendor there in the desert?

I am trying to understand Aaron. What motivated him to do such a wicked thing? Was it fear? Did he assume that Moses died on the barren Mount Sinai? There was probably an element of dread in Aaron's heart. But there was something else at work. Aaron was bonded to the people, and his sympathy for them trumped everything. But it was not counterbalanced by a similar sympathy for God. Aaron had not learned the secret of a personal walk with God.

I recall another low point in Aaron's life. His sister, Miriam, became jealous because Moses took an Egyptian woman as his second wife. Aaron should have challenged Miriam's attitude. Instead he joined in her criticism. God could not let her critical spirit spread venom through the camp, so she became leprous. Aaron saw his own sister joining the lepers outside the camp. He was severely flawed.

> *Lord, is it possible that Aaron can be forgiven for such huge sins?*
> *You not only forgave him,*
> > *but also appointed him to be the high priest.*
> *This is nothing but grace at work.*

Jesus Meets My Need

Such a high priest meets our need—one who is holy, blameless, pure, set apart from sinners, exalted above the heavens (7:26)

At Sinai God directed Moses to construct the tabernacle, which was an elaborate affair and took some time to build. But when the day came to institute the priesthood, who would be the first Jewish high priest? God chose none other than the flawed Aaron. I see in this the mighty grace of God that extends to sinners like me.

Aaron presaged Peter who, having denied Christ, repented and wept in utter brokenness. That same Peter wrote, "You were redeemed . . . with the precious blood of Christ, a lamb without blemish or defect" (1 Peter 1:18-19). Peter experienced the cleansing power of the blood of the Lamb, the perfect sacrifice.

Unlike Aaron, who had to first confess his own sin before he could intercede for all Israel, Jesus knew no sin. He walked with his heavenly Father in perfect fellowship without a moment of interruption. That is how he lived and that is how he died. Jesus is certainly qualified to be my high priest. He is "holy, blameless, pure, set apart from sinners, exalted above the heavens." There is no flaw to sully his perfection.

> *My Lord, what more could my heart desire than a perfect high priest,*
> *offering for me, a sinner, the perfect sacrifice—God's chosen,*
> *precious Paschal Lamb?*
> *Be still, my soul. Gaze again at the wondrous sight—Jesus,*
> *my high priest, is offering the sacrifice*
> *of his own precious blood for me.*
> *Praise him to eternity.*

July 27

Jesus, the Real Object of Worship

**Unlike the other high priests, he does not need to offer sacrifices
day after day, first for his own sins, and then for the sins of the people**
(7:27)

I vividly recall a day in Nepal, a Hindu nation, when a missionary friend joined my wife and me on a hike to the top of a hill just outside the town of Pochra. We found a walled enclosure at the summit. Worshipers were selecting their spots inside the walls, where the animals they had brought would be offered as sacrifice. We left before the slaughter began but as we descended the hill we met worshipers coming up with their protesting animals. I tried to imagine the scene up there as the worshipers slit the throats of those innocent animals, flooding the floor with blood. Then what? They had to go home and prepare for the next sacrifice. And so it goes month after month, year after year, century after century. They live under constant condemnation.

The Jews lived under the same condemnation. No sooner was one sacrifice slaughtered than another was set aside for the next slaughter. In the meanwhile, what about their sins? Were they taken away or not? This entire sacrificial system, while promising remission for sin, was a frustrating affair. Yet every sacrifice was a sign of hope that some day a way would be found to deal with sin once and for all. Each sacrifice was branded, "Not yet."

This dream, Lord Jesus, was realized when you poured out your life,
thus opening the way for me and all who love you
to have peace with God.
Your sacrifice need not be repeated; in fact,
cannot be repeated. It is once for all! Amen.

Jesus Offered the Perfect Sacrifice

**Unlike the other high priests, he does not need to offer sacrifices
day after day, first for his own sins, and then for the sins of the people
(7:27)**

Jewish high priests longed for the day when they could offer the perfect sacrifice. We noted earlier that some Jews believed that if one perfect red heifer could be found, that would be the end of the sacrificial parade. So they bred almost-perfect animals in the hope of getting one with 100-percent red hair. Imagine their anticipation as they examined a newly born calf of near-perfect parents, only to discover around the ears a few white or black hairs. So they went on breeding one generation after another, in search of the perfect red heifer.

When Jesus, the sinless one, took on himself the sin of the world and then on the cross poured out his lifeblood, it was done. The perfect red heifer had appeared! As Matthew wrote, "She will give birth to a son, and you are to give him the name Jesus, because he will save his people from their sins" (Matthew 1:21).

The world is full of religions. Having studied many of them, I have come to one conclusion: The best of all religions point to Jesus Christ. Every prayer ever prayed has in it the yearning that someday the gap between people and God will be bridged. Every animal that people present to their deity points to the Lamb, offered by God himself, to take away sin once and for all. Every philosopher who ponders the mystery of life indicates that people need a purpose in life. All signs point to Jesus.

*Jesus Christ, you are the ultimate and sure answer
to the prayer of every worshipping heart.
May many place their faith in you today.*

Jesus, Seated at God's Right Hand

The point of what we are saying is this: We do have such a high priest (8:1)

People need a priest, someone to connect them with the supernatural.

I lived among the Wakuria people of Tanzania for many years. Their priests established phenomenally elaborate procedures and rituals in attempts to ensure supernatural aid. From our house we could see the Bugoshi hill, their sacred mountain, a mile or so away. When a crisis occurred, such as the threat of famine, the tribal elders climbed Bugoshi with animal sacrifices and the local "beer." Following ancient tradition, they presented their offerings to the spirits. They believed that their sacred totem animal, the leopard, which lived on the hill, would eat the offerings and answer their prayers.

The tribal elders performed the ritual on Bugoshi only on special occasions—to fend off famine and misfortune. All the while the people visited their local medicine men and women who served a priestly function. They consulted ancestral spirits for protection from evil spirits.

The point here is that every culture provides some access to the supernatural. That desire was placed in the human heart by God, the Creator, the Father of Jesus Christ, who fulfills perfectly the role of great high priest. The gospel announces that God has provided a high priest named Jesus Christ. He is at God's right hand, the position of sovereign authority.

Jesus, my intercessor, stretch out your strong arm
to enable me to walk in the presence of God today.

Jesus, More Than a Shadow

They serve at a sanctuary that is a copy and shadow of what is in heaven
(8:5)

The entire Aaronic priesthood with its elaborate ceremonies, though impressive, was but a shadow cast by the "real thing," which is not on earth but in heaven.

This strikes me as contrary to my usual way of thinking. I tend to see heavenly things through earthly eyes. I need to learn to see earthly things through heavenly eyes. The real is in heaven; the shadow of the heavenly real is seen on earth.

The author of Hebrews assumed that in heaven there is a tabernacle, so to speak, that is the real thing. The earthly one is but a shadow or copy. So Moses did not invent something new. God revealed to Moses what he should do to represent on earth what already exists in heaven. The tabernacle with all its paraphernalia was not the real thing, but it accurately represented in iconic form what exists in heaven.

I find it a challenge to get used to this kind of thinking. The heavenlies know nothing of time and space as I know them. Heaven is not a physical place and what I call history is *now* in heaven. That helps me to understand statements like Revelation 13:8: "The Lamb . . . was slain from the creation of the world." In heavenly "time," Jesus was always the slain Lamb of God. Earth had to "wait" until that reality could be realized.

> *Lord Jesus, you taught us that what we see on earth*
> *is connected with heavenly realities.*
> *You know that my heart longs for reality, not shadows.*
> *Give me eyes to see.*

Jesus, the Real Word

They serve at a sanctuary that is a copy and shadow of what is in heaven
(8:5)

Plato taught that what we see is not real, but only the shadows of what is real. The philosopher's job is to figure out what is real by examining the shadows.

The Bible invites us to consider the shadows too. The difference, however, is that it is not up to us to figure out what is casting the shadows. We gain that knowledge by divine revelation, particularly through the person Jesus Christ. Plato, with all his wisdom and knowledge, never saw what I see clear as crystal.

A book I consider precious is Roy Hession's *From Shadow to Substance*. It is a brilliant exposition of the book of Hebrews in which he sees Jesus as the reality behind everything in the Law and the Prophets. He starts with the shadow that points to the substance.

I do not despise the shadows, for they assure me that the real thing is there. One shadow is the tabernacle itself. Every silver fitting, every badger skin, in fact every aspect of the tabernacle and of the Aaronic priesthood reminds me of the sufficiency of the atoning work of Jesus.

As a young man I saw how excited some preachers got when they spoke on "types of Christ" in the old covenant. That puzzled me, but I understand it now.

> *Lord Jesus, as I focus on the details of each item of the tabernacle*
> *and the priesthood, I see all of them pointing to you.*
> *Each is an icon in which I see your face.*
> *Thank you for enlightening my eyes to see you*
> *in every detail in the earthly tabernacle.*

Jesus Has a Superior Ministry

**But the ministry Jesus has received is as superior to theirs as the covenant
of which he is mediator is superior to the old one (8:6)**

Old Testament prophets reminded the people that all the blood of all the sheep, oxen, goats, and doves—billions of gallons of sacrificial blood—cannot take away one single sin. Yet the people kept bringing their animal sacrifices to the priest and the priests kept on slaughtering them. So what is the worth of all those sacrifices?

This question often came up as I interacted with African church leaders. Their ancestors had made both blood sacrifices and offerings of food from time immemorial. Was all of it futile?

We agreed that the sacrifices sincerely given all pointed to Jesus, the one and only Lamb of God. That is why God put it into their hearts to offer sacrifices. We also agreed that if, after being introduced to Jesus, people reject him and continue to believe that their sacrifices benefit them, they abandon their only hope of eternal life.

We also agreed that it is our responsibility and our great joy to announce that Jesus Christ is the end of the sacrificial system for every culture, whether Jewish or African or whatever.

The new covenant is a blood covenant, and Jesus, God's select lamb, has established it to fulfill the promise of the former one.

> *God, you alone can determine the validity of past sacrifices.*
> *One thing we do know: When people embrace the gospel,*
>   *all other sacrifices simply stop.*
> *If people continue to offer sacrifice to their gods,*
>   *Jesus is of no worth at all. Jesus,*
>   *you are the fulfillment of the law,*
>   *for you are grace and truth.*

Jesus, Mediator of the Superior Covenant

I will make a new covenant with the house of Israel (8:8)

What did the Wakuria, the people among whom we lived, expect when they climbed the Bugoshi hill with their sacrificial animals in tow?

If there was famine, they prayed for rain. If witches plagued their communities, they prayed for ways to overcome their power. If quarreling reached such a pitch that it threatened the welfare of the group, they prayed for power to reconcile. Their ancient worship was based on the hope that if they cooperate with the good ancestral spirits, those spirits would look after them.

I have studied their sacrificial ritual and find little evidence that they gave sacrifice to remove sin. Their sacrifices were their way to get what they needed to avert tragedy.

How different the old covenant from the new, which was sealed by Jesus' blood. The new promises forgiveness of sins, companionship of the Holy Spirit, a renewed, born-again, regenerated life, peace with God and with God's people, and much, much more.

The covenant inaugurated by Jesus' atoning work is superior to anything promised by any other religion. It seems odd that anyone would hesitate to reach out and embrace it wholeheartedly. The gospel of Jesus Christ is more comprehensive, more all-encompassing than any religious or secular system.

> *Jesus, you are the better promise,*
> *the new covenant made possible through your atoning work.*

Jesus, My New Conscience

**Nothing wrong with that first covenant . . . but God found fault
with the people (8:7-8)**

The least that can be said of the law is that there was nothing wrong with it. In that it resembles my conscience, there is nothing wrong with it.

I believe that my conscience is good. But if it is so good, why do I not always obey what it tells me? It seems that, instead of being a help, it stands over me with its judgmental finger pointing to what I already know is wrong. To relieve this pressure, I can either obey my conscience down to the scruple or reeducate it so that it will wink at my frequent slips and falls. In my heart of hearts, I know that neither approach is right.

What I really need is a power within me that always says yes to God. My natural inclination is to do my very best to do the right, just, and most gracious thing all the time. Good luck! The ghost of inadequacy and failure constantly haunts me. My moral self wants to please God but fails time and again. This is the anguish of all religions, for religions are mankind's attempts to please a deity of one kind or another.

The new covenant promises a new heart, a gift of God's marvelous grace. Is that a reality or a hope?

*Thank you, Jesus, for inaugurating a new covenant
    based on your perfect atoning work.
There was nothing wrong with the first covenant.
The problem was how to obey it.
You always pleased the Father,
    and you came to live in us
        to show us that you are the way to please him.
Now, blessed Jesus, aided by the Holy Spirit,
    enthuse me with that same desire.
I know that I am flawed; you are not.
Be in me my desire to obey.*

Jesus in Me

**Nothing wrong with that first covenant . . . but God found fault
with the people (8:7-8)**

The problem is not the law. How could it be? The law is nothing less than God's description of the nature of all things. I am the problem. The Jews were the problem. Everyone who reads this is the problem.

Only Jesus Christ embodied the law, for he was the preexisting Word. In a sense, he is the law. That is why he pleased the Father in all things. And that is why the Scriptures remind us again and again that Jesus pleased his Father perfectly. He confided that he always did the will of the Father, and the Father on several occasions announced that Jesus satisfied him in every regard.

Now we come to the point. Knowing that in our natural state we cannot please God, Jesus devised a way to live within believers so that he himself could obey his Father in them, just as he did as the Son of man on earth. This is such an overwhelming thought that it takes a while to sink in, but when we open our hearts in complete surrender to Jesus and the blessed Holy Spirit, an amazing thing happens. We find ourselves slowly comprehending what God wants and we discover that we also begin to want what he wants. The apostle Paul knew and experienced this. The supernatural becomes natural.

Jesus, it is a glorious truth!
You take up residence in our souls,
and then you do what you always do
—you please your Father.

Jesus, the New Law

I will put my laws in their minds and write them on their hearts (8:10)

Saul grew up in a Pharisee home in Tarsus, a small town in southern Turkey. He actually believed that he never broke God's law from infancy. Hear his testimony: "Circumcised the eighth day, of the people of Israel, of the tribe of Benjamin, a Hebrew of Hebrews; in regard to the law, a Pharisee; as for zeal, persecuting the church; as for legalistic righteousness, faultless" (Philippians 3:5-6).

When the risen Jesus Christ met Saul on the road to Damascus, the bewildered Pharisee began to discover that God never assumes that people can obey the law on their own.

The Old Testament prophet Jeremiah, who is quoted in this section of Hebrews, wrote, "'This is the covenant I will make with the house of Israel after that time,' declares the LORD. 'I will put my law in their minds and write it on their hearts. I will be their God, and they will be my people'" (Jeremiah 31:33). This prophecy was fulfilled in its entirety by Jesus taking upon himself the demands of the law, carrying our sins to the cross as God's atoning Lamb, and then promising to all believers that the Holy Spirit will enable us to lead holy lives, well-pleasing to God. This is the gospel in a nutshell. It is possible to please God, not by dint of exertion, or by obeying each detail of the law, but by allowing Jesus to obey his Father in us.

> *Praise be to God, who established the new covenant*
> *in which the law still stands but is now written on our hearts.*
> *Thank God for the presence of Jesus and the Holy Spirit*
> *to enable us to fulfill it.*

August 6

Jesus, My Obedience

I will put my laws in their minds and write them on their hearts (8:10)

My earliest experience of civil law came when I turned sixteen, the age to apply for a driver's license. I remember that little book of laws—how far you must park from a fire hydrant and what you must do in case of an accident. I found out that it was up to me to learn the law. My conscience can tell me to obey the law but it does not tell me what the law is. That I must find out for myself

When I think of the Israelites as they heard Moses reading the Law for the first time, they were stunned and frightened. It was so painful that they covered their ears and demanded that Moses stop. But Moses could not stop. He did not invent it; rather, God was speaking.

Their dread came from the fact that they were incapable of obeying what they were hearing. To make matters worse, the law came from God, who would ultimately judge them. It terrifies the human heart.

At the time of Christ, the Pharisees started with the assumption that the law could be obeyed, so they devised a culture of holiness. They established a detailed set of rules that controlled every human activity. That is the tradition in which Saul of Tarsus was raised. Paul, as we noted, believed that a human being could obey the law by self effort.

He wrote of his life as a Jew, "As for legalistic righteousness, [I was] faultless" (Philippians 3:6). I believe he was telling the truth.

> *Jesus, you devised a better way:*
> *you bore our sins in your own body on the cross*
> *and then offered to take up residence in our lives*
> *to please the Father.*
> *Rule in my heart as it is in heaven.*

Jesus, Never Obsolete

**By calling this covenant "new," he has made the first one obsolete; and
what is obsolete and aging will soon disappear (8:13)**

I just purchased a car. It's not new, but it's better than the one I had. The old car served us well, but it's obsolete and needs to be replaced. The newly purchased one is better than the old one, but I am under no illusion that it will never be obsolete too.

Not so with Jesus. Most religions serve a good purpose, especially Judaism, which so far exceeds all others that there is no comparison. However, even that magnificent religion was temporary. God never intended it to produce life. As Paul said, the law served as a schoolmaster to bring us to the place where we despair of the old legalism and reach out for Jesus.

When automakers design and produce cars, they assume that the new ones will be superseded by newer ones before long. All religions are like that. Each is flawed. Their logic might be flawless, but if the fundamental assumptions on which they are based are faulty, it cannot possibly come out right. Our Muslim friends, for example, begin with the assumption that God cannot suffer. This makes it difficult for them to see the meaning of the cross of Christ, where God in Christ suffered. Their religion is based upon some false assumptions.

The Gospel promises a better way because it is based on new assumptions. Jesus is the Son of God and the Son of man. He died so that all that believe might live.

> *Thank you, Lord Jesus, for the "better way,"*
> *which is based on the hard reality*
> *that we cannot obey the law by human effort.*
> *Your atoning work changes everything.*
> *You become our desire to obey and the power to obey.*
> *Thank you, Jesus.*

Jesus Is Entirely New

**By calling this covenant "new," he has made the first one obsolete;
and what is obsolete and aging will soon disappear (8:13)**

That is what makes Christianity so fundamentally different from other religions. Jesus Christ is new and is perfect. He will never be superseded, because the atonement he won for us is without flaw or deficiency.

"Worthy is the Lamb" is the song of our heavenly Father and all the hosts of heaven. "This is my Son, whom I love," he announced from heaven. "With him I am well pleased" (Matthew 3:17). No qualifiers!

In the course of my teaching career I taught a class on comparative religion. The textbooks tend to compare various aspects of religions, such as ethics and observances. For example, they examined how each religion dealt with charity or worship.

As I look back, I believe such comparative studies serve very little useful purpose. The exercise becomes ridiculous when Christian religious phenomena are compared to those of the religions of the world. To be sure, followers of Christ do develop religious practices, so to speak. But Jesus did not come among us to establish a new religious system. He came from heaven to redeem us from the dominion of Satan. That is absolutely unique. There is only one Jesus Christ, Lord and Savior of all.

Jesus will never be obsolete, because he alone accomplished the atoning work that brings God and people together.

*Thank you, Jesus, for who you are
and for what you have done for me.*

Jesus, Our Way of Worship and Our Sanctuary

**Now the first covenant had regulations for worship
and also an earthly sanctuary (9:1)**

The Jews of the temple period were fastidious about each tiny detail of their worship because they wanted to do everything exactly as God revealed it. No detail was too small for them. They were driven by the commitment to get it precisely right. This was important because the tabernacle was God's sanctuary on earth.

In my mind's eye I see a craftsperson selecting two special onyx stones for the robe of the high priest and on them inscribing the names of each of the tribes. It must have been an act of profound, heartfelt worship to do exactly as God instructed. Obedience and worship kissed one another. Jesus did exactly that. A far greater hand selected two eternal onyx stones for Jesus and, with the utmost care, carved my name there, to be worn close to his heart.

For each tabernacle item, I can ponder the grace and love of God for a lifetime and still stand in amazement before the beauty and wonder of the free salvation that is mine in Jesus Christ.

Or the brazen altar might catch my attention. I hear the innocent animals bleat as they give their lives as a substitute for sinful people. I see their blood being sprinkled reverently on the altar. Were I to ponder that scene for all eternity, I would catch only a glimpse of God's justice and mercy. Each detail reveals yet another facet of Jesus' redeeming work.

*Lord Jesus, as I read Old Testament prophecy concerning you,
I bow in wonder as I see that you fulfilled all prophecy
in every detail.*

Jesus, the Light

**A tabernacle was set up. In its first room were the lampstand,
the table and the consecrated bread (9:2)**

There is something to be said for orderly worship and a beautiful sanctuary, as prescribed under the old covenant. As I read Hebrews, however, I am reminded time and again that none of this is real, but only a shadow of the real.

Yet each item carries profound meaning. For example, on entering the tabernacle, the first item to catch the eye was the elaborate lampstand, burning brightly, the only source of light in the windowless first room. It was fashioned of pure gold, hammered into an ornate arrangement of seven lamps. Each lamp had a wick and a small supply of oil. It burned continually, day and night, giving light so the priests could go about their duties.

I see Jesus here. He enlightens all my life. As Isaiah prophesied, "The people walking in darkness have seen a great light" (Isaiah 9:2).

One of the priestly duties was to replenish the oil and trim the wick. In a way, I am a lamp. After trimming the wick, the priest—Jesus—carefully lifts and tilts the pitcher and fills me to the brim with pure olive oil. I need the daily infilling of the Holy Spirit of God. Only as I am tended by the affectionate hand of Jesus can my light shine in this world and for ages to come. Jesus is the holy light.

Jesus, you announced that you are the light of the world.
Without you, there is no light at all.
You are not one of the many lights but the only light.
Without you, Jesus, all is darkness and death,
but with you is brilliant light and exuberant life.

Jesus, My Unleavened Bread

A tabernacle was set up. In its first room were the lampstand, the table and the consecrated bread (9:2)

Also in the first room is the bread: twelve loaves arranged in two rows of six each, representing Israel's tribes. The bread supply was replenished each week. As the priests worked, they were free to eat this bread. To highlight the bread's importance, the table was overlaid with gold, an uncharacteristic setting for common, everyday bread.

I see Jesus standing on the shores of the Sea of Galilee. After he fed the five thousand in a miraculous display of grace, he invited his listeners to eat of him. He reminded them of the manna, which means "what is it." Jesus gave the answer, "It is me." The true manna that comes down from heaven is Jesus.

Think about Jesus as bread. He is my energy, sustaining me no matter where the pilgrimage takes me. He is my fresh supply, new every morning, as Jeremiah testified: "Because of the LORD's great love we are not consumed, for his compassions never fail. They are new every morning; great is your faithfulness" (Lamentations 3:22-23).

Jesus is within reach, available to me and to all—old, young, poor, rich, man, woman, black, white—everyone. He satisfies every need in every person and in every fellowship. In him are all the vitamins and minerals we need, so there is no need to supplement him with other foods.

Food is to be eaten with others. So we commune with our Lord Jesus as he feeds us, his children. We rejoice because Jesus, the heavenly manna, is given without cost to us. The food of grace is a free gift from above. All of this points to Jesus. In the first room is the bread.

Jesus, you are my bread for this day.
And you are my hunger for that bread.
Be in me that living bread,
*   which satisfies for time and eternity.*

Jesus Brings Meaning to the First Room

A tabernacle was set up. In its first room (9:2)

Before considering the wonder and delight of entering the holiest of holies, I pause in the outer first room, surveying all that is happening there, so that I miss nothing that will assist me in the way of holiness.

As dawn breaks, the priests enter the outer room eager to perform their duties. First, the lamps must be trimmed because during the night's burning, carbon has built up, hindering the full brilliance of the holy fire. With the sharp scissors, the priest trims each wick, being ever so careful to remove the hard, charred bits, thus exposing the new, fresh wick that can burn with full brilliance.

Learn, my soul, the need for your morning trimming, because sin always dims the light. I submit my wick to the cleansing blood of Jesus. That atoning blood clips the fouled wick and renews it so that it can once again burn brightly. Were I to overlook this morning trimming, the wick would become harder and harder until it would scarcely burn at all.

Soul, do not fear the sharpness of the cleansing scissors. The pain of repentance is part of my walk with God. Let the scissors do its work. Remember, the One who holds the scissors has pierced hands. Those hands also tilt the pitcher out of which flows the abundance of the Holy Spirit, the oil that keeps me burning. Those are hands of love.

> *Renew my lamp, Jesus.*
> *As you prune the vine,*
> > *remove from me the hindrances to fruitfulness*
> > *and then fill me with the wonder-working power*
> > > *of the Holy Spirit so that I might serve you with joy.*

Jesus, Our Intercessor

**Behind the second curtain was a room called the Most Holy Place, which
had the golden altar of incense (9:3-4)**

Linger at the golden altar of prayer. The way to the seat of mercy passes the golden altar of incense, the place of prayer. Prior to entering the Most Holy Place, where the Shekinah glory resides between the cherubim, the high priest tarries first at the altar of prayer before proceeding to the throne of God almighty. No one dare simply rush in, for divine worship requires supplication. Prayer prepares the heart.

God provided the way by which worshipers can approach him. It is through Jesus Christ, the golden altar. When Jesus ascended to the Father, he assumed the position of intercessor.

The Holy Spirit is also involved, because he interprets those things that we feel but cannot adequately express. So the Father, Son, and Holy Spirit enable me to pray. If efficacy in prayer depends on me, I am undone. I pray because Jesus is in me by the Holy Spirit, and he is the source and object of my prayers. In prayer I am with Father, Son, and Holy Spirit. As I enter into the holiest place I am surrounded by the godhead.

While visiting a Buddhist shrine in Thailand, I saw people brush past banks of brass prayer spools. As they hurried along they reached out and spun the spools. I can still hear the whirring sound of those spinning cylinders. I was told that each spool had a prayer of some sort engraved on it. Instead of praying the prayer, the worshiper simply gave it a spin and quickly moved to the next and spun that one as well. If I am not careful, I can be just as perfunctory as that.

Remind me, Lord, of the sanctity of prayer.

Jesus, the Ark of the New Covenant

The gold-covered ark of the covenant (9:4)

The ark began as a plain acacia-wood box, a common wood of the wilderness. I like to think that Jesus' body was like that. Had all the men of Nazareth lined up for inspection, Jesus, as a human being, would not have stood out as different. He was ordinary and nondescript, with a body like all the others. None of the biblical writers thought it important to picture Jesus' human body.

He was indeed the Son of man, but he was also the Son of God. I admit that the incarnation defies human logic. John wrote that "the Word was God" (John 1:1), then declared, "The Word became flesh" (1:14). Simply put, God clothed himself in flesh, real flesh, and lived among us. The Son of God became the Son of man.

The incarnation makes all man-made religions, which are merely ways to pursue God, obsolete. The good news is that God pursues me! Religion promises that people can be more like God; the gospel boldly announces that God in Christ seeks to be like us to save us from ourselves. That's what happened when the Son of God became Jesus of Nazareth. God became human, not to confirm us in our sin, but to rescue us from our sinful nature.

No human being could have invented this way of salvation. It defies logic. It is truth revealed and makes eternal sense when I believe it.

> *Jesus, you had a body like my body.*
> *You know every drive and inclination of human nature.*
> *Thank you, Jesus, for identifying with me*
> *   so that I can identify with you, my Lord, my Savior, my friend.*

Jesus, God's Mercy and Grace

This ark contained the gold jar of manna (9:4)

God chose items to be placed in the "chest of promise" (my translation of "ark of the covenant"). Each item in that chest marked a special outpouring of God's mercy and grace.

First, the manna. After six weeks in the wilderness, the Israelites had consumed the food they had brought with them from Egypt. Then "the whole community grumbled against Moses and Aaron" (Exodus 16:2).

God hates grumbling because it is the expression of unbelief. One heart cannot contain both faith and grumbling. The two are mutually exclusive. And grumbling is a deadly sin. In Exodus we find that "the LORD said to Moses, 'I have heard the grumbling of the Israelites'" (16:11). Was it not time to abandon these unbelievers? That is what I would have done. But God listened, then surprised them with an outpouring of grace and generosity:

"In the morning there was a layer of dew around the camp" (verse 13). How like God! Instead of lashes of punishment, he poured out bread from heaven. God's mercy saved them from destruction. His grace provided them with ample bread to sustain life.

To remind future generations of his love, he directed Moses to fashion a vessel of pure gold to hold a portion of manna for as long as the ark would last. Moses did so and placed it permanently in the chest of promise. It speaks of God's saving grace.

> *God, may the manna remind me of your love,*
> *which seeks a way to bless ordinary sinners.*

Jesus' Cross, Like Aaron's Staff

This ark contained ... Aaron's rod that had budded (9:4)

Beside the manna of grace lay Aaron's rod, which budded. It too spoke of mercy and grace.

We pick up the story in the wilderness. "The next day the whole Israelite community grumbled against Moses and Aaron" (Numbers 16:41). Grumbling again! "Suddenly the cloud covered [the tent of meeting] and the glory of the LORD appeared.... The LORD said to Moses, 'Get away from this assembly so I can put an end to them at once'" (verses 42, 45). A plague broke out and 14,700 people perished. Moses and Aaron appealed to God to stop it. Moses and Aaron could not make excuses for the people who had sinned grievously by grumbling against the very One who was sustaining them. Perhaps the people thought they were grumbling against Moses and Aaron. No, it was against God.

God devised a way to stop the plague. He directed that the elder of each of the twelve tribes bring his staff, with the tribe's name inscribed on each. Then, "the next day Moses ... saw that Aaron's staff, which represented the house of Levi, had not only sprouted but had budded, blossomed and produced almonds.... The Israelites said to Moses, 'We will die! We are lost, we are all lost! ... Are we all going to die?'" (17:8, 12-13). They broke in repentance.

Then the plague stopped. Moses placed Aaron's staff beside the golden jar of manna in the "chest of promise"—another strong reminder of God's love, mercy, and grace. It speaks of grace from within the box for all generations.

> Lord, may I never, ever forget Calvary,
>   the staff that budded, bloomed, and produced eternal fruit for me.
> You devised a way, the way of the cross,
>   to bring me to yourself.

Jesus, the Truth

This ark contained ... the stone tablets of the covenant (9:4)

The ark is God's throne. He sits on it and judges according to the stone tablets under the seat. God does not judge according to impulse, but on the basis of immutable law, which cannot be altered, because it is the manifestation of God's character. The law is not external to God, as something he created. It is God's Word, a window in readable form into who God is.

God might change in the way he goes about doing something, but there is one thing God cannot change—his character. So no matter how much people may want to modify the law of God, they can never do so, because God cannot change who he is.

I find it interesting to hear people say, "Times have changed. Catch up, stupid." They are really saying that truth is a wax nose that can be bent to suit the whim of the bender. Western culture, now in the twenty-first century since Christ, has little time for the law of God. It determines morality by voting on what's moral, and the outcome of this "voting" is predictable. In this culture individual rights trumps everything else. Democracy is a good way to govern society but it does not work in the area of morality.

It is not easy to live as followers of Jesus in a culture that despises Jesus, the truth. I fear that western culture has abandoned the search for truth altogether. That is a mark of postmodernism.

> *Lord, enable me to be ever vigilant,*
> *keenly aware of the allure of this age with all its idols,*
> *so that my heart may be fully set on you.*

Jesus, Our Source of Obedience

This ark contained . . . the stone tablets of the covenant (9:4)

Jesus did not remove the Law from the ark. Yet he never expected us to obey it on our own. Jesus obeys the law, and he has promised to be in his believers to enable them to live lives that please the Father.

I have come to this: the law does not tell me what I *should* do, but what I *will* do if the Spirit of the Lord is in me. This is true of both the Mosaic Law and the teaching of Jesus. Jesus confounded his audience when he taught, for example, that not committing adultery means little if one harbors lustful thoughts and that hate is on the same level as murder. Jesus insisted that God's standard exceeds the standards of the strictest Jews, the Pharisees. Jesus was making the point that without being born again and being led by the gracious Holy Spirit, no one can please the Father.

So the law serves to describe how a redeemed child of God will think and act. It both describes and urges holiness in believers. But these laws, whether that of Moses or the teachings of Jesus were never meant to redeem sinners.

Surely, I often fail. I resist the Holy Spirit and go my own way,
but thank you, Jesus,
because your redeeming blood is always there
to cleanse me and restore me as your humble servant.
As I give the Holy Spirit unrestricted access to all of my life,
I discover to my delight that, like you,
I want to please the Father.
By your redeeming power I find myself doing so.

Jesus, the Center of Attention

**Above the ark were the cherubim of the Glory,
overshadowing the place of atonement (9:5)**

The magnificent golden cherubim served a single purpose: to stare at God's marvelous grace. They do nothing but gaze. Their wings are unfurled, prepared for flight, but they fly nowhere, for the place where they are is the center of all reality. They are absolutely transfixed by what they see. They face one another, but their eyes are riveted on the centerpiece of God's grace, the spot where the blood of God's very own Lamb is applied.

I need to be more like those cherubim, gazing in wonder at what it cost heaven to find a way whereby the demands of God's justice and mercy can be fully met. As I see the Son of glory pouring out his lifeblood so I can be reconciled to God, I suspend my breathing, for I stand before the mystery of mysteries: the deep, deep love of God giving all, even his own beloved Son, emptying heaven itself, so that I can become a son of God.

The greatest act of worship is to fix all attention on Jesus Christ, on his person, his teaching, his miraculous power, but most of all on his atoning blood, poured out for me. As I see him, risen from the dead, I know that all he accomplished for me pleased his Father. Now all the blessings that flow from that great redemption, including the fellowship of the Holy Spirit, are mine. I can "scarcely take it in," as the hymn puts it.

*Lord, every day I stand with those marvelous cherubim,
newly amazed at the glories of Jesus Christ.*

Jesus, Where Justice and Grace Blend

The place of atonement (9:5)

Be still my soul, before this most profound of all divine mysteries. See reflected in the mercy seat what happened on that dreadful hill outside Jerusalem, where Jesus Christ poured out his lifeblood to make atonement for my sin.

Heaven had to find a way to reconcile two aspects of God's character: his righteous justice and his perfect love, usually considered contradictory. I find comfort in 2 Samuel 14:14: "God does not take away life; instead, he devises ways so that a banished person may not remain estranged from him." This verse is a challenge to King David to deal mercifully with his rebellious son, Absalom, but it speaks an eternal truth. God devised ways to bring people to himself. He did that in Jesus.

That is why the apostle John could proclaim in the opening section of his Gospel, "We have seen his glory . . . full of grace and truth" (John 1:14). On the cross, "mercy and truth are met together; righteousness and peace have kissed each other" (Psalms 85:10 KJV).

I see all of Jesus' atoning work in the picture before us—the mercy seat, where God receives sinners. I join the cherubim as they gaze on the solution of the seeming irreconcilability of God's justice and love—the blood of the new covenant, shed for me. The demands of divine justice and divine love are met in him.

> *Jesus, you met all the claims of divine justice and love.*
> *That is the basis of my salvation*
> *and of my daily walk in the Holy Spirit.*

August 21

Jesus Serves in the Outer Room

**The priests entered regularly into the outer room to carry on
their ministry (9:6)**

I sometimes find myself serving in the "outer room." It is a good room, with light and bread and incense. It is all so nice because I know precisely what to do. I have done my service hundreds of times in the many sermons I have preached. I have learned how to break down a text into three points, add an illustration or two, and preach with a holy demeanor. Like the priests, I "entered regularly." I love routine and thrive on predictability. The outer room suits me just fine, because there I am in control. I am not in the least threatened by my fellow priests either, because they are occupied with similar routines.

How easy it is to get adjusted to serving God in the outer room. It is not that I am a stranger to the inner room, for there I first met my Savior. There on the altar I saw his blood poured out for me. I know the warmth of intimacy with God.

But I do love the outer room. It's where I can feel good about serving God. It is the room of activity, and I flourish on that. But it's not where Shekinah glory dwells.

I suppose life in the outer room is for good people who have no need for blood cleansing. Life there is centered on doing good things for the Lord. There the goal is to get the job done well as one of a team of priests. It requires meticulous service that concentrates on doing things absolutely right. But there is a better room, the holiest of all, where God dwells. Maybe I should learn the lesson of shuttling back and forth between these two rooms.

Jesus, may my heart be restless until it enters the inner room.

August 22

Jesus Ushers Me In

**The priests entered regularly into the outer room
to carry on their ministry (9:6)**

How well I recall my early days as a missionary, serving in the outer room.

God, in his mercy, made me ill at ease in service; he frustrated my diligent attempts to get things right. It was as though, as a fumbling priest, I couldn't find the incense, and when I did finally find it, I could not locate the matches. In the meantime, some of the lamps began to flicker and demand my attention. Then I remembered that I forgot to ask someone to bake the special bread for the table. While all this was happening, I kept wondering what my fellow priests thought of my hectic efforts to succeed. I was in a frazzle.

To heap insult on injury, I saw a steady stream of people coming out of the inner room, where the blood was applied to the mercy seat for them, where they confessed their sin and found the infilling of the Holy Spirit. They sang, "The cleansing blood has reached me, glory, glory to the Lamb." That unnerved me because I had convinced myself that I was more mature than they. Furthermore, was I not dead serious about giving my all to serve God? I must confess, serving God as a missionary in the outer room was tough going.

Thanks be to God, the mercy seat, Calvary's cross,
is but a few steps away.
I am eternally grateful to you, Lord,
and to the brothers and sisters who walked with me
into the place where sinners meet you,
at the mercy seat where the blood of the Lamb
proclaims freedom and forgiveness.

Jesus Entered the Inner Room—Once

**Only the high priest entered the inner room, and that only once a year
(9:7)**

Awake, O Israel, it is the tenth day of the seventh month, the annual Day of Atonement, the most holy day of the year. The high priest lays aside his magnificent raiment, dons a common linen tunic and takes three animals—a bullock and two male goats. He slays the bullock outright, but he casts lots to see which of the two goats will be slain and which one will carry Israel's sins into the wilderness.

The high priest first has to seek cleansing from sin for himself and for his household. For that, he enters the holiest place with incense from the altar and a container holding the blood of the bullock. He waves the censor above the ark until the mercy seat is shrouded with aroma. Then he sprinkles some of the blood on it for his own sin and for the sin of his household.

Having applied the bullock's blood, he departs, then returns with the national sacrifice, the blood of the male goat, which he sprinkles on the mercy seat with great reverence. That is the blood of the atonement. Then he goes out and in full view of the multitude places his hands on the head of the remaining goat. This transfers to the goat all Israel's "wickedness and rebellion." An appointed person then leads the scapegoat into the desert, never to be seen again by Israel. And "the goat will carry on itself all their sins to a solitary place" (Leviticus 16:22).

I see dimly the contours of justice, mercy, and grace. A blessed trinity.

Thank you, Jesus, for carrying away my sin.

Jesus Remains in the Holiest Place

**Never without blood, which he offered for himself and for the sins
the people had committed in ignorance (9:7)**

The Day of Atonement ended in song. A great hymn of thanks filled the nation as Israel saw their sins forgiven, taken away by the sacrificial blood and by the scapegoat. It is written, "Then, before the Lord, you will be clean from all your sins" (Leviticus 16:30).

We hasten to the new covenant. Unlike Israel's high priests, Jesus was without sin, so he had the right to enter in without a moment's hesitation. Jesus, the perfect high priest, presented the perfect sacrifice. Satan surely threw a fit as all heaven shouted, "He is worthy!"

Jesus entered never to come out again, ever. He is with the Father and the blessed Holy Spirit. There is no need for him to go through all that again. He did it once and for all, and that changed everything. The cross and the empty tomb stand as witnesses.

Today's verse speaks of sins committed in ignorance. What about those sins we commit with our eyes wide open? In the new covenant we are assured that all confessed sin is taken away by the blood of Christ. And that is supremely good news.

I see you, my Jesus, in every act, every gesture,
every scene in the tabernacle.
My spirit responds with a resounding note of praise.
You are my high priest, my bullock,
my sacrificial goat, my scapegoat.
Why should not my heart rejoice,
for I know that I need not wait for
the Day of Atonement every year.
Your blood avails for me this morning as I write these lines.
To God be the glory!

Jesus Was Always Jesus

**The Holy Spirit was showing by this that the way into the Most Holy Place
had not yet been disclosed (9:8)**

I taught biblical theology in Africa for many years. Often my students wondered about their many ancestors who had tried to please God. They wanted to know when God shifted from saving people because they were good to saving them because of the atoning sacrifice of Jesus. I chuckled at that. Did God change?

I think the answer is found in today's verse: "The way ... had not yet been disclosed." The way was already there but they had not yet seen it. The way was determined before the stars were flung into space, before day was divided from night. The way was eternally in the timeless heart of God, waiting for the precise moment when it should be revealed. There was never a time when mankind could earn salvation by good works.

It is easy to imagine that God created mankind, hoping that they would not sin. When they did so, then he had to come up with a plan to redeem them. But then I saw phrases like "the Lamb slain from the creation of the world" (Revelation 13:8). The cross and all it stood for was not an afterthought. Jesus Christ has always been "the way." He is the "I Am" of the burning bush and of the cross of Calvary. God does not change, but he reveals himself to mankind as he deems appropriate.

Jesus, you came at just the right time.
Praise God, the "not yet" is replaced by "now."
The way is fully revealed.
You were there all the time, waiting to be revealed.
That revelation is now complete.
I rest all my hope on you, both now and forever.

Jesus, the Way

The way into the Most Holy Place had not yet been disclosed (9:8)

"There are many ways to reach the summit of Mount Fuji." This old adage has come down through the ages in Japan. That may be true when it comes to climbing a mountain, but it cannot be applied to salvation.

The gospel is not another way to climb the mountain. Rather it is a sure declaration that there is a way into the presence of God. All other ways fail. "Oh," scoffers say, "you are intolerant because you insist that Christianity is the only way." We respond, "The point is, there *is* a way! His name is Jesus of Nazareth."

I used to teach a comparative religion course. It was just that, comparing one religion with another. I found it interesting and insightful but realized that the gospel is not a religion. It is a person. Unbelieving students could not grasp that. They liked to compare religions. They would say, "I like this part of Hinduism. I do not like this part of Christianity. Islam is best on this point."

I believe it is fruitless to talk about the superiority of Christianity over all other religions. I realize only too well that some people have made Christianity into a religion. Jesus came among us to save us by his life, death, and resurrection. That is not religion; it is history. It is what God did, whether I approve of it or not.

> *God, accept my humble thanks.*
> *I am thrilled beyond words*
> > *that I have found the way to true happiness*
> > *and peace in your Son, Jesus.*
> *Help me to announce with solid confidence,*
> *"There is a way. His name is Jesus."*

Jesus' Blood Removes Sin and Cleanses the Conscience

The gifts and sacrifices being offered were not able to clear the conscience of the worshiper (9:9)

The sun sets as night falls on the great Day of Atonement. I take a moment to sit with the high priest. I ask him to reflect on what happened that day as he applied the blood of the bullock for his own sin and the blood of the goat for the sin of all Israel.

What changes did that day bring about in his life? I hear him say, "I was in the presence of God and he did not slay me! We must have done everything according to the letter of the law. Now, that is done for another year." He breathes a sigh of relief.

I then ask, "How is what you did today going to change your life?" He hadn't thought of that. "What hope do you have that your sins are forgiven?"

He had thought of that. "I believe that if I do everything just as it is written in the law, God will turn his eye away from my sin."

"But," I ask, "are your sins taken away?"

"I am not sure about that. The sacrifices ameliorate God's anger so that I am not condemned. If it were not for God's great mercy, I would be dead! God told us to offer blood sacrifices but it is a mystery to me to see how the blood of a common goat can take away sin. For now, that is the best we can do."

That is certainly true. But is it enough? Judgment is thwarted but what about the conscience of the high priest? The sacrifice and offerings fend off God's wrath, but they do not clear the conscience of sin. On the day after the great Day of Atonement, the high priest must find a way to live with a troubled conscience for another year.

Lord Jesus, your sacrifice not only saves me from destruction but also cleanses my conscience. Marvelous!

Jesus' Blood Deals with Real Sin

**The gifts and sacrifices being offered were not able to clear the conscience
of the worshiper (9:9)**

While I am not a trained psychologist, I know that mental and emotional health is enhanced when a person's conscience does not condemn him or her. How can the conscience be quieted? One way is to convince it that there is nothing like sin, just bad choices. If that is so, then counseling takes the line of trying to find out why a person makes bad choices. That should calm the conscience.

Were the gospel to be but another palliative for a troubled conscience, why should anyone consider it? What is the use of calming the conscience if the sin remains?

The good news is that Jesus poured out his blood on the cross, not to cover sin, but to remove it completely. Nothing can clear the conscience but the atoning sacrifice of Jesus Christ because that blood first cleanses away the sin, then sets the conscience free.

I praise God that the Holy Spirit reveals my sin to me so that I can take it to Jesus for cleansing. Furthermore, I praise God for the knowledge that the atoning blood of Jesus cleanses my conscience at the deepest level, where I cannot reach. The blood is doing its work there. By the grace of God, I am free of known and unknown sin.

Unlike the high priest who must settle for a troubled conscience, I can serve God with a clear conscience, not because I do not sin, but because the cleansing blood of Christ continues to do its gracious work in my life, cleansing my conscience. What a blessing!

Lord Jesus, thank you for making all this possible.

Jesus Changes the Heart

**They are only ... external regulations applying until the time
of the new order (9:10)**

I must admit I like "external regulations." I want clear laws to obey. I am pleased when governments enact laws that are in line with Christian principles. I believe that even nonbelievers are better off with "Christian laws" than with laws that run contrary to the mind of God.

It is disturbing to see laws passed that are contrary to the God's law. I think of the discrimination against African-Americans in the Civil Rights Movement in the United States. That kind of discrimination was blatantly contrary to biblical principles, and the United States is better off because of legislation that conforms to Christian principles by outlawing discrimination.

But legislation can only set boundaries. It cannot change the intent of the heart. The Law delivered to Moses did not set boundaries; it required a change of heart. Unfortunately it had no ability to do that. Laws are only external regulations.

How does Jesus see all this? He said that he did not come to destroy the law but to fulfill it. This is what our verse for today says. Under the new order, the kingdom of Christ, the law will be written on the heart by the Holy Spirit. External law may have sociological advantages, but it is of little help in reforming human behavior.

I believe that laws that reflect Christ's values are better than laws based on popular consent. Nevertheless, even good laws have absolutely no saving power.

> *My God, give me the proper perspective*
> *about external rules and regulations.*
> *They are good but can never save.*

Jesus, My Internal Regulator

External regulations applying until the time of the new order (9:10)

It pained Jesus to see God's chosen people, the Jews, living exclusively in the external. They had a tendency to reduce everything to a series of dos and don'ts. Jesus got so frustrated with this behavior that he likened them to painted tombs. The Jews refused to deal with internal problems like the rebellious heart, preferring to apply yet another fresh coat of paint to embellish the casket.

How about me? Do I not also hesitate to get to the root of a besetting sin in my life? Instead of uncovering the evil in my life, I tend to control things by the dint of self-discipline, or I just try to ignore my hard heart and press on bravely. In the flesh, I will do anything rather than admit I am a sinner.

The way of grace that lives in the shadow of the cross and the glory of the empty tomb breaks through all the externals into a reality where the light penetrates every corner. All is revealed; nothing is hidden. That is where I meet God.

God told Israel that, on the mercy seat, "I will meet with you and give you all my commands" (Exodus 25:22). This is the place where God's brokenness in Christ Jesus meets my brokenness as a repentant sinner.

This is not to discount aids to worship, such as soul-lifting music or art that reveals the heart of God. They are good but they are only the vestibule, the outer court, which is resplendent with its own beauty. The outer court is meant to prepare the worshiper to enter the inner sanctuary of the soul where Father, Son, and Holy Spirit abide in love.

Lord, I enter with thanksgiving!

August 31

Jesus Is the Best Thing

**When Christ came as high priest of the good things that are already here
(9:11)**

Life is brimming with good things. For me, nature is one of them. Few things lift my spirit like a glowing sunset or droplets of sunlit dew on rose petals. I just videoed the underside of the wing of a red-spotted purple butterfly. The brilliant, brick-colored spots against the indigo background took my breath away. And just this week I videoed a miracle—a bright green, two-inch-long parsley worm as it began the process of becoming a dazzling, black swallowtail butterfly. The psalmist said it well: "The heavens declare the glory of God; and the firmament showeth his handiwork" (Psalms 19:1 KJV).

Another one of my good things is art in its various forms, including music. I almost leave the earth as I soar with a Bach oratorio or an animated African choir harmonizing around one of my favorite African hymns, "There is no one like Jesus." Music invites me to go beyond sound and sequence to harmony with God when my song blends with the song of heaven, "Worthy is the Lamb who was slain." Few things cheer my heart like music.

Nature and the arts cheer me. They are good things. I also draw immense inspiration from philosophy, science, history, and the world of ideas. These are "good things that are already here." I thank God for them. They all aid me in my adoration of Jesus Christ, the giver of these good things.

Lord, why do I love these things so much?
I believe it is because they all point beyond to that which is better,
to you. Good things are signs pointing to the best.

Jesus Removes Old Barriers

**When Christ came as high priest of the good things that are already here,
he went through (9:11)**

Christ came as high priest. The Jewish scholars tended to ignore the Scriptures that refer to the promised Messiah as a priest. They much preferred to dwell on the promise that the Messiah would be a king, like the renowned King David.

What does it mean that Jesus is the high priest? It means that I need a savior as much if not more than I need a king, because unless my sins are forgiven and my rebellious condition broken, no king would have much success ruling over me. Before I can be a good citizen in God's kingdom, I must be at peace with God and with my fellow citizens. Jesus is king, that we know, because he is Lord over all principalities and powers. The central question is whether Jesus is, first and foremost, my priest or my king. We know he is both. For me, I want to know him primarily as my savior, my priest, and then as my king. He can only reign in my life if I bring my rebellious nature to the mercy seat where I find forgiveness and power.

Jesus' high priestly function is coupled with the fact that he is also the sacrifice. That is powerful beyond words. Can it be that Jesus is both the perfect high priest and the perfect Lamb of God? I believe he is, and I base my faith life on that knowledge.

> *Jesus, thank you for your high-priestly work,*
> *which broke open the way for me to be reconciled to God.*
> *I am yours eternally. Amen.*

Jesus Went Through

**He went through the greater and more perfect tabernacle
that is not man-made (9:11)**

Jesus never served as high priest in the temple in Jerusalem. He was not interested in dealing with appearances. He pressed through to reality itself. He did not try to reform Judaism. That would have been a meaningless triumph. No, Jesus "went through" all the walls of the heavenly tabernacle, vanquishing our two menacing enemies: sin and death.

Satan surely knew he had no leg to stand on if Jesus died as God's perfect Paschal Lamb. So Satan employed every ordnance he had against Jesus at every step, hoping beyond hope that Jesus would disobey his heavenly Father, thus disqualifying him as the perfect sacrifice. To Satan's consternation, Jesus maintained his fellowship with his Father through to the end. His atoning work opened the way for sinners.

What looked like Satan's victory—Jesus Christ dying on the cross—was in fact the victory of the Lamb, for when he gave his life on the cross and rose from the dead, he broke death's tyranny of fear. He became the first fruits of those who would rise to newness of life.

He "went through" every problem that keeps me from God and keeps me bound. Now I can "go through" with him. There are no half-measures with Jesus. He goes right through!

*Jesus, by your willing death on the cross,
  you broke the fear of death for all who will believe.*

September 3

Jesus Undaunted

He went through (9:11)

Jesus Christ went through. But I suppose he was tempted a hundred times not to go through.

Did he hesitate for a moment on the threshold of heaven as he was about to cast off his glorious heavenly robes, knowing full well that he would take on human flesh and be subject to pain and death? Did he hesitate when, after thirty comfortable years in Nazareth, he began that descent down, down, down to the River Jordan, where John the Baptist baptized him and announced him as God's Lamb who had come to earth as our sin-bearer? Did he flinch when he faced his life work? Did he hesitate when the Holy Spirit led him into the wilderness, where he knew Satan would tempt him sorely?

Did he hesitate when, after three years of ministry, he was led to the Mount of Transfiguration, which marked the beginning of the journey to Jerusalem to pay the ultimate price for our sin? Did he hesitate when Satan, through Peter, hurled at him a lance of fear about his impending crucifixion? Did he hesitate when, after singing his final hymn with his disciples in the upper room, he walked into the waiting arms of his assassins?

Praise God. He went through with it.

Thank you, Jesus, that even if you hesitated for a moment,
you "went through" and with great joy
rushed to heaven where you entered
by the merits of your own shed blood. For me.

Jesus, Adequate Savior

Once for all by his own blood (9:12)

I see millions of animals—cows, bulls, sheep, goats, even chickens, and not a few marked people, some of them but innocent children—being slaughtered in religious rituals in all cultures. My heart cries out, "There has to be a better way."

Then I see something new. The Son of God hangs on a cross outside Jerusalem. He then takes his poured-out blood, which represents all of his atoning work, and appears in God's heavenly presence. His work is pronounced finished. That is the end of blood sacrifice.

"Once for all." *Once* means that it need never be repeated, for it is complete and perfect. *For all* means for all time and for all people. Jesus' sacrifice is sufficient for all time and for all cultures.

By his own blood means that Jesus did not sacrifice an innocent animal as did the priests. He sacrificed his own body and poured out his own blood. And wonder of wonders, he did it for me!

I was struggling as a young missionary in Tanzania. The moment I saw Jesus' atoning sacrifice as "once for all," grace flooded my being and I was at rest, relying completely on Jesus' finished work.

That did not mean I stopped working. I think I worked harder than ever. But my driving motive changed from working to please God to working with God, empowered and led by his Spirit. Serving mankind became a wonderful expression of worship. Every glass of cold water that I shared with the poor was an act of thanksgiving to Jesus.

By your grace, my God, I hope to sustain that faith
until I meet Jesus face to face in his glory.

September 5

Jesus, God's Lamb

He did not enter by means of the blood of goats and calves; but he entered the Most Holy Place once for all by his own blood (9:12)

As Jesus appeared in the heavenlies, bearing his own blood, the Father must have broken out in song, "Worthy is the Lamb who was slain." The Holy Spirit who was part of it all joined the song, for now he could do what he had hoped to do for years—take up his residence in people whose sins are forgiven. Before he was an honored visitor, now he can take up residence. Not only the Father and the Holy Spirit but all those who died in faith, hoping for complete salvation, eagerly joined the singing throng, for Jesus had done it!

All the hosts of heaven converged on the holy sight as Jesus Christ of Nazareth, crucified, buried, and raised from the dead, appeared in heaven, bearing his own precious blood, which he placed on the eternal seat of mercy to atone once and for all for all the sins of mankind.

God is just. It was prophesied that he would pour out his fierce anger against sin in the last days. We need not wait for that, because he already poured out that wrath against our sin, in Jesus Christ on the cross of Calvary. Jesus received the just penalty for sin so the demands of divine justice were satisfied.

God is love. If I wish to see love in its purest form, I kneel at the foot of the cross and see the wounded hands of Jesus, open to embrace me as his brother, a precious child of God.

> *My saving Lord, if all heaven rejoices,*
> *is it not right for me to lift my soul in heartfelt thanksgiving*
> *as I utter these holy words:*
> *"Worthy is the Lamb who was slain, for me"?*

Jesus, Ashes to Cleanse

The ashes of a heifer sprinkled (9:13)

The law says that anyone who touches a dead body is ritually unclean and is therefore barred from the community. But the quarantine alone did not take away the defilement; that was done by ritual cleansing on the third and seventh day following the offense, when the priest applied a prescribed cleansing water that contained the ashes of a red heifer.

The origin of that practice is instructive. Knowing full well that people must handle the dead now and again, God made a way, saying to Moses, "Tell the Israelites to bring you a red heifer without defect or blemish" (Numbers 19:2). They were directed to slay it outside the camp. The priest took the blood and sprinkled it with his finger toward the door of the tent, then ordered the heifer completely burned. Into the blaze he threw cedar wood, hyssop, and scarlet wool. The priest then gathered the ashes and carefully placed them in a jar kept "outside the camp." According to the law, the ashes "shall be kept by the Israelite community for use in the water of cleansing; it is for purification from sin" (19:9).

On the third and seventh day, as an unclean person approached the tent for cleansing, the priest took a pinch of the ashes and some water, and sprinkled the defiled person with it. That ritual of cleansing canceled the uncleanness. The cleansed person was then reunited with the community.

Jesus, you are the precious red heifer given for me.
May I find cleansing in those Calvary ashes!

Back in the Camp

The ashes of a heifer sprinkled (9:13)

My soul, consider Jesus. He was the red heifer, perfect in all ways. Driven by divine love, he gave himself to that horrifying death on the cross as the eternal Paschal Lamb. He took on himself my sin and the sin of all mankind and agreed to carry it in his own body. The fire of the wrath of God incinerated my sin in the body of Jesus Christ. The sky darkened. The pilings of the earth shook. In that sacred moment the wrath of God burned our sin in Jesus. Our sins have been judged in his body on the cross.

I love this juxtaposition of texts. "Who knows the power of your anger?" (Psalms 90:11). The answer is, "From the sixth hour until the ninth hour darkness came over all the land. About the ninth hour Jesus cried out in a loud voice . . . 'My God, my God, why have you forsaken me?'" (Matthew 27:45-46).

Jesus knew precisely the intensity of God's hate for sin. He experienced the power and wrath of God on sin that he carried in his own holy body. God's very own red heifer paid the price for my salvation. His ashes, as it were, are now stored up in a golden vial of grace for all those who are contaminated by sin. We can wash and be at peace again. We can be reinstated back into the community of faith.

> *Lord, when Jesus' blood is applied, I am reunited with you*
> *and with the community of faith.*
> *Your blood makes me outwardly clean and inwardly clean,*
> *cleansing heart and conscience.*
> *When I am defiled by sin, please, Jesus,*
> *stir the ashes of cleansing with the blessed water of the Holy Spirit,*
> *and wash me clean for time and eternity.*
> *That is real cleansing for real sin.*

Jesus, Unblemished

Christ ... offered himself unblemished to God (9:14)

We noted several times that the Jews were never able to present a perfect red heifer for the yearly sacrifice. None existed in all the herds of Israel. Knowledgeable breeders must have known that it was highly unlikely because imperfection cannot beget perfection. They also knew that all their stock was imperfect. So they offered their almost perfect ones—and hoped.

Israel's longing for the perfect sacrifice was fulfilled in Jesus Christ. The twelve apostles who lived with him for three years could not point to a single sin in Jesus' life. John summed it up for all the disciples: "The Word became flesh and lived for a while among us. We have seen his glory, the glory of the one and only Son, who came from the Father, full of grace and truth" (John 1:14).

Nothing Jesus did compromised either grace or truth. He was the perfect red heifer. That is why his death on the cross, outside the camp, has the power to save with eternal effect.

The rulers of the Jews sought to find a defect in Jesus. The only thing they could come up with is that he claimed to be the Son of God and that he played loose with tradition. The Romans found no fault whatsoever in him.

I add my personal witness. Having lived with Jesus for these sixty years, I have found no fault in him. He has proved to be exactly who he said he is! He was unblemished here on earth and is now my perfect intercessor.

I believe, Jesus, that you were unblemished in every way.
Accept my praise and adoration, precious Lamb of God.

God, Pleased with Jesus

Christ . . . offered himself unblemished to God (9:14)

From heaven God spoke clearly to those who gathered on Jordan's banks after Jesus' baptism: "This is my Son, whom I love; with him I am well pleased" (Matthew 3:17). In a sense, this covered Jesus' life up to that point—thirty years. He pleased the Father in every way as he grew and matured. The Father found no fault in him.

Likewise, as the days drew near for his death and resurrection, Jesus took three of the disciples high into the mountain, where he was transfigured before them. Once again God spoke from heaven, "This is my Son, whom I love, with him I am well pleased. Listen to him!" (Matthew 17:5). That put the Father's stamp of approval on all Jesus taught and did. In the Father's eyes, he was perfect as Son of God and as Son of man.

However, the most convincing proof that Jesus pleased the Father was the coming of the Holy Spirit. During the Last Supper Jesus promised the disciples, "I will ask the Father, and he will give you another Counselor to be with you forever" (John 14:16). On the day of Pentecost, as the 120 gathered, it happened: "All of them were filled with the Holy Spirit and began to speak in other tongues as the Spirit enabled them" (Acts 2:4).

Jesus had asked the Father to send the Holy Spirit to be with them, and the Father did exactly that. What further proof did they need to prove that Jesus pleased the Father in every way? They received the Holy Spirit just like Jesus promised!

> *Jesus, I see you asking the Father to pour out the Holy Spirit*
> *on those who love you.*
> *He did it. Bless your name.*

Jesus, Enabled by the Holy Spirit

**How much more, then, will the blood of Christ,
who through the eternal Spirit offered himself
unblemished to God (9:14)**

Father, Son, and Holy Spirit, each with a specific office to fulfill, brought about our salvation. Each was intently at work as Jesus presented himself as the unblemished offering.

I see each member of the blessed Trinity in today's verse: "the blood of Christ," "the eternal Spirit," and "God," denoting the Father. What we see on Calvary's cross was the divine blending of the efforts of our triune God. The blood of Jesus is the announcement to all the world that Father, Son, and Holy Spirit, in absolute unity of purpose and virtue, established the basis on which all who wish may be saved and inherit eternal life.

Likewise, at Jesus' baptism in the Jordan, the inauguration of his earthly ministry, we see the triune God, joined as one, in announcing the coming of eternal life. The Son came up out of the water, and the Holy Spirit rested as a dove on him. The Father's voice from heaven said, "This is my Son, whom I love; with him I am well pleased" (Matthew 3:17). I adore the blessed unity of Father, Son, and Holy Spirit and observe them working with a common heart and goal, to save us from our sin.

> *Our God, you have revealed yourself to me in three persons*
> *with identical virtues but with different offices.*
> *I accept that by faith.*
> *But I have not found words*
> *to convince our Muslim friends on that point.*
> *Come to think of it, I could not conceive of such a thing either*
> *until I was born again.*
> *Give me grace to believe what this world considers*
> *absurdly ridiculous.*

September 11

Jesus Keeps My Conscience Alert

**How much more, then, will the blood of Christ . . . cleanse our consciences
(9:14)**

If I am not careful, I end up bending my conscience to suit what I think instead of allowing it to guide me. For example, my conscience tells me it is wrong to carry a grudge. I know that. I can even preach sermons about it. But then someone says something or does something that really hurts me, and the war is on. My ego forms a little grudge. Then my ego comes up with flimsy arguments to make the grudge seem legitimate. I console myself with arguments that I am obliged to carry the grudge. Such arguments for me are usually along this line: "Unless I straighten this person out, who will do it? If I do not confront him, he will hurt others." Grudges are never removed that way.

As grudges mature, they trigger ungodly behavior. For example, when I was doing some family tree work recently, I asked why a particular ancestor stopped going to church. The answer was that he got hurt by someone in the church. That grudge caused the poor fellow to do something terrible. He cut off his relationship with the church—until death, I understand. He must have compromised his conscience to the point that he could barely hear what it was saying, all because he nursed a grudge. And he died like that.

Lord Jesus, as I bring my compromised conscience to you,
cleanse it with your atoning blood.
A corrupted conscience produces "acts that lead to death."
Purge my conscience, Lord Jesus,
so that it speaks to me with the authority of your Holy Spirit,
giving life.

September 12

Jesus Produces Life-Giving Fruit

So that we may serve the living God! (9:14)

When I received the gift of regeneration, made possible by the sacrifice of our Lord Jesus, my conscience was cleared and reprogrammed to conform to his character. The Holy Spirit became the guardian of my newly cleansed conscience. When I transgress, the Holy Spirit is faithful to send me an alarm. When that alert sign flashes, I know that I should stop, examine my attitudes and actions, and if the Holy Spirit puts his finger on something in my life that displeased God, I rush to Calvary for cleansing. Then I am free again.

My cleansed conscience then produces acts that lead to life. My prayer life becomes real, and worship thrills my heart once again. Even my service for him becomes more enjoyable. By God's grace, I am in alignment with his will and character, and I love once again. It all means that I can serve the living God with a pure heart, no matter what is before me—a chore, a bore, or a delight.

That is the way it should work. But I must admit that I find it hard to do, because my ego does not like to admit wrong. I dread it, so I rationalize myself right out of taking the sinner's place. It is little wonder, then, that at times my relationship with the Lord is strained and I produce bad fruit, such as a critical spirit or a judgmental attitude. Instead of producing life-giving fruit, I too often produce bitter fruit that kills grace. I should not be surprised if others spit me out.

God, I see it clearly.
My part is to make sure I respond quickly
when the Holy Spirit alerts me that something is wrong.
Jesus' part is to cleanse me and to renew my spirit within me.
In that way I can serve you, my Lord,
with my whole heart, seeking only your glory.

Jesus Mediates the New Covenant

For this reason Christ is the mediator of a new covenant (9:15)

Under the old covenant, the worshipers were greatly relieved after offering blood sacrifice, because it proclaimed them ritually clean and enabled them to reunite with the community. The social consequences of sin were dealt with. That was good, but a debilitating problem remained: the conscience was left untouched.

Jesus Christ instituted a new covenant in his blood that cleanses the inner person, the soul and heart. It is real cleansing, not ritual cleansing, which deals only with the externals. Does that mean the worshipers under the old covenant who repented and offered their animal sacrifices were not truly cleansed? The answer is that they are cleansed by the atoning work of Jesus Christ. Had it not been for the atonement, their sins would remain.

I am eternally grateful for the blood of Jesus, which cleanses my conscience from sin. That is precious. However, the blood does an even greater work: it updates and renews my conscience and gives me a desire to walk with God. That desire is related to eternal life, which is mine as a free gift. I know this is true because, even though I do sin, I am not ruled by a desire to sin. I am ruled by a desire to serve God with my whole heart. That is a miracle. The new covenant makes it possible for me to live at peace with God.

Thank you, Jesus, for finally making it possible
for human beings to live with cleansed consciences.
This is entirely new. It is surely the basis of the new covenant
you established through your atoning blood,
opening the door to the possibility of a holy life.

September 14

Jesus Gives Me a New Heart

**That those who are called may receive the promised eternal inheritance
—now that he has died as a ransom to set them free from the sins
committed under the first covenant (9:15)**

I am writing this on the anniversary of my conversion as a sixteen-year-old. My life was a mess. I had no idea who I was or where I was going. While I was floundering, Jesus crept up on me and invited me to give my life to him. That startled me, for I was not looking for him.

As I recall, I was not even troubled about my accumulating mountain of sin. But when he made himself real to me, I became painfully aware of my sinfulness. All my defenses dropped and I yielded my life to him, just like that. I soon found myself at the foot of the cross, broken and penitent, and there discovered that Jesus paid the price to ransom my soul. I could safely transfer all my sin to his account.

It was as though the walls of my prison crumbled, my chains fell off, and I was free. Jesus had paid the full price for my ransom, my freedom, so why not cast all on him? In all candor, I thought little about how I was going to sustain a holy life in the future, but I was absolutely sure of one thing: Jesus had lifted the burden of sin from my life and I was set free, "free from the sins committed under the first covenant."

Jesus, my Savior, it is awesome to know that you forgive all past sin
as I take the sinner's place and repent.
But there is something even more marvelous:
you gave me a new heart, a new disposition that seeks to obey God.
This is the gift of God that makes the new covenant possible.
I got a new heart! Thank God.

September 15

Jesus, My Ransom

**That those who are called may receive the promised eternal inheritance
—now that he has died as a ransom to set them free from the sins
committed under the first covenant (9:15)**

As I look back over the many years since I was born anew, several things amaze me. The first is that when Jesus met me at my point of need, he met that need marvelously. The second is that, unknown to me, the Lord had plans for me, and he set me on a path I have walked as a hopeful pilgrim for more than half a century. I did not see my path then, but I see it now, and it is marvelous.

I have found that Jesus' covenant with me, made possible by his atoning blood, is the anchor of my soul. What began as a halting step to follow him as a teenager was no less than the beginning of a journey of an entire lifetime of service in God's kingdom. I am astounded by Jesus' patience with me. He never left me. There were times when I followed from afar, yet I followed because he never let me out of his sight.

Today's verse speaks of "eternal inheritance." My inheritance is written in God's will. God has willed to me one blessing after another. I live by grace alone.

When my mother died, it did not take long to read her will, which was short and to the point. It is not like that with the will Jesus prepared, which is voluminous! Each day I find new and marvelous gifts of grace that are mine because Jesus "wrote them" into his will. As I live with the Lord, I receive his manifold grace, freely given for my welfare. To him be the glory forever.

> *As I ponder my life, Lord,*
> *I believe that the greatest thing you willed to me is salvation,*
> *"the promised eternal inheritance."*
> *With that gift is bundled hundreds of gifts that you willed to me.*

Jesus Died

**In the case of a will, it is necessary to prove the death of the one
who made it (9:16)**

Did Jesus really die? Muslims, Hindus, Buddhists, atheists and New Agers pay no heed to the death of Jesus. Muslims believe Jesus' body died, not his spirit. Other religions dismiss Jesus' death as insignificant. Yet his death and resurrection dominate the New Testament and are at the heart of the good news.

Who can fully understand the mystery of Christ's death? He is God in the flesh, but he died. That stumps the imagination because by definition God cannot die, in the human sense of the word. On the other hand, if he did not die, there is still no sacrifice for sin. So by faith I believe that Christ Jesus died. Furthermore, I believe that he died as Son of God as well as Son of man.

We have already noted that a will is of no real benefit to the heir until the one who prepared it dies. Jesus wrote his will brimming full of great and marvelous promises, including the promise of salvation and the gift of the Holy Spirit. But that will has effect only because Jesus died. And it has meaning to us only if we are his heirs.

The Scriptures leave no doubt about the death of Jesus. He was physically dead for three nights. Who can explain the mystery of the death of Jesus, who is Son of God and Son of man?

Jesus, my Lord, I cannot explain it, but I believe it
because it was prophesied and it is attested to by eyewitnesses,
both your friends and your foes.
Jesus, I believe that you died, so now the will is in effect for me.

Jesus' Will Is Open to His Heirs

**In the case of a will, it is necessary to prove the death of the one
who made it (9:16)**

I find this focus on the death of Christ to be mind stretching. Why don't the Scriptures place primary emphasis on Jesus' resurrection from the dead? I would prefer it that way. That is of vital importance also, but as I think of it I realize that the resurrection has no real meaning unless Jesus really died.

That a human being died on that cross is entirely understandable. That God died in Christ is quite another matter. One thing is sure: the legal will God prepared, full of benefits, is now in effect because Jesus Christ died. I know this because I am enjoying what was written in that will. I am enjoying my inheritance already. Jesus died.

The writer of Hebrews illustrates the point by referring to the law. He reminds us that the will had no effect until the law, the tabernacle, and all the paraphernalia were sprinkled with blood, denoting death. Then and then only did the grace flow to the people.

One of my great privileges is living in light of all the benefits that the atoning work of Christ bestows on me. If I am unsettled about one of the promises, maybe doubting whether Jesus really cares for me, all I need do is proceed to Calvary's brow, where the blood of God's Paschal Lamb was poured out. All that he willed to me is now mine!

I love you, Lord Jesus, for revealing this to me,
the least of all your children—and in my humble opinion,
the most blessed.

Jesus' Blood Opens the Door to Blessing

[Moses] said, "This is the blood of the covenant" (9:20)

In the top drawer of my filing cabinet lies my will. It is just so much ink and paper, because the people and charities to which I willed money cannot touch my assets. The reason is quite simple, I am still alive and in control of my faculties, as they say. It is only after I am pronounced dead that my will benefits people.

So when I see the blood of Jesus Christ, proof of his death, I know that all he promised is now mine. This is an aspect of the death of Jesus Christ that I am just now comprehending. It is awesome. That blood announces the death of Jesus, but it also ushers in an exciting new covenant that promises and delivers resurrection life. In that way, the blood of Christ, God's Paschal Lamb, is the source of all my life.

Moses took the blood of the covenant and sprinkled all the people and "the scroll," to proclaim God's gracious covenant. Taking that same blood, he sprinkled the tabernacle and everything that was used in the ceremonies. That sprinkling gave everyone access to the wide-ranging benefits of the covenant that God had sworn to Abraham, Isaac, and Jacob, and that was renewed in the wilderness. It was a blood covenant.

> *My God, open my eyes to see this mystery revealed.*
> *I am only beginning to understand why it is so important*
> *   to believe that Jesus died.*
> *By confessing his death I open my life to the power of his resurrection.*
> *That is promised in his most holy will.*

Jesus' Blood Announces Life

[Moses] said, "This is the blood of the covenant" (9:20)

I have been known to emphasize the blood of Christ now and again in my preaching. How well I remember a brother challenging me, saying, "That blood talk is morbid." I hadn't realized I was stirring such feelings. Perhaps I failed to make it clear that far from being a morbid event, the sprinkling of the blood announced life. The death is over.

I doubt that Moses commiserated with the slaughtered lamb whose blood he was sprinkling. There is little to be gained by commiserating with a sacrificed sheep. He rejoiced in the fact that God had provided the lamb in the first place and that, by the mercy of God, the blood of the lamb sealed the life-giving blessings of God.

The sprinkling of the blood was a solemn moment, no doubt, but it was at the same time a celebrative moment, rather like what happened in heaven when Jesus appeared with his own blood. All heaven broke into singing, "Worthy is the Lamb who was slain to receive power and wealth and wisdom and strength and honor and glory and praise!" (Revelation 5:12).

As I tarry at the foot of the cross and gaze on God's Lamb dying for me, I join the heavenly choir. When I see the blood, I melt in praise and thanksgiving, for it speaks life to me. I commiserate with Jesus, certainly, but soon move on to praise.

Jesus called the cup at the Last Supper "the new covenant in my blood" (Luke 22:20). How can I keep from praising, because now all the resources of heaven are available to me!

Praise God for the precious blood of Jesus Christ,
the Paschal Lamb, given that I might have life in abundance.
All the fullness of the Godhead bodily dwells in Jesus Christ,
and I am complete in him.

Jesus' Blood Announces Forgiveness

Without the shedding of blood there is no forgiveness (9:22)

Having examined many of the religions of the world, I am struck by the universality of blood sacrifice. For example, before the Kekchi people of Guatemala plant the first grain of corn, they sprinkle the field with the blood of a freshly killed cock. In Hinduism, blood sacrifice plays a central role. And in African traditional religions, blood sacrifice was an essential feature.

Where did this idea come from? Who first came up with the idea that when there is a problem between people and their gods, it is helpful to offer a sacrifice?

I believe that blood sacrifice is a basic human archetype. We are born with it. God stamped the human race with this archetype because he was preparing us to recognize Jesus Christ as God's Paschal Lamb. All the animal sacrifices offered by religious devotees through the centuries point to Jesus.

I see another truth in this text. It was not sufficient simply to slay the sacrifice; the blood had to be applied. At the first Passover, the Jews slew the animals, and then they applied the blood to the doorposts. The blood did no good until it was applied. What saves the soul is not the knowledge that Jesus Christ died on a cross 2000 years ago. Rather salvation is assured when we apply the atoning work of Christ to our lives.

> *So, Lord Jesus, help me to understand that it is not just enough*
> *that you died for me.*
> *Encourage me to apply that blood*
> *to whatever needs to be atoned for in my life.*
> *Your precious blood must be applied!*

Jesus Is Substance, Not Shadow

Copies of the heavenly things (9:23)

If I read this passage correctly, there is a holy of holies in heaven similar to the one in the tabernacle. Both remind me that God is holy and I am a notorious rebel. In order to shield me, the rebel, from being destroyed, God isolated himself in a place where he could not be approached. It was for my own good.

Before Adam and Eve sinned, they had open access to God, enjoying fellowship with him and he with them. It was only after they willfully disobeyed God that they had to leave. Their sin of rebellion and unbelief clouded their relationship with him.

This estrangement from God is echoed in many cultures of the world. The people we lived with in Tanzania told of how God and people did have fellowship long ago. But something went wrong. According to the story, a woman was pounding grain in her mortar when God looked over her shoulder to see if she was grinding fine enough. Annoyed by this, she let go and popped God in the eye with the pestle. He left, never to return. I have heard similar stories, all sharing the belief that God was close to mankind early on, but that day is gone. They also agree that people chased God away.

The biblical account tells of God in his garden, which he enclosed with a wall after the Fall. He placed a guard with a flaming sword at the only gate to warn people not to enter. God protected humans from his justified wrath by erecting a dividing wall.

> *Lord, I do not see a sword-wielding soldier at the gate,*
> *but my beloved Jesus stands there inviting me to come in.*
> *I enter with joy, reentering the garden of communion with God.*

Jesus, the Better Sacrifice

The heavenly things themselves with better sacrifices than these (9:23)

It is difficult to imagine how the Jewish society would have survived had there not been a provision for reinstating unclean people back into the community. The law was full of ways to be pronounced ritually unclean. Most people would have been barred from the community quite often because of some defilement. Using the blood of sheep, goats, doves, and heifers for ceremonial cleansing was a superb way to enable transgressors to take their place in community life once again. I marvel at the wisdom of that practice. It is an ingenious way to reinstate a repentant scofflaw.

However, real sin cannot be cleansed away by blood sacrifice only meant for ceremonial cleansing. If I am to have peace with God, I need a sacrifice that actually takes away sin. I need a "better sacrifice," not just more sacrifices for my many offenses. I need one that breaks my will and takes away all sin, and then imparts to me a new heart that longs to serve my Lord and Savior.

Animal sacrifices cannot possibly cleanse anything in heaven. They are not meant to do that. Only one sacrifice changes things in heaven, that of heaven's own Son, Jesus Christ. He is the "better sacrifice."

> *Jesus, my Lord, you are that "better sacrifice."*
> *You came among us in the form of a person*
> *—both Son of God and Son of man.*
> *You gave your life as a sacrifice without spot or blemish.*
> *That sacrifice is not only better,*
> *it is also the only one with any real merit at all,*
> *because you alone can cleanse me of sin*
> *and renew a right spirit within me.*
> *Thank you, Jesus, for becoming the real sacrifice*
> *that cleanses real sin from real hearts, like mine.*
> *You are my real Savior and real Lord.*

September 23

As Jesus Entered, So May I

**Christ . . . entered heaven itself, now to appear for us in God's presence
(9:24)**

In these meditations I am reminded of how attractive it is to live among religious icons, without ever experiencing what is real. The icons—shadows and grand stories—lift me up and inspire me—to a degree. For instance, I have been blessed in these studies by the beauty and the symmetry in the tabernacle. Religious life is full of symbols and wonderful representations of holy things. Nevertheless they remain as aids to worship.

Icons cannot fully satisfy, for they only represent the real; they have no reality in themselves. I am not meant to live among icons alone. They are valuable when they remind me of the real, but they can never bring me into the realm of reality. For that I need to hide myself in Jesus Christ, my real Savior and Lord and, covered by his righteousness, enjoy fellowship with the Father as freely as the Son does.

When Jesus was crucified, the veil in the temple in Jerusalem was torn open, top to bottom. That also happened in heaven. Jesus entered by the power of his own blood. His grateful Father received him with open arms and gave him the name above every name, Jesus Christ, our Lord and Savior.

Jesus cleansed the Temple in Jerusalem but he did not enter the holiest place there. That would have had no value. When he shed his blood he did not bother to go to Jerusalem, he entered heaven itself. That changed everything.

> *Jesus, I am drawn to religious symbolism,*
> *but symbols are but pointers to the real.*
> *You have a much better way.*
> *You invite me to enter into what is eternally real.*
> *You entered first, on the merits of your atoning work.*
> *That entrance was also "for us."*
> *Now you invite me to enter, just like that,*
> *and so to live in peace with God forever and ever.*

Jesus, My Real Savior and Lord

Christ ... entered heaven itself, now to appear for us in God's presence
(9:24)

God is not one bit happy about the fact that the people he created cannot enter his presence. He must surely remember the time when he and Adam and Eve walked in the garden together in the cool of the day, relating as friends. Could that ever happen again?

"God so loved the world that he gave his one and only Son" (John 3:16) to be the real and perfect sacrifice. Jesus gave himself freely as the real Paschal Lamb, which can take away the sin of the world. His poured-out life had real worth. His blood was precious beyond measure. Because it was real, not a shadow, it was the actual life of the Son of glory, the holy one.

All heaven realized the reality of the atoning work of Jesus. The choirs of heaven swelled with that song of the ages, "Worthy is the Lamb, who was slain, to receive power and wealth and wisdom and strength and honor and glory and praise!" (Revelation 5:12).

The real Lamb offered his life; the real High Priest presented the sacrifice; the real God declared forgiveness for all who plead that blood; and the real Holy Spirit filled real hearts with power and light. The shadows are replaced by the substance. The icons come to life! The blood shed for me is now in God's presence.

Dear Lord, thank you for all the signs and reminders of your grace,
but thank you even more that, in your mercy,
you have allowed me to know and experience what is real
—eternal life in the Son.

September 25

Jesus, Our Sin Bearer

Now he has appeared . . . to do away with sin (9:26)

The Jews agonized over the problem of sin. They realized that what went wrong in Eden is what is wrong with everyone. Adam and Eve preferred to do precisely what God told them not to do.

Adam and Eve were then on the horns of a dilemma. They wanted two things: first, they wanted to do what they wanted to do, and second, they wanted the blessing of God to rest on their lives. It must have occurred to them that these two desires are irreconcilable. The decision was theirs: do they take their own way or God's way?

Every religion must address the problem of the persistent, perplexing compulsion to disobey God. The writer of Hebrews asserts that sin is real and that it remains as the basic human flaw. There is no merit in trying to rename sin as something else. It is red-handed rebellion against God.

The good news is that Jesus "has appeared . . . to do away with sin" and remove it so completely that humans can enjoy unbroken fellowship with almighty God. It was Jesus who broke the power of sin. His atoning sacrifice canceled not only my sin, but also all the sin of those who trust God to save them. This includes Adam and Eve and all who would ever live and sin until the end of the age. Jesus did not come to cover sin but to "do away with sin" once and for all.

> *Jesus, I see it clearly.*
> *You came among us for one compelling reason,*
> *to do away with sin.*
> *Continue that good work in me.*

Jesus, One Sacrifice for All

Christ was sacrificed once to take away the sins of many people (9:28)

I try to imagine what it would be like if I had to offer a costly sacrifice each time I loused up. The truth is, I would have been broke long ago and would be woefully in debt by now.

Because Jesus was a perfect and willing sacrifice, he needed to die only once for all sinners. Because Jesus died for my sin, it is futile for me to conjure up excuses for sin so that I can avoid its consequences. All I need to do is agree with the Holy Spirit; when he graciously points out sin in my life, I need to admit it and then drop it at the foot of the cross, where the atoning power of Jesus' blood wipes it out forever.

It does no good to feel miserable and to castigate myself as though there is some merit in my repentance. I am not forgiven because I repent, but because Jesus shed his atoning blood. If I am not careful, I can think of my penitence as good works which deserve some heavenly merit. My repentance is simply accepting what is already done.

No, there is only one way for sin to be removed—by the sacrifice of Jesus Christ.

Lord Jesus, give me the grace to leave it there.
I ask for a contrite and broken spirit as I come to you for cleansing,
but forbid that I should add to my sins the additional sin of unbelief,
which hopes that my contrition somehow
contributes to your willingness to forgive me.
The moment I come to you, the sin is obliterated,
no matter how I feel.
My feelings have nothing at all to do with it.
Jesus, you died for me. I rest on that now and forever.

Jesus Is Coming Again

Christ ... will appear a second time, not to bear sin, but to bring salvation to those who are waiting for him (9:28)

Jesus will appear a second time, but we will not see him on the cross again to accomplish a better atonement. No one can find a flaw in Jesus' atoning work. His finished work is perfect. He is the end of all sacrifice.

But that does not mean he is inactive. He is interceding for me before the Father, even as I write these words. When the time is right, he will indeed make his second appearance, not to die again, but to take to himself those who love him and are waiting for him.

Only those who believe that Jesus came the first time can believe that he will come again. Those of us who place our hope on him know he will reappear. We are counting on that with all our hearts. The moment we see him, our hearts will burst with exuberant joy, because all we ever dreamed of or hoped for will be reality. We were right! We wagered everything on the belief that Jesus is who he said he is. When he appears the second time it will be a day of great celebration for all believers, for their faith will have been proved right and their hope will have found its ultimate fulfillment.

The disciples must have felt something of this when they gathered in the upper room on the day of Pentecost. The coming of the Spirit proved that Jesus' atoning work was complete. The disciples then announced that Jesus will return again. They lived in the hope that he might appear at any time. This motivated them to spread the gospel to the ends of the earth.

So, come, Lord Jesus. Hasten your appearing.

Jesus Offers the Good Things

**The law is only a shadow of the good things that are coming
—not the reality themselves (10:1)**

I recall those delightful days of childhood when the mail-order catalogues arrived. I spent hours looking at items I dreamed of getting. One year it was a baseball glove. I pored over the picture of that glove. I studied it carefully, every stitch in the soft leather, all the webbed rawhide. Everything was right there for me to drool over. And I read and reread dozens of times the description of the glove that I hoped to buy. Then I sent for it. And I waited those agonizing but hopeful days for its arrival.

That excitement reached its height when the mailman delivered the glove. Then I had the real thing. The picture had meaning only because it described a reality. I almost forgot the picture and description as I donned the glove and snagged some grounders in the front yard.

Likewise all those marvelous things the Israelites did under the law excited the imagination, because everything pointed to the probability that the real thing would some day appear, and the prophets delighted in announcing what God had promised.

For us who believe, sure enough "good things are coming." Praise God.

> *I was ready at 8:30 p.m. the other night*
>   *to video a total eclipse of the moon.*
> *It happened just as predicted.*
> *Lord, you are stunningly predictable.*
> *What you have promised,*
>   *you will do precisely as you told us.*
> *All the "good things" will come.*

Jesus Makes Us Perfect

**[The law] can never ... make perfect those who draw near to worship
(10:1)**

I want to be the perfect husband, the perfect preacher, the perfect father and grandfather. I want to be a perfect Christian. The dream of perfection is good, but it eludes me. What does it mean that Jesus makes me perfect?

The perfection spoken of in today's verse does not speak of my perfection but of my position before God. As a result of Jesus' atoning work, my access to my heavenly Father is wide open. The door has been removed from its jamb. As I enter, my unworthiness is covered by the worthiness of Jesus Christ, in whom I am hidden. Jesus made it possible for me to have unhindered fellowship with my heavenly Father. All that is perfect. I am imperfect but because of the atoning work of Jesus my relationship with God is perfect. I need only to embrace that perfection.

Seen in this light, I receive the perfect work of Jesus and rely on his atoning sacrifice as the basis of my relationship with God. The work he did is perfect. The result is that as I approach my heavenly Father in Jesus' name, covered by his righteousness, I have perfect access to God.

All perfection is imputed. This means that my flaws do not stand in the way of my perfection. As I repent and open myself to the riches of Jesus' atoning sacrifice, in an instant I am before the Father, fully accepted because of the perfect work of Jesus.

Jesus, my dreams for perfection can come true
not through self-effort but through my abandonment to you,
for you are truly my perfection.

Jesus, the Willing Sacrifice

It is impossible for the blood of bulls and goats to take away sins (10:4)

While in Nepal, my wife and I had a few hours of free time, so we climbed a hill outside the town. A dozen or so Hindu worshipers were also climbing that hill with cantankerous goats and sheep on ropes. They were yanking them about, literally pulling the protesting animals up the hill. The poor animals did not know what lay in store for them. On the summit, they were to be sacrificed in worship. The whole scene seemed ludicrous to me.

I agree with the writer of Hebrews that animal blood cannot remove sin, because animals have no comprehension at all about what is going on. I cannot imagine one of those squirming goats in Nepal breaking out into song, "I am carrying the sin of my master. I am overjoyed by the fact that I can die so that the effect of a sin that he has committed against his gods can be canceled." Never!

But Jesus knew precisely what was going on. "When Christ came into the world he said: 'Sacrifice and offering you did not desire but a body you prepared for me'" (verse 5). In that body Jesus said, "Here I am. . . . I have come to do your will, O God" (verse 7). Jesus knew exactly what he came to earth to do. It was not an easy path he took; it was the way of the cross. But he despised the pain of it all to bring full salvation to all who believe.

> *Thank you, Father, for sending Jesus for this arduous task*
> *and thank you, Jesus, for never flinching.*
> *And thank you, Holy Spirit of God,*
> *for revealing this eternal truth to me.*

Jesus, My Willingness

**By that will, we have been made holy through the sacrifice
of the body of Jesus Christ once for all (10:10)**

I believe an appropriate paraphrase of today's verse would be, "Because Jesus willed to obey the Father, we are made holy."

This refutes my earlier belief that my salvation hinges on my willingness to believe. Not so. It hinges on Jesus' willingness to pay the price to save me. I realize that if Jesus had not died for me, no amount of "deciding" on my part would make any difference. Everything hinges on the fact that Jesus sustained his willingness to die for me.

It all begins by Jesus deciding for me. I say "me" because, had I been the only sinner in the universe, I could have been saved in no other way. Therefore I stand before the awesome fact that Jesus decided to do what it took to save me.

Of course, before Jesus can invade my life I must decide to let him. But that decision cannot save; it simply opens the door for the Savior. The only reason my decision for Christ is a life-changing event is because Jesus already decided in my favor. He received me long before I decided to receive him.

As I consider that, a spirit of gratitude wells up within me.

Jesus, everything I experience, everything I preach,
every deed of mercy I do is anchored in the bedrock truth that you,
my Lord, willed to obey your Father.

Jesus Victorious

But when this priest had offered for all time one sacrifice for sins,
he sat down at the right hand of God (10:12)

We have many, many chairs in our house. We needed seating for twenty-four guests recently and managed to provide some kind of a suitable chair for each person. It amazed me that ours is a house of chairs!

Not so the holy place of the tabernacle. We see tables and lamps and bread, but not a chair. What does that mean? The obvious meaning is that the tabernacle was a workplace with priests leaving and entering, always moving, always performing tasks. They may have completed their turn of service but the work of the priests went on and on.

The author of Hebrews wrote, "Day after day every priest stands and performs his religious duties; again and again he offers the same sacrifices" (10:11). But when Jesus offered himself once for all for sins for all time, he sat down. There is a chair in heaven for him. This passage shows Jesus as having won the decisive victory and as now seated with his Father, watching the effects of his victory over Satan.

That is a lesson pregnant with meaning for me. If Jesus can relax in the presence of God, I should be able to do the same because I have accepted his atoning sacrifice as my own. I can add nothing to and take nothing from the victory Jesus won for me.

Jesus Christ, you offer me the joy of all joys,
the privilege of sitting with you in the heavenlies with your Father,
our God, clothed with victorious power.

Jesus, My Perfecter

**By one sacrifice he has made perfect forever those who are
being made holy (10:14)**

Today's verse summarizes the good news. There is only one Jesus, one incarnation, one Redeemer, one Lord and Savior.

The work is done; all is prepared. There is nothing I can add or subtract from the great salvation Jesus Christ has earned for me. For me, salvation is free. For God, salvation meant the death of his Son, Jesus. He has done it, and it is flawless.

Jesus removed every barrier that impedes full communion with his Father. The way in is "perfect." Nothing can keep God from forgiving a sinner. I am not insinuating that God would ever want to withhold forgiveness from anyone. I am making the point that the work of Jesus is so complete that when a sinner pleads for forgiveness, God must forgive because he has promised to do so. It is impossible for God to forbid entrance to a penitent sinner because, by doing so, he would declare the work of Jesus to be insufficient.

Lord, it is hard for me to fully comprehend what you are saying here.
Me, perfect? The only way this is possible is if holiness is a gift.
I see that you did not say
perfection is for "those who are attaining holiness,"
but "for those who are being made holy."
I am beginning to understand.
I am being made holy by the atoning power of Jesus,
which releases mercy and grace
so that I begin to think and act like him.
I am blessed, Lord, because you are making me holy,
not because I have attained a holy state.

Jesus Modifies the Heart

**The Holy Spirit ... testifies ... "I will put my laws in their hearts,
and I will write them on their minds" (10:15-16)**

When I first gave my heart to the Lord, a love for God welled up within me. It startled me. Something entirely new had happened in my soul. I wanted to bathe in God's love and never get out. God was so real.

The same thing happened in my attitude toward people. That too amazed me. Upon conversion, it was as though God broke down the walls between me and other people. I was different. I could scarcely believe the change that had come over me.

As I look back on those days, my new attitudes were not learned behavior or the results of my striving to be better. Come to think of it, no one counseled with me to challenge my bad attitudes either. Little did I know that the prophecies of Jeremiah, quoted in today's verse, were being fulfilled. Jesus put his laws in my heart and wrote them in my mind.

This radical change of heart and mind is the direct result of the power of the atonement in my life. That does not mean that all my attitudes are Jesus-like all of the time. Far from it. I still regret bad attitudes after all these years of walking with him. The wonder is not that I might slip into a bad attitude; the wonder is that my heart and mind have been so dramatically changed that I often think like Jesus and, now and again, act like him. Now, that is a miracle!

Thank you, Jesus!

Jesus Enables God to Forget Sin

Their sins and lawless acts I will remember no more. And where these have been forgiven, there is no longer any sacrifice for sin (10:17-18)

Not only does the sacrifice of Jesus cancel out the sin against us, it enables God to actually forget our sin.

When I forgive someone, I still remember it and maybe even feel a twinge of guilt or pain in connection with it. I suppose forgiveness would be much more complete if the incident could be deleted entirely from my memory. My delete button fails on that one.

Not so with God. Because of the power of the atonement, when Jesus forgives, God forgets. We might say the blood of Christ accomplishes these two works of grace: it cancels sin and removes the memory of that sin in the heart of God. We might retain it as a vestige in our minds, but God has the ability to wipe it out of his mind, once and for all.

I have often pondered the words of Jesus on the cross: "Father, forgive them" (Luke 23:34). He did not say, "Father, I forgive them." Had he said that, it would have put the onus on God to punish those who did it. True forgiveness forgives completely. As I search my heart, I find that I secretly hope that God will remember those who hurt me and punish them good and proper. I register that in my memory. Shame!

Calvary forgiveness forfeits all rights to retaliate because, by forgiving, I have really told God he is free now to forget the whole thing. By so doing, I relinquish any power over the one I forgave. That spells divine, Christlike forgiveness.

> *Lord Jesus, teach me the lesson deeper than just forgiving;*
> *teach me forgetting as well.*
> *Jesus, be my forgiver and my forgetter!*

Jesus, Our Ticket

Therefore . . . we have confidence to enter the Most Holy Place (10:19)

Now and again someone gives me a ticket to something—a concert, a sporting event, or a banquet. That ticket gives me the right to go in.

When I am there because someone gave me a ticket, I do not feel the same as if I paid for the ticket myself. If I pay for it, I expect certain things to happen. When it is a gift, I take what comes.

That is how the grace of God works. The only way I can get a "ticket" is by receiving it as a free gift. That runs against the grain of human nature, certainly my human nature. I cannot buy tickets to grace.

If tickets to peace with God could be bought, people would line up in endless rows to pay the price, while only a few would be humble enough to stand in the line for free tickets. Churches are full of people who believe they are owed a ticket to peace with God because they have paid the price by their upright lives or their deed of kindness or sacrifice. This could be said of all religions.

I hear the call of the water seller in Isaiah 55:1, who was like a true preacher of the gospel. "Come, all you who are thirsty, come to the waters; and you who have no money, come, buy and eat! Come, buy wine and milk without money and without cost." It echoes Mary's song: "He has filled the hungry with good things but has sent the rich away empty" (Luke 1:53).

> *Jesus, you are not for sale.*
> *Your abundant benefits are available only by grace.*
> *I receive you either by faith or not at all.*

October 7

Jesus, Our Confidence

We have confidence to enter into the Most Holy Place (10:19)

The moment God approved Jesus' sacrifice, the veil was split top to bottom so that all believers can have open access to God almighty. What an awesome privilege! It changes everything.

My own spiritual ancestors, the Anabaptists of the early sixteenth century, discovered that Jesus' sacrifice was sufficient for them. They realized on the basis of the Bible that they had direct access to God and need not go through the saints or the priests. This was not good news to the powers of the Catholic Church at the time. And the reformers had to rethink the role of the church.

That sixteenth-century protest reshaped the religious landscape of Northern Europe. It broke the back of a religious system that claimed it held the keys to salvation. Every authentic revival threatens those who "administer" salvation. True revival puts ordinary people in touch with God almighty through the merits of Jesus' atoning work. No church or institution holds the keys to the salvation of a human being. God holds that key.

As a missionary, I saw something similar happen. When local believers discovered that they had open access to God as repentant sinners, it did not matter much what we missionaries said. They had just as much access to God as the missionaries because of the all-sufficient atoning work of Jesus. Glory be.

Jesus, on the basis of your perfect sacrifice
I can walk through the door into God's awesome presence.

By Jesus' Blood, the Only Way

Enter the Most Holy Place by the blood of Jesus (10:19)

Some of my friends find the thought of Jesus' blood to be abhorrent. So do I. But I feel sorry for them because this natural revulsion keeps them from a glorious spiritual discovery: there is a way to peace with God. They choke on the notion that the only way to have peace with God is through the atoning work of Christ.

I too would prefer to believe that there are many ways to approach God. I can think thoughts like that only if I convince myself that I am not a sinner. If I do not see myself as an incurable sinner, any god or guru will do. But if the Holy Spirit turns his penetrating spotlight on my sinful nature, I am greatly relieved to know that Jesus gave his life as God's perfect Paschal Lamb so that my sinful nature can be broken and a new power can and will invade my life.

If the thought of Jesus' blood is abhorrent to me, imagine how much more abhorrent it is to our heavenly Father. Jesus is his Son. That is the price God paid to save me from utter loss. Perhaps some believers abuse the blood of Christ, employing it as a fetish. That is an erroneous way to think of the atonement. When the writer to the Hebrews refers to the "blood of Jesus," he includes the expansive totality of all that has been made available to us through the atonement, including salvation, justification, sanctification, the power to do good and many other truths named with big words.

Jesus, teach me to value your blood as much as God almighty does.

October 9

Jesus, New and Living

By the blood of Jesus, by a new and living way (10:19-20)

The atonement blends the unblendable. Life blends with death.

Today's verse begins with death: "by the blood of Jesus." The atoning work of Jesus embraces death. In his case, it was a cruel, murderous death. Jesus' atonement conquered death. After that comes the word *new*. I understand that it literally means "newly killed" or a "just-now sacrificed," as though the shed blood is crimson red. Finally, the word *living* unfolds like a spring tulip. This sequence is important; death precedes life but is also caught up in or swallowed by life.

Jesus spoke often about dying to self in order to live for God. For instance, he said, "If anyone would come after me, he must deny himself and take up his cross and follow me" (Matthew 16:24). And "unless a kernel of wheat falls to the ground and dies, it remains only a single seed. But if it dies, it produces many seeds" (John 12:24).

I recall an African brother who, when learning English idioms, pondered the phrase *life has its ups and downs*. I still hear his holy chuckle when he said, "That is backward. For believers, life has its downs and ups." He saw that when we die to our demanding egos, life bursts forth in extraordinary power. We live "by the blood of Jesus, by a new and living way."

The way up is down.

> *Jesus, you surprise me by the way you braided*
> *into one strand both death and life*
> *in your marvelous atoning work.*
> *Dying to self, I live in you.*

Jesus, the Curtain

Through the curtain, that is, his body (10:20)

Curtain signifies a wall, a separator, a hindrance. The idea is that I am separated from God by something I cannot remove.

As noted throughout these meditations, Adam and Eve had full and open fellowship with God before they were banished from the garden. After they rebelled, the garden was encompassed by a high wall to ensure that people did not stray into the presence of the Holy One, whose wrath was fierce.

That's how it was when God instructed the Jews to build the tabernacle to "house" the presence of God. The curtain protected the people from the holy wrath of God against sin. This restriction was relaxed once each year, on the Day of Atonement, when the high priest, bearing blood for his sins and those of the nation, dared to lift the curtain enough to place the blood before God.

Then Jesus came. He placed his body between the presence of God and the people, like the curtain in the tabernacle. In his body he received the full, white-hot wrath of God against sin. He became in that moment our sin-bearer. I like to think the searing wrath wracked Jesus' body on the cross and tore, as it were, a hole in him—a hole large enough to enable all who will to enter in. By his sacrificial death he became the open door.

> *Jesus, your body was the curtain,*
> *now blessedly torn so that I might enter in.*
> *The seeming tragedy on Calvary's hill is my door to God.*

Jesus Opened the Door

By a new and living way opened for us (10:20)

Jesus returned to glory not only as God's Son but also as the eternal Savior bearing his own poured-out blood, his very life. As he approached heaven's gate, we hear the song of the ages ring out, "Worthy is the Lamb. Come right in, Jesus of Nazareth, for you have conquered death and hell." We enter God's presence in exactly the same way, bearing the blood of Jesus Christ. It is only by the blood of Jesus that we have access to the Father, for it is heaven's only way to save sinners.

Jesus opened the new and living way for us. I can scarcely take that in. There was no reason for Jesus to go through everything he did for himself. He had full access to heaven already. He did it for you and me. If that is true, I owe everything to him. I understand why the writer of Hebrews is so excited about Jesus.

As I began to plumb the depths of this precious letter, I was astonished at the way Jesus is elevated and exalted in a way that seems extreme. Was Jesus actually all that the writer claims him to be? Is he really that crucial in the history of heaven and earth? Does he deserve all the praise he receives from the author of this book and from every tongue in heaven and on earth?

I have come to believe that Jesus is the person the writer depicts him to be. Remove Jesus, and all that is left is the old, dreary, worn-out dictum, "Try to do better."

> *Like you, Jesus, I enter the presence of God,*
> *pleading the merits of your redeeming blood.*
> *It was shed for me.*

Jesus, Our Confidence

**Let us draw near to God with a sincere heart in full assurance of faith
(10:22)**

Why tarry? Come in. Me? Is it possible that I, a sinful mortal, can stand in the presence of almighty God? Can a guilty person enjoy the presence of the judge who is well aware of his offenses? Will Jesus, who always did the will of his Father, ever smile on me, a rebel?

The answer is yes. But it is not because God pities me so much that he decides to lay aside his justice and set me free. If that were the case, there would be no need for Jesus to give his life as a ransom for sinners like me.

The writer of the letter to the Hebrews, who I assume was a normal human being, knows he can approach God without fear. He hides himself in Jesus, in the cleft of the rock that was split to receive such sinners. Trusting completely the merits of Jesus and fully embracing them as his very own, the writer pauses, looks at me and says, "Let's go in!" He enters by faith.

Do I have the same confidence in the completed atoning work of Jesus as he has? If not, I need to banish any confidence in myself and believe.

I have a choice. I can go in or stay out. I cannot set the conditions of my own salvation. Salvation is not something that I fashion for myself. It is made for me by the triune God. I can say either yes or no. God will never force me to go in. The invitation stands. The response is up to me.

Why tarry?

Lord, I come.

October 13

Jesus Desires Sincerity

With a sincere heart in full assurance of faith (10:22)

I remember my mother talking about not doing things half-heartedly. I suppose I provided her with many opportunities for such admonition. Through life I have discovered that it takes intense concentration to do anything really well.

As we approach God, we should do so with sincere hearts. I understand that the root meaning of *sincere* is "without wax." Sometimes a sculptor would use wax to fill in a flaw. If it is well done, it looks like marble. The way to check for wax was to hold the sculpture up to the sun. Light easily passes through high-grade marble, but not through wax. The dark spots showed where wax was used.

Sincere hearts allow no falsehood or duplicity. Jesus called hypocrites whitewashed graves. He knew the destructive power of mixed motives and insincerity.

When I first came to Christ, I had no defense. I was a condemned sinner, and I knew it. How is it, now that I have walked with Jesus for many years, that I come to God with my pockets full of righteousness? That is "wax," to be sure. I use my self-righteousness to defend myself, unwilling to place myself in the hands of Jesus Christ. That will show up as a dark spot under God's examination.

> *O, Lord, give to me a sincere, pure, and undivided heart.*
> *Forbid that I should approach you half-heartedly.*
> *Melt all the wax out of your good work in my life.*

Trust Jesus

Let us draw near . . . in full assurance of faith (10:22)

Faith in what? Faith in Jesus.

I am invited to believe that everything Jesus said and everything the Bible says about him is incontestable fact. That includes everything Jesus said about himself, about his Father in heaven, about his world, and about me. Faith is putting my full weight on him. It might be difficult to give good reasons for believing so completely in Jesus, but the heart has reasons to which the head must ultimately adapt.

This letter insists on one thing. If I believe in Jesus, I have full access to his bountiful supplies in this life and in the life to come. The flipside is, if I choose not to believe, then I have no legitimate rights to life here and hereafter.

I live in an age and a culture that war against this kind of faith. The well-known Jesus Seminar, in which skeptical scholars meet, has concluded that no one knows what Jesus said. Each decade or so a new book comes out flatly denying the uniqueness of Christ. Each of these heresies attacks the divine nature of Jesus.

The most difficult thing is to believe. When Jesus fed the multitude, someone asked him what good work pleases God. With razor-sharp perception, Jesus replied, "The work of God is this: to believe in the one he has sent" (John 6:29).

Trust me, that is *work*. I know that and all believers know it. It is work to believe, but worth it.

Lord, I believe!

Jesus Is Truth

In full assurance of faith (10:22)

I learned in a rather roundabout way that Jesus is truth. When Jesus made himself known to me at age sixteen, I was flailing about, living entirely for self, oblivious to all things spiritual. He met me, I opened my heart to him, and he came in. It was as simple as that.

As I recall, I had no intellectual hurdles to overcome. It had not occurred to me that I should doubt and struggle. I needed to be saved from my headlong plunge into egoism; that was about it.

Several years passed before I began to face the intellectual challenges of faith. Higher education in western culture is not a friend to faith. Faith is considered an indication of intellectual shallowness. So I told myself that any belief I held that could not stand up under painstaking logical scrutiny must be abandoned. So I cobbled together a personal theology that defended religion but criticized faith.

Fast-forward to Tanzania. My so-called enlightened scientific worldview did not serve me well there. Frustration built up within me. Which worldview was right, my "enlightened" one or the one Jesus talked about? I recall the Holy Spirit pressing me to decide whether I believed that the statements attributed to Jesus in the Scriptures were his.

After a painful struggle, I replied simply, "My God, by faith I do." In a moment the heavy cloud of unbelief lifted, and Jesus and I became close friends once again. I have struggled with moments of doubt since then, but I have never abandoned my determination to believe.

Lord Jesus, many of the things you say about yourself,
your Father in heaven, and the Holy Spirit baffle me.
But I choose to believe.

Jesus Cleanses the Heart

Having our hearts sprinkled to cleanse us from a guilty conscience (10:22)

The idea that people should be cleansed before they worship is universal.

The tabernacle reinforced this. At the entrance stood the laver, a large basin filled with water for the cleansing of all who entered. Muslims are fastidious in this regard. As they enter the mosque, they remove their shoes, which are considered "unclean," and wash face, hands, and feet. I asked a nomadic Muslim what he does when he is herding his camels in the desert and it is time for prayer but there is no water for miles. He said, "No problem. We wash with the sand."

Cleansing is a must. As we come to God through Jesus Christ, we enjoy genuine cleansing. Jesus cleanses our hearts with the sprinkling of his own atoning blood. This cleansing so penetrates the depths of our soul that all guilt is gone—an amazing thing. The Scriptures remind us that all our righteousness, or accumulated merit, is nothing but filthy rags, not at all fit to wear as we go before the holy God. Jesus provided the answer in his atoning work. He sprinkles our entire being with his blood, which covers sin.

> *Jesus, when I came to you for salvation,*
> *   you plunged me into a most remarkable bath,*
> *   head to toe.*
> *I do not need to go through all that again,*
> *   but I do need daily sprinkling.*
> *I praise you for your loving hand, which takes the hyssop*
> *   and sprinkles the precise spot in my heart that needs cleansing.*
> *Because of you, Jesus, I can approach God without guilt.*
> *You have paid my debt fully.*
> *The least I can offer you is my devoted, grateful, joyful heart.*

October 17

Jesus Purifies the Body

Our bodies washed with pure water (10:22)

First we are cleansed on the inside, then on the outside. That is always God's way. The apostle James reminded the religious leaders that pure water is not to be found in contaminated springs (see James 3:12).

That is why it is so important to be cleansed, first on the inside, because that is the throne room of the self. It is at that level that true brokenness occurs. When I die to my self-centered life and see the Lord on his throne, everything changes from the inside out. It is futile to try to change from the outside in.

I saw this clearly in Africa. People wanted to change, and we missionaries wanted to help them, so we stressed dos and don'ts. We added baptism to their ancient puberty rituals and encouraged them to add Sunday worship to ancestral veneration. They did that. Why, then, did we see so little change? Unless a person breaks before God and invites Jesus to take over, all is frustration and futility, because in the end we cannot serve two masters. Why should it be any different for Africans than for me? It is not a matter of ceremonies, but of powerful purification.

Lord Jesus, seeing how your atoning power revolutionizes lives
helps to make a believer out of me!
Such life-changing dynamics can be set in motion
only by your atoning blood,
which takes effect in the inner sanctum of the human heart
and ultimately judges every aspect of life.
Lord, continue this inside-out work in my life
for my good and for your glory.

Jesus Created Bodies

Our bodies washed with pure water (10:22)

Can my body, with its needs and passions, ever be like Jesus? The apostle Paul viewed his body as something he must tame. He confessed that its demands could threaten his relationship with God, writing, "I beat my body and make it my slave so that after I have preached to others, I myself will not be disqualified for the prize" (1 Corinthians 9:27).

As I ponder the message of the entire Bible, I see no support for the notion that the body is evil and the spirit is good. Did not Jesus make our bodies? The biblical revelation does not support the Gnostic view, which dismisses the body as of no consequence at all because it is essentially amoral.

Hindus try to rise above bodily needs by squelching all appetites. On the other extreme, western cultures tend to coddle the body, making it an idol to be served.

Our text reminds us that the body can indeed lead to uncleanness; otherwise it would not need to be washed. Even though the body is not—in itself—unclean, it does get dirty, so it needs cleansing. The atonement provides for that. Jesus sprinkles our consciences on the inside and washes our bodies on the outside!

My Lord, when I present myself to you,
I need to leave no part of myself behind.
You want me to come just as I am, all of me.
In this way I can bring all my spiritual and physical needs
before you.
Shower me, Lord, with all your mercy and grace.

Jesus, My Hope

Let us hold unswervingly to the hope we profess (10:23)

What is the hope that sets my heart to singing and stirs my faith? The answer is simply Jesus. For faith and hope to have any reality in my life, I must have complete confidence in him.

Jesus is my one hope. If what the Scriptures reveal about him is nothing more than pious imagination, as some enemies of Christ contend, then my faith and hope are no more than wishful thinking. But if what the Scriptures reveal is actually true, then I have done well to pin all my hope on Jesus. Jesus cannot be half right. I believe that he is in me, hoping in God without wavering.

Sometimes I hear or read about someone who, looking back on a time of crisis, says, "My faith sustained me." Good. But my question is, Faith in what? Faith in faith? In your own determination? In others? Or just faith that it would all work out in the end?

I too have gone through searing fires, but I was not sustained by my faith. I was sustained by Jesus' faith. I have no intrinsic faith. I am sustained by the faith of Jesus Christ himself.

Our verse says, "Hold on to hope."
Jesus, I can do so only if I tighten my grasp on you,
*   for "he who promised is faithful."*
If I abandon all to a person who is not faithful to his promises,
*   I am headed for shocking disappointment.*
You, Jesus, promised to be faithful.
Now, at this stage of my life, I can say, "You are faithful."
As Pilate said, "I find no fault in you." You are my hope.

Cling to Jesus

Let us hold unswervingly (10:23)

"Orpha kissed her mother-in-law good-by, but Ruth clung to her" (Ruth 1:14). Naomi loved both of her daughters-in-law, Ruth and Orpha. Orpha loved her devoted mother-in-law dearly, but she loved security more. She stayed behind in Moab.

Ruth, on the other hand, decided to throw her lot in with Naomi. The Bible is so expressive here: Ruth "clung to her." There is a note of desperation in what she did, and a note of hope. She had no idea how important that decision was. By the grace of God, this Moabite woman—not a Jewish woman— had the rare privilege of being the grandmother of King David and a direct ancestor of Jesus Christ. It all happened because she clung to her mother-in-law, Naomi.

I must confess that at times, like Orpha, a kiss of gratitude is about all I have to give to Jesus. Would that I had the courage of Ruth to cling to him with all my might. To do that I must turn my back on everything else and follow him into the unknown.

The writer of Hebrews is very much aware of the human tendency to follow Jesus with early enthusiasm but then drift away from or lose a grip on Jesus. The antidote is to "hold unswervingly" to him and to the gospel in its entirety. No matter what life throws at me, I must hold on tenaciously, without any loosening of my grip.

Jesus, inevitably life's swerves will come.
May they result in me gripping you more vigorously.

Hold on to Jesus

Let us hold unswervingly (10:23)

The apostle Paul tells us about his struggles to cling to Jesus through all the "swervings" of life. In his letter to the Philippians, he gave his testimony clearly and simply. As Saul, the persecuting Jew, was making his way to Damascus to stem the spread of the gospel among the Jews there, Jesus appeared to him. Paul looked back on this event and described it as Jesus Christ *taking hold* of him. Jesus *apprehended* him and in effect arrested Saul and held him in custody. Then, Paul confides, he took hold of Jesus. What an embrace! The words of Paul echo throughout all time: "I press on to take hold of that for which Christ Jesus took hold of me" (Philippians 3:12).

How do I take hold of Jesus? First, it is a matter of the will. Do I trust Jesus enough to let my entire weight down on him? If I do, then I must put that into practice. Be gone, self-sufficiency!

The best way for this to happen is to be acutely aware of my sinnerhood. At the same time, I must fix my eyes on Jesus and follow him without question. Then, each time I see him do a new thing in my life, I note it in my heart. In this way my knowledge of Jesus expands dramatically.

> *Jesus, I tighten my hold on you*
> *as you tighten your hold on me.*
> *As I grasp you more firmly,*
> *I relax my grip on all but you.*

Jesus, the Faithful One

Let us hold unswervingly to the hope we profess, for he who promised is faithful (10:23)

When I hear, "Hold on to your hope," I wobble. In myself I cannot hold on. I know that, even at my very best, I am a stumbling, bungling, exhausted human being. As long as I trust in my own strength, I have no peace, because in my heart of hearts I know I am no better than Peter who, under fire, discovered his true nature to be self-centered and proud.

As a young missionary in Tanzania, driven by the need to succeed, I kept telling myself, "You can. You will overcome this and accomplish that." The Lord allowed me to flail away, only to fall exhausted in a heap of disappointments. In my desperation I cried out, "I can't."

That was when I heard the voice of Jesus, saying, "You can't, but I can. Abandon self-effort and let me work out my will in your life." In hindsight, what I did was transfer my hope from self to Jesus. It makes all the difference.

I am not dependable; Jesus is. I am not worthy of trust; Jesus is supremely trustworthy. I cannot fulfill the simplest of my promises to God; Jesus pleased his Father in heaven in every regard.

The answer is as clear as the noonday sun. I hope only in Jesus Christ, for I am hopeless. I often feel pangs of despair as I serve my Lord. I also admit that those feelings sprout from the root of self-sufficiency and self-confidence. Great, my Lord, is your faithfulness.

> *Lord, lay the axe to this root.*
> *Remind me always, "I, who promised, am faithful."*
> *Everything I lean on fails, but you.*

October 23

Jesus Desires Fellowship

**And let us consider how we may spur one another on
toward love and good deeds (10:24)**

The message gets down-to-earth practical at this point. "Come up with workable ideas," Jesus says, "so that I can use you to help people love and serve one another."

I am not very good at this. It seems to me that I need all my energy just to prod little me to love and serve others, let alone try to figure out how to spur others to get on with serving God.

I believe that today's text means that, left alone, I accomplish very little. I need someone to prod me to serve others. To live the life of Christ, I must be accountable to some brother or sister on a regular basis. Furthermore, if I can team with others to do the work Christ wants us to do, my effort is multiplied.

For more than twenty years, my wife and I have had the rare privilege of meeting regularly with a small group of people who attempt to hold one another accountable. Knowing the grace of God, they gently spur me on to love and serve. I may resist their spurring, but, to be honest, I need every bit of their encouragement.

I recall several times when African brothers and sisters put their fingers on things that I was not willing to give up. "Stay out of my business, please!" was often my first response. But as I prayed about their challenges, I realized it was the Holy Spirit speaking into my life.

> *Lord, thank you for faithful brothers and sisters*
> *who care enough to challenge me.*
> *I admit that I need to be spurred on to love more*
> *and to do more for you.*
> *They help!*

Jesus, Our Meeting Place

**Let us not give up meeting together, as some are in the habit of doing
(10:25)**

How vividly I recall the life-changing, dynamic prayer meetings at Eastern Mennonite School. A few of us had given our hearts to Jesus for the first time, and a few had just rededicated their lives to him. We began to meet on a regular basis. As we climbed that narrow attic stairway to a place we called "the upper room," a hush came over us. We knew that Jesus was there. The awesome power of the Holy Spirit filled that room. As we read the Bible, every word and comma was pregnant with meaning.

I attended those meetings for almost two years before I left that college. I learned things there that shaped my life. Years later, while at the University of Maryland, the Lord provided an equally meaningful group, then we were off to Africa.

My heart often yearned to have that kind of Christ-centered fellowship again. As a young missionary, I resisted the Holy Spirit, who was at work in the great revival in East Africa. Eventually I broke before God, repented of my hard, sinful heart, and to my utter amazement and delight, I was once again in that familiar "upper room," this time in Africa with a mixture of all sorts of people opening their hearts to Jesus. Different place, different people but the same spirit.

Of course, Anna Ruth and I had our own precious "upper room," which grows deeper and deeper every year. I have no idea how I would have made it without that sweet fellowship God has given me with her. The Lord designed us all for fellowship. I pity a Christian who has given up meeting with others on the Way.

> *Jesus, you promised to be there*
> *when two or three gather in your name.*
> *I can prove that by my own experience.*

Jesus, the Only Sacrifice for Sin

**If we deliberately keep on sinning after we have received the knowledge
of the truth, no sacrifice for sins is left (10:26)**

I recall thinking that if Jesus went to all that trouble to atone for my sins and give me his Holy Spirit, why didn't he just finish the task by eradicating from my being any possibility of sinning?

As a young missionary the total eradication doctrine tantalized me. Some of my missionary colleagues (not of my own mission, by the way) taught this doctrine, which says we die to sin as Jesus did, so now we reckon ourselves to be dead to sin. I did my share of reckoning, believe me, but I still found myself harboring resentment or holding to prideful thoughts.

Slowly I discovered that even though sin no longer had dominion over me because of the atoning work of Christ, the desire to take my own way to please myself was alive in me. Does that mean Jesus did not complete the work in me? Of course not; I am complete in Jesus. But living in a world that scorns the Jesus I love is not a picnic. It is super hard to stay on the way of holiness. I discovered to my joy that no matter what, his blood is sufficient to keep me from sin and to cleanse me from it when I inadvertently fall.

Today's verse does not speak of inadvertent sin but of sustaining a rebellious attitude toward Jesus after believing in him initially. The possibility of becoming insensitive to sin is a daily peril. It is spiritual leprosy that desensitizes the nerves.

*Lord Jesus, forbid that I should coddle any sin whatsoever
and lose my sensitivity to the horrid nature of sin
as you view it.*

October 26

Jesus Deserves Honor

How much more severely do you think a man deserves to be punished . . .
who has insulted the Spirit of grace? (10:29)

This passage urges people who were sanctified by the blood of the covenant to take stock lest they "insult the Spirit of grace." This is serious. I insult the Spirit of grace when I know that grace is sufficient but then try to get on in my own strength. I also insult the Spirit of grace when I profess that Jesus is my Lord and Savior, then act as I always did.

This is a warning to me. I know the restoring, energizing, renewing power of the Lord Jesus and the Holy Spirit. I can look back on a blizzard of activity in ministry when I saw the Lord at work enabling remarkable victories in my days. But what about now, in my "maturing years"?

This is a crucial moment. Am I going to lose the focus I had when the battle was raging, when spiritual adrenalin was flowing? Or will I inadvertently shift attention to my own needs rather than being responsive to the needs of others? Will the physical and mental slowdown that commonly accompanies aging collapse my world into the small space I occupy? How am I to handle my dwindling world?

I am greatly encouraged by the warning I read here, because the one who wrote it must have been speaking from experience. The warning is to beware of the dangers but get on with walking with Jesus. This word of the Holy Spirit is not designed to paralyze me but to energize me. When I am in Jesus my world expands, never contracts.

You, Jesus, began the good work. Now complete it!

October 27

Jesus, Our Memory

Remember those earlier days (10:32)

How can I describe my earlier days? I was in my mid-teens and a bundle of bewilderment. Two of my brothers excelled in their studies in the newly consolidated high school I attended, and I was expected to do the same.

Not a chance! I was determined to do it my way. This landed me in heaps of trouble. I began to run with friends who encouraged my self-centered ways. A part of me sneered at authority, but another part warned me of doom if I were to persist in making decisions that isolated me more and more from all foundations and structure.

The boom fell as I finished eleventh grade. I was fifteen years old, and the school authorities put pressure on my parents to "do something." Bless them, they did. They offered to pay my way to the Mennonite high school in Harrisonburg, Virginia. That was a real risk for them, because they were certainly not flush with money. And what assurance had they that I was not going to proceed on my merry way there? They took the risk and prayed that I would be helped. My heart rejoices when I think of their determination to do what they could to arrest my downward slide. I will be eternally grateful for that.

But as I packed my bags and headed off to Virginia, I was determined to establish my independence in a big way. That was August 1944. Six weeks later, on October 10, Jesus appeared to me. I had no idea what was going on, but I knew I had met Jesus. Period!

Jesus, I recall my own earlier days with gratitude.

Jesus, the Same in the Present Days

Remember those earlier days (10:32)

Jesus found me as a headstrong individualist. He broke my heart and poured in his love. I dread to think what would have become of me had Jesus not encountered me "on the way." I do well to remember that truth every day of my life, lest I become self-sufficient once again.

There is another chapter to my story that I must share. As I pursued my studies in developmental psychology and comparative religions, I had to rethink the idea of conversion. I recall reading Sigmund Freud, William James, Carl Jung, and others who described conversion as nothing more than a puberty ritual. So what had happened to me? Was I converted, or was I just growing up? This doubt clouded my thinking for some time.

That all changed when I came to the end of myself as a struggling missionary in Africa. For there the Holy Spirit led me into one crisis after another and revealed my sinful, self-centered nature in a most damning but redeeming way. At that point I cried out for cleansing and healing.

Jesus poured forgiveness, love, peace, and mercy into my heart, and I knew without a shadow of a doubt that he had met me that night on October 10, 1944. It was the same Jesus and the same Holy Spirit. My conversion was real, if I may say it like that. I have never doubted it since.

> *Jesus, thank you for allowing me to revisit*
> *the time you first flooded my life with light and joy.*
> *May I never forget!*

Jesus, My Lasting Possession

**You stood your ground ... because you knew that you yourselves
had better and lasting possessions (10:32, 34)**

In giving my testimony one day, I surprised myself by saying, "I believe I was most mature as a Christian the first day I was saved." What I meant was that I came as a sinner pleading nothing but the blood of Christ. I had childlike faith. I was needy, and Jesus told me that he would meet my every need. That did it.

To faith he added love. I loved my parents once again. I even felt love for my teachers and administrators. Instead of squirming under their authority, I saw them as friends because they too loved Jesus.

The driving force in my life had been to express my independence and make my own way. It was replaced by a profound desire to follow Christ. I had found a "better and lasting possession." I was ready to sell all to secure the priceless pearl, Jesus. That is why I said that I was most mature as a Christian the day I was saved. Of course, that faith, love, and hope had to be tested. And it was.

In all candor, I must admit that doubts sometimes crept in and my love for some cooled. I began to value things that were not of lasting value. The antidote to this spiritual confusion is to revisit my "earlier days." By so doing, I again become a little child. What changed me that day can change me today.

Lord, I embrace anew my first love, Jesus.

Jesus, Priority Number One

You knew that you yourselves had better and lasting possessions (10:34)

Almost everyone who has been born again wants to shout from the housetops, "Jesus is the most important thing in my life." I did. I had found the hidden treasure, the costliest pearl, the largest diamond, the richest bank, the King of all kings. I had found the living bread, the water of life, God's only begotten Son. I determined to live for him only. He would have absolute priority in my life, and I would allow nothing to challenge his supremacy.

These are lofty sentiments, well spoken and heartily believed. What happened, then? I discovered that Jesus has many rivals, each promising some kind of security or hope or just plain fun. I will spare you my list of rivals, each of which had its day with me. My heart became a battlefield.

I praise God that he allowed things to happen to challenge the worth of those rivals. Most notable was dropping me down on the shores of Lake Victoria in the heart of Africa, where my carefully constructed critical spirit shattered under the impact of the Holy Spirit.

I realized that I had been chasing the second best, and it broke my heart. Jesus is better and Jesus lasts.

> *Jesus, I need to be alert every day to the possibility*
> *that a rival will arise to bring you into second place.*
> *May it never be so.*

October 31

Jesus, My Confidence

So do not throw away your confidence (10:35)

Jesus never lost confidence in his Father. That fellowship anchored him as the storms of rejection and hate battered him mercilessly. As I hear him cry out in Gethsemane, I do not detect a hint of lack of confidence in his Father. His problem had to do with how to obey the Father, not whether the will of the Father was justified. He believed implicitly in the wisdom and love of his Father in heaven.

I am tempted to doubt whether God really concerns himself with my every need, and I speak as a believer. That sounds ridiculous, but it is true. I would much prefer to see the way ahead, rather than to live by faith.

A few years ago I went through a fire of testing when the enemy tempted me to doubt God's love and providential care. I could not reconcile the hurt and suffering I was feeling with his promise to be with me. The enemy of my soul was ready to solve my problem. In his insidious way he whispered, "Throw away your confidence in Jesus."

I am so thankful that I heeded the advice of the Holy Spirit: "Do not throw away your confidence; it will be richly rewarded. You need to persevere so that when you have done the will of God, you will receive what he has promised" (Hebrews 10:35-36).

Lord Jesus, thank you for reminding me
of a line from that old hymn:
"Trust and obey,
for there's no other way to be happy in Jesus."

Jesus, My Perseverance

We are not of those who shrink back and are destroyed, but of those who believe and are saved (10:39)

Christians are not equipped to turn tail and run when the battle gets hot. They forfeit their divine protection when they do that. As long as they have full trust in the power and wisdom of their captain, they can be assured of victory in the battle over the evil one. Were they to entertain thoughts which cast doubt on the hope that their captain will prevail, they may well "shrink back" and by so doing place themselves in mortal danger.

The key to perseverance is unshakable trust in Jesus Christ. We read, "My righteous one will live by faith" (10:38). Today's verse indicates that the contrast is drawn, and the choice is mine. I can either persevere in the battle or cut and run.

We are about to enter chapter 11, often called the faith chapter. As my mind races back over everything the Holy Spirit has revealed so far, the outstanding thing is the elevation and exaltation of Jesus Christ. It seems as though the writer of Hebrews cannot find words and illustrations to adequately describe the glory of Jesus.

Time and again I stood breathless as the Holy Spirit revealed yet another aspect of the manifold grace of God in Christ. As I reflect on all that, I am challenged to believe that it is true and that Jesus is for me. This section concludes, "Those who believe . . . are saved." I might add *were* saved, *are* saved, and *will be* saved eternally.

Embolden my heart, O God,
by unshakable faith in your infinite love.

Jesus Makes Faith Real

**Now faith is being sure of what we hope for and
certain of what we do not see (11:1)**

Jesus had absolute confidence in his Father in heaven, whom he saw with the eyes of faith. Our culture has serious problems with that.

All my life I've been told that what the senses experience is real, and everything else is fantasy or poetry. I've been taught that if something cannot be proved by scientific methods, it is not real. How, then, am I to deal with a verse like this?

The Spirit of God describes a different view. He has been teaching us through the first ten chapters of Hebrews that Jesus is the trustworthy object of our hope. We can depend entirely on him.

But I ask, is Jesus real? The answer comes back: Before anything we call real was created, Jesus was. When the universe finally disintegrates, Jesus will remain. Jesus is real. Heaven is real. God the Father is real. The Holy Spirit is real. The atonement is real. God's love is real. That which can be tested by scientific method will vanish. It will simply be no more.

When my wife and I recently visited Africa, where we had spent twenty years of our life, we found that what remained of our efforts was not building projects and structures, but friendships, love, and the church. These are eternal realities, and we saw some things that we scarcely could have hoped for. People were walking with Jesus in determined hope. That lasts!

> *God, deliver me from the illusion*
> *that the material world will last.*
> *Faith is being sure of something we cannot prove.*
> *That is why it is such a stretch.*

God, the Eternal Creator

**By faith we understand that the universe was formed at God's command
(11:3)**

God's question to Job echoes through all time: "Where were you when I laid the earth's foundation?" (Job 38:4). The answer is obvious. No scientist was there when the chemical compounds were formed and pulsing energy brought order out of chaos. No historian, scientist, or philosopher was there to ask the Creator why he was doing what he was doing.

The writer of Hebrews begins by laying the foundations of faith. First, God is the Creator of the universe. He is not embedded in it but has a separate existence entirely. Second, all matter has a beginning point. Third, matter is temporal. Finally, material cannot create material. As it is stated later in Hebrews 11:3, "What is seen was not made out of what was visible." Atheism is remarkable in that it believes that the material universe sustains itself. Now, that is hard to believe. The laws of thermodynamics blast that theory.

Today's text declares that God commanded the universe to form. I believe that it is impossible to understand the gospel of Jesus Christ without believing that God created the universe. As a graduate student I faced this challenge every day, because I was surrounded by staff and colleagues who did not believe that. By grace, my faith in God never wavered. Today I can state without a shadow of a doubt, "God created the universe."

*My God, that same creating power was at work in Jesus
    as he lived on Earth, died on the cross and rose again.
Thank you for your creating power!
Enthuse me with it.*

Jesus Foretold

By faith Abel offered God a better sacrifice (11:4)

Why was Abel's sacrifice better than Cain's? I get a clue from Romans 10:17. The Greek reads, literally, "So faith (comes) by report but the report by word of God." Most translations use the wording "faith comes by hearing, and hearing comes from the word, which comes from God."

If that is a universal truth, both Abel and Cain knew the kind of sacrifice that was pleasing to God. Cain rejected God's way and Abel accepted it. That is at the heart of the matter. It had little to do with the relative worth of pumpkins or sheep.

Be that as it may, I see nothing in Cain's sacrifice that reminds me of Jesus at all, while Abel's sacrifice speaks eloquently of God offering his only begotten Son so the world through him might be saved. Abel's offering was a faith offering, sealed by blood.

All of us who follow Jesus know we must bring offerings to God. In all candor, I sometimes bring the offering of Cain, bloodless and unbroken. I know what the sacrifice is that truly pleases God—the sacrifice of a willing spirit. That is true, but I would much prefer to offer him the work of my hands. He is doubtlessly pleased with both.

> *My Father in heaven,*
> *my desire is to offer you the better sacrifice.*
> *Thank you for revealing to me*
> *that the better sacrifice is Jesus Christ.*
> *I offer myself as a fulfilled, contented, happy disciple.*
> *Fill me with your faith.*

Jesus Walked with God

By faith Enoch (11:5)

Genesis 5 is a list of who begat whom, until we come to Enoch. In verses 22 and 24, we read, "Enoch walked with God." Only Enoch is described as more than simply the father of someone, even though he was the father of an exceptional son, Methuselah. It is written simply that he walked with God.

I come from a generation of doers. We know one another because of our achievements. When I meet someone new, I find myself asking, "What do you do?" I suppose I want to know what he or she produces. To be sure, when I find out a person's vocation it helps me to remember. But is there a better way to know people?

I once overheard a conversation between two Tanzanians who were discussing missionaries. "So and so helps us a lot. Another one is selfish. But that one, he loves Jesus." I felt good that among all us missionaries, at least one was known as loving Jesus. I hasten to say they were not referring to me. However, I began to wonder what is the most important thing that a missionary can do. It must certainly be to walk with God.

Enoch did not just visit with God on occasion or pray to him only in dire circumstances. He walked every step of the way with God, day in and day out, whether fathering Methuselah or plowing the fields. Enoch obviously trusted God. By faith he walked with God.

> *Lord Jesus, my heart's desire is to walk with you,*
> *because I have absolute confidence that you*
> *will never ever lead me astray or into situations*
> *from which you cannot deliver me.*
> *I do not live for an epitaph,*
> *but may that little sentence describe my life this way:*
> *"He walked with God."*

By Faith Jesus Pleased His Father

**Without faith it is impossible to please God, because anyone
who comes to him must believe that he exists and that he rewards
those who earnestly seek him (11:6)**

"Without faith it is impossible to please God." This is the theme of this chapter. Enoch's translation to glory indicates that God is highly pleased when a normal human being chooses to live entirely by faith in him.

This does not mean that people who live by faith in God will enter glory without tasting physical death. That is not the point. The Holy Spirit is teaching us that in order to receive the fullness of God in our lives we must exercise faith in who God is and what he can do.

True faith believes that God exists. That is fundamental. It also believes that those who seek him are rewarded. True faith focuses on seeking God earnestly, as a shepherd seeks a wayward sheep or a woman seeks a missing coin or a father seeks a lost son.

Conversion marks the beginning of the journey. What follows is a lifetime of learning who Jesus is, how the Holy Spirit ministers, and the extent of God's love, grace, and justice. This requires a lifetime of being conformed to the image of Christ. Slowly but surely I find myself desiring to live as he lived, in the presence of the Father.

Father God, my heart eagerly seeks you.
You promised through the prophet Jeremiah
that "you will seek me and find me
when you seek me with all your heart."
If I look for you and you look for me,
what will hinder our getting together?

Jesus Loved His Father and Did His Will

By faith Noah ... in holy fear built an ark (11:7)

The debate goes on: what is the relationship between faith and works? Some claim that too much emphasis on grace leads to wooly ethics. Others warn that too much emphasis on doing good breeds legalism and "salvation by works."

Noah had it right. By faith he built. He believed that whatever God said was true. The text says God warned him about something that no one had ever seen. Noah saw an "unseen" vision.

The key to it all was Noah's holy fear. The opposite of holy fear is unholy complacency. Holy fear prompts holy living; unholy complacency or outright rebellion results in tragedy. Jesus told us how sanctification works: "If you love me, you will obey what I command" (John 14:15). Holy fear is a reverential awe of God. If as a disciple of Jesus I act or think contrary to what I know about Jesus, I cannot claim to stand in awe of God.

A Tanzanian friend, the son of a godly pastor, in reflecting on his growing-up years, said, "We do not have the fear of God any more like we had in our home." He was lamenting the fact that it is hard to sustain a close walk with Jesus if we treat God as inconsequential. He determined to teach his family to live in the fear of the Lord, like his father taught him.

> *My God, through Christ you invite me to be in your presence.*
> *You paid a heavy price for that—*
> *the death of your only begotten Son.*
> *May I never take lightly what cost you so much*
> *or take my access to your presence casually.*
> *Teach me holy fear as I live my life of service before you.*

Jesus, My Vision

**By faith Abraham . . . was looking forward to the city with foundations,
whose architect and builder is God (11:8, 10)**

I see the sequence in Abraham's life story. First, he believed God. Then he walked so closely with God that he could hear God speak. Then he caught a vision of God's promise, which led to obedience based on implicit faith in God. Abraham followed the call of God. The rest is history. His walk with God changed the world.

I find it compelling that Abraham saw something no one else could see, and he saw it by faith. He saw a city "whose architect and builder is God." His entire life then moved in the direction of that vision. It enabled him to leave the familiar and predictable, to move out by faith into challenging circumstances. Having been a citizen of the prosperous and powerful Ur, he became a stranger in a foreign land. Having lived in convenient Persian housing in one of the greatest nations of the time, he was willing to live in tents in strange places. No loss was too great for Abraham, because he yearned to see the city of his dreams become a reality.

This is the journey of faith. It is difficult to sustain a purpose-driven life if there is no vision on which to focus energy. And it must be a vision given by God and not a selfish vision with self as the center of it all. Followers of Jesus are always "looking forward."

> *Jesus, I believe by faith you saw Jews and Gentiles*
> *streaming into the church,*
> *the kingdom expanding to cover the Earth.*
> *I think you had an earthly vision and a heavenly one.*
> *Re-envision me! I need to see what you see, by faith.*

November 9

Jesus, a Stranger on Earth

**[Abraham] was looking forward to the city with foundations,
whose architect and builder is God (11:10)**

One of the most disturbing verses in the entire Bible is, "[Jesus] came unto his own, and his own received him not" (John 1:11 KJV). Isaiah saw this by divine revelation seven hundred years before it happened, and prophesied, "He is despised and rejected of men; a man of sorrows, and acquainted with grief" (Isaiah 53:3 KJV). Jesus was pronounced an unwanted foreigner by the people he created.

Jesus steeled himself to be scorned, mocked, and rejected. Knowing that his disciples would face similar rejection, he prayed in the upper room, "I have given them your word and the world has hated them, for they are not of the world any more than I am of the world" (John 17:14). The world that rejected Jesus would surely reject Peter, John, and all of them. All of the eleven remaining disciples met a martyr's death except John who suffered imprisonment.

Through the years I have discovered one thing about myself: I depend heavily on the approval of people. I too often get my perspective by listening to what people think of me. This is ingrained in my ego. When someone applauds something I have done, I work even harder to make sure the compliments keep flowing my way. Unwittingly I shape my life around human approval.

But not Abraham. He sought only God's approval.

God, I need help on this.
Through my life, at times I feared being rejected by people
more than I feared being rejected by you.
Forgive me for that.

November 10

Jesus Believed God

By faith Abraham ... was enabled to become a father (11:11)

The writer of Hebrews skips right over a major glitch in Abraham's life. Or was it? God promised Abraham that he would be the father of a nation that would bless all nations. The problem was that Sarah could not conceive. So she proposed a good way to help God fulfill his promise. She urged Abraham to have a child by Hagar, their Egyptian maidservant. He did and Hagar produced a son, Ishmael.

The human solution seemed to be working, so when Ishmael was thirteen years old, he and Abraham were circumcised on the same day. But that very year, it seems, Sarah got pregnant and produced Isaac. Who, then, was the legitimate heir, the son of Hagar or the son of Sarah? According to ancient primogeniture it should have been Ishmael. The battle was on. Their descendants fight to this day. The Muslims insist it is Ishmael, their ancestor.

Was conceiving Ishmael a slip on Abraham's part? Probably so, but is Abraham not like us? Do we not at times employ human effort to help God realize his promise? It is so easy as a Christian worker to figure out ways to get the job done without submitting every decision to God's judgment.

I think of you, Jesus, led into the wilderness by the Holy Spirit,
 just after John identified you as God's Lamb.
There Satan did not test your vision
 but how you would realize that vision.
You knew that you would feed the people.
Satan presented a nifty way to do that: turn stones into bread.
You knew that you would perform signs and wonders.
Satan said, "Jump now."
You knew that you would inherit and rule the world.
Satan had a shortcut in place:
 "Worship me and you will have it, without the cross."
Jesus, I want to be like you.

Jesus Trusted God to the End

All these people were still living by faith when they died (11:13)

It is one thing to have faith when we first believe, but quite another to weather the storms of life and still cling to that same faith when it comes time to die. My faith should grow stronger as I put to the test the promises of God. My aim is to still be living by faith when I die.

The writer of Hebrews reminded his readers that it is possible that some people who begin the journey by faith will fall along the way because for some reason or other they did not sustain a living faith in God. Satan is determined to confuse every believer by deceiving him or her that God is unjust, unwise, capricious, or just not at all interested. We recall what Jesus said to Peter: "I have prayed for you, Simon, that your faith may not fail" (Luke 22:32).

The last words of Jesus on the cross were, "Father, into your hands I commit my spirit" (Luke 23:46). He knew the hands of his Father. He died believing. By then he had left the question of why in the hands of his heavenly Father.

Years ago I visited with an old African brother in the Lord. "My one desire," he confided, "is to have a repentant heart until I die." His only fear was that he might die with a hard heart. That is a godly fear.

My Lord Jesus, give me the grace to live by faith,
and when it is my hour to be with you in glory,
may I enter with the very same faith by which I lived.

November 12

Jesus, God's Only Son

By faith Abraham, when God tested him, offered Isaac as a sacrifice (11:17)

It takes faith to believe in a God whose ways are completely incomprehensible. Abraham faced that when God asked him to give up Isaac. Was not this the God who promised that through Isaac a nation would arise to bless all nations?

In his commentary on Hebrews, William Barclay wrote, "Abraham is the pattern of the man who accepts what he cannot understand." Abraham was able to do what he had to do because he had faith that God would find a way to get his promises fulfilled.

Abraham did not abandon reason; he "reasoned that God could raise the dead" (Hebrews 11:19). He found a deeper level on which to reason: the wisdom and power of God. He believed God could raise the dead!

Facing a rather hopeless situation as a missionary in Africa, I blurted out, "I see no way through this." My friend asked, "Did God raise Jesus from the dead?" He was right; I had no reason to doubt God's power. I could see no way forward, but God could.

The words of Habakkuk reverberate through the corridors of faith: "Though the fig tree does not bud and there are no grapes on the vines, though the olive crop fails and the fields produce no food, though there are no sheep in the pen and no cattle in the stall, yet I will rejoice in the LORD, I will be joyful in God my Savior. The Sovereign LORD is my strength" (Habakkuk 3:17-19).

He advised the doubters, "Though it linger, wait for [the revelation]; it will certainly come and will not delay" (Habakkuk 2:3). Faith is ours only after it is tested.

God, when I face a situation that seems hopeless,
remind me of the cross of despair
and the open tomb of hope.

Jesus Knows the Future

By faith Isaac blessed Jacob and Esau in regard to their future (11:20)

What about Isaac? Unlike Abraham, his father, Isaac accomplished little. The writer of Genesis was hard put to fill even one chapter with Isaac's achievements. Married when he was over forty, he and Rebecca failed to produce offspring for more than twenty years. Tension marked their marriage. When Rebecca finally became pregnant and gave birth to twins, Isaac favored Esau, the firstborn, and Rebecca favored Jacob. So they fought through their children.

As I read about Isaac, I see that he had very little spiritual discernment. His appetites ruled his life. The Scriptures tell us his eyes grew dim. Might this refer to his spiritual eyes as well?

God must have been aware of Isaac's spiritual semi-deafness. Rebecca, his wife, was more open to the voice of God. He told her, "Two nations are in your womb . . . and the older will serve the younger" (Genesis 25:23). She had gone "to inquire of the LORD" about the future of her offspring. Isaac exhibited no such spiritual sensitivity, as far as we know.

So why is Isaac on this list of heroes of faith? The test for him came late in life, when he discovered that because of his blindness he had inadvertently blessed the younger Jacob, thinking he was Esau. Now what? Esau pleaded with his father to correct his "mistake." Isaac stood firm, saying, "I blessed [Jacob]—and indeed he will be blessed!" (Genesis 27:33).

Amazing. The grace of God operates in spite of, or maybe even in light of, human frailty. God finally got through to Isaac.

Jesus, may my eyes never dim.
Grant me the grace to discern
the things of the Spirit.

By Faith, Jesus Blesses Us

By faith Jacob, when he was dying, blessed each of Joseph's sons (11:21)

The story of Jacob is riveting drama. I have spent hours walking alongside him, learning deep lessons of what it means to be educated in God's school of grace. I cannot begin to list the spiritual lessons I have learned. Having been so blessed by Jacob's tutelage in grace, I stand amazed that the writer of Hebrews highlights an aspect of Jacob's faith that on the surface seems to be of lesser value than many others.

Evidently from God's point of view, the true test of Jacob's faith was whether in the twilight of his life he would bless Joseph's two sons, Ephraim and Manasseh—both born of an Egyptian mother outside the Holy Land.

Is it possible these grandchildren, raised as Egyptian princes, could be incorporated into the future nation of Israel alongside Reuben, Judah, and the others? By faith Jacob embraced them, saying that they "will be reckoned as mine" (Genesis 48:5). By blessing them as he did, Jacob accepted them as equal to his biological sons.

Jacob also knew that God wanted the younger son, Ephraim, to receive the primary blessing. Joseph, their father, wanted to follow the rules of primogeniture. So when Jacob placed his right hand of blessing on the younger Ephraim, Joseph, assuming that his father had made a mistake, tried to stop him. At this Jacob protested, "I know!" Our text says that Jacob then died, having faith.

Lord God, may I have faith that prompts obedience.

Jesus, Always Full of Faith

By faith Joseph . . . gave instructions about his bones (11:22)

What will become of the young Jew, Joseph, sold as a slave in Egypt? By faith he was a trustworthy slave. By faith he counseled his fellow prisoners. By faith he entered the strange Egyptian culture as a government officer. By faith he fled the temptations of his youth. By faith he organized Egypt's food supply. He did astounding things—by faith in God.

Egypt was a mighty nation. When Joseph was sold into Egypt, the pyramids were already a thousand years old. The little piles of stone that his great-grandfather Abraham had thrown together as temporary altars were nothing compared to the awesome pyramids and the perpetually staring lion god, the Sphinx. I stood on that spot myself and felt the power of those symbols.

By faith Joseph discerned that the powerful sun god, Ra, universally worshipped in Egypt, was not really God, but an idol.

I am struck by the contrast between the power of Egypt and those eleven quarrelsome sons of Israel back home in the highlands of Judah. Yet Joseph believed that Yahweh had made a covenant with his great-grandfather Abraham, his grandfather Isaac, and his father, Jacob. The gods of Egypt never claimed his soul or his body, even though he served that nation. By faith he asked that his bones be taken to where his soul was all the time: in the land of promise. His bones found their resting place.

> *So may I, by faith,*
> *pursue the vision of the better land that you, Lord,*
> *have prepared for me and all your redeemed ones.*

Jesus, Hidden for Three Days

By faith Moses' parents hid him for three months (11:23)

Joseph lived by faith in a friendly Egypt. About four hundred years later, Amram and Jochebed, Moses' parents, lived by faith in a hostile Egypt. Faith is needed in good times and bad.

Times were bad for the Jews when Moses was born. While many newborn Israelite boys were slaughtered by a tyrannical Pharaoh, Moses' parents hid him for ninety anxious days. Each day they had to renew their faith. They knew that if the authorities discovered the boy, the entire family would be killed, along with many others. By faith they entrusted themselves to God. Each day became more difficult as Moses grew.

What sustained their faith? I believe they knew what God wanted and they cooperated with him, for they walked with God. This act of faith went beyond parental instinct. God was in it for a definite purpose: to bring light and life to all people.

Is it not like God that he relied on two ordinary people, Amram and Jochebed, to risk their lives to carry out God's purposes? God always relies on the faith of the few to bless the multitudes.

Their faith was rewarded, even in the short run. I see mother Jochebed with baby Moses on her knee and Miriam by her side, praising God for his faithfulness.

Eighty years later it was Moses' turn, as he, like his parents, was called to live by faith.

Lord, increase my faith! I need it today.

Jesus Renounced All Privilege

By faith Moses . . . refused to be known as the son of Pharaoh's daughter
(11:24)

Moses owed his life to Pharaoh's daughter, who had rescued him from certain death. He was then raised to take his place among the princes of fabled Egypt. All the privileges of royalty were his. Mighty Egypt would be his. Who could possibly renounce that?

Moses did, at about forty years of age. With his gifts of leadership he could have been a respected ruler of the greatest nation on earth at that time. But he renounced it all. To the royal court, this surely looked like gross ingratitude. Moses had a sensitive spirit, as is evident in his later life, so walking away from those who had given him "everything" must have been terribly difficult.

When I was completing my doctorate work at New York University, an adviser who had helped me a great deal offered me a teaching position at the university. You can imagine how he felt when as tactfully as possible I turned down his generous offer. He could not comprehend how I could do that, especially when I told him I would return to a struggling Bible school in Tanzania. Maybe he felt that he had cast his pearls before swine.

Every follower of Jesus gets to a point when he or she is called on to renounce something of great potential benefit in order to serve the Lord. That's when faith in God is tested.

Lord, as Moses "by faith" agreed to renounce worldly gain
to live in complete dependency on God,
so may I lay my all on the altar.

Jesus Knew His Father

[Moses] persevered because he saw him who is invisible (11:27)

No one could mistake the power of Pharaoh. He had absolute control over his own people and over the Jews who lived among them. He had money beyond counting and chariots of war to strike fright into the enemy. His might was awesome.

Moses knew the power of the Pharaoh, who had everything. In contrast, Moses had nothing. This was obvious to everyone. But what the people could not see was that "the LORD would speak to Moses face to face, as a man speaks to his friend" (Exodus 33:11).

Moses saw God. Pharaoh did not. Moses knew the love and the power of God. That is the reason he could persevere in the face of what looked impossible.

I see Moses standing before Pharaoh with nothing more than his herdsman's staff. Does he not see that Pharaoh can crush him in a moment? Moses, do you not see Pharaoh's might? Yes, Moses was aware of Pharaoh's power, but he saw something greater—the Lord of heaven and earth, the One who covenanted to never abandon his people. It was only in the periphery of his vision that Moses saw Pharaoh. At the center he saw Yahweh, mighty to deliver.

Thank you, Lord God, for helping me to stand
before overwhelming odds when Satan insinuated,
"What makes you think you can do that?"
I moved forward because I saw you, my God,
who promised again never to leave me.
You have been faithful and will be so into eternity.

Jesus Knows the Power of the Atonement

By faith he kept the Passover and the sprinkling of blood (11:28)

God spoke to Moses, "I will bring judgment on all the gods of Egypt. I am the LORD" (Exodus 12:12). He carefully prescribed the means he would use for their salvation. Take a lamb. . . . Remove the yeast. . . . Apply the blood.

The story of the Exodus is familiar. After nine plagues, the crisis came. The firstborn of Egypt—of cattle and people—would die. The earlier plagues did not depend on Israel's faith; God brought them. This one would be different. This one required faith and obedience on the part of the people. Would the families of Israel believe and show faith in the word of Yahweh?

God set the night of judgment, but did not tell the people what he was about to do. He simply told each household to take a lamb from among the flock on the tenth day of the first month and keep it for four days, then slaughter it at twilight on the fourteenth day. Likewise God instructed them to cleanse their homes of all leaven and to keep them clean for seven days.

All of this was a test of faith, leading up to the night of decision. Did it occur to them that dead sheep and tasteless bread would hardly conquer the might of the Egyptian Pharaoh? It seemed ridiculous, but it was the way God had chosen. They had a choice—follow God's way or perish in slavery.

> *Jesus, you truly "kept the Passover"*
> 　　*when you broke the bread and poured out the wine.*
> *You astonished your disciples.*
> *Your blood and your body, broken on the cross,*
> 　　*is the power of the new covenant.*
> *You knew that,*
> 　　*but it took the disciples some time to believe it.*
> *By faith in God, new things happen on the earth.*

Jesus Splits the Waters

By faith the people passed through the Red Sea as on dry land (11:29)

Because Moses believed, the people believed. Had Moses been a doubter, Israel would have faltered. A leader cannot have faith *for* the people but *with* the people. In face of the overwhelming power of Egypt, they had faith and they acted on it. They obeyed God. In the wilderness, it was another story. What happened to their faith?

This sounds familiar. I pray for physical healing for someone, for example, and the person is healed. Glory! My faith is soaring. I sing, "God does mighty things." Later on, someone speaks ill of me and I fuss and fume. Where then is my faith? I cross the mighty Red Sea and drown in a mere streamlet because I lack faith in my Lord.

Moses sustained his faith by walking closely with God, which enabled him to act by faith in each circumstance without argument. Often there was no time for debate. I think of that moment when Moses was shut in on every side by the sea and the desert, with the Egyptian war machines fast approaching. To be sure, their condition was hopeless.

Once again, God's grace came to the rescue! "Stand firm and you will see the deliverance the LORD will bring you today," Moses told the people. Then the Lord told Moses, "Raise your staff and stretch out your hand over the sea to divide the water" (Exodus 14:13, 16).

By faith Moses stepped in, then all Israel entered the jaws of death, where they experienced not only their own deliverance but also the destruction of their enemy. By faith they crossed over.

Thank you, Lord,
that by faith I can pass through the highest waters.

Jesus Keeps Us Believing

**By faith the walls of Jericho fell, after the people had marched
around them for seven days (11:30)**

One of my heroes is William Carey of England, the father of modern missions. In 1793, when he was in his late twenties, he abandoned his shoemaking business to do something that took immense courage. He went as a "nobody" to evangelize India.

"By faith" Carey left home and nation because he heard God's call. He had little more than a vision, nothing impressive. From that feeble beginning grew the modern missionary movement, which advanced the world's Christian population three-fold between 1800 and 1900. I feel honored to have played a small part, embarrassingly small, in this venture of faith called missions.

Carey issued a challenge that still rings through the years and reverberates in our souls: "Ask great things of God; expect great things from God; undertake great things for God." I do fairly well on the first two parts but hesitate on the third, for it implies a risk, abandonment to God. Lord, help me.

No doubt Carey renewed that faith every day, continuously, as did Joshua and his believing band, who for seven days called forth faith. Then the victory!

> *Lord, I have learned from you*
> *that faith that does not march in obedience to you*
> *is no faith at all.*
> *Lord, seven times seems like a lot.*
> *Increase my faith,*
> *and enthuse me to keep going around.*

Jesus Leads the Parade

By faith the prostitute Rahab ... was not killed (11:31)

I am impressed as the parade of faith passes. Abel, Enoch, Noah, Abraham, Isaac, Jacob, Joseph, Moses, Joshua—all were exemplary Hebrews who represent the best of the lot. Then, surprise, Rahab! This Canaanite woman was a harlot. How did she get a place among Israel's elite?

It seems odd that shortly after Moses told the Jews not to mix with the Canaanite population, behold, Rahab! This questionable Canaanite woman steals the limelight. If we read this text correctly. She had faith just like Joshua, a son of the covenant.

What motivated Rahab to provide sanctuary for the two Jewish spies? I believe the Spirit of God surely gave her some understanding of what was happening. Her knowledge was limited, as might be expected, but she had faith that Yahweh would protect her. She had no idea how it would happen, but somehow God's grace was extended to her, and she acted on the basis of her belief.

As I reflect on this, I also see a similar missionary parade of faith. The apostle Paul, St. Augustine, St. Francis, Menno Simons, William Carey, E. Stanley Jones, Mother Teresa and Lesslie Newbigin and thousands more. They were all mighty men and women, full of faith, and then, *me!* How did this renegade lad ever get into this parade? Good question. Happily, there's a good answer: by faith!

> *Lord, you surprise me all over again.*
> *You are marvelous.*

Jesus Loved His Heavenly Father

Barak, Samson, Jephtah, David, Samuel (11:32)

Israel again suffered under Canaanite rule, this time under Sisera, whose army contained nine hundred iron chariots and thousands of soldiers. Though greatly outnumbered, the Jewish band, under the leadership of Barak, overpowered Sisera and destroyed his great army—by faith.

Samson was endowed with extraordinary strength and was quite successful in his exploits of deliverance. But those victories were short-lived. It was only when he was stripped of his strength that he discovered God's power, and with faith in that power he went out. He died bringing destruction to Israel's foes, by faith.

Many in this parade of faith were of noble birth. Not so with Jephtah, an illegitimate son. But he learned to walk with God. Out of that grew a strong, unwavering faith. By faith he defeated the enemies of Israel, the Ammonites.

David sang the old songs of faith and added new ones, each pulsing with the glory of walking by faith. By faith he slew Goliath. By faith he refused to kill King Saul. By faith he prepared to build the temple. By faith he was victorious in battle. By faith he cried out for forgiveness when he sinned before God and before Israel. David lived by faith and wrote his hymns of faith.

Samuel walked with God, and all Israel looked to him for a word of prophecy from God. He listened to God and received messages, by faith.

> *In my weakness, Lord,*
> *show your almighty power as I live by faith.*

Jesus Empowers the Weak Faithful

Who through faith conquered kingdoms, administered justice ...
shut the mouths of lions, quenched the fury of the flames,
and escaped the edge of the sword (11:33-34)

By faith David slew the menacing Philistine, Goliath. Later, as king he extended Israel's borders from the sea to the rivers of Persia. We think of King David as primarily a warrior. When God called him to battle he went out by faith and was usually victorious. But as we see from this reference in Hebrews, he excelled in the way he administered justice as well. The text indicates that it takes as much faith to administer justice as it does to defeat armies. By faith he "reigned over all Israel, doing what was just and right for all his people" (2 Samuel 8:15). He believed that God was involved in every case he had to settle.

By faith Daniel believed God would protect him among the fierce lions that could have torn him apart.

By faith Shadrach, Meshach, and Abednego cast their lives into the hands of God and passed through fire. In their weakness, God showed himself strong to save.

By faith both Elijah and Elisha escaped the swords of King Ahab and Jezebel. Those prophets of God confronted the evil king and queen with nothing but faith. Humanly speaking, Ahab and his queen, Jezebel, had the power to crush Elijah and Elisha in an instant. God provided a way of escape. In their weakness, God showed himself strong to deliver.

So the refrain goes—by faith, by faith, by faith. I note that there is not one reference to personal power and acumen. It is all God.

> *I see, Lord, that in each case,*
> *weakness was turned to strength by faith.*
> *I recall times when I trembled in the face of daunting challenges.*
> *As I look back over my life,*
> *I praise you for showing me the simple way*
> *of walking with you by faith.*

Jesus, the Way to Life

**They were stoned, they were sawed in two, they were put to death
by the sword (11:37)**

Yes, some "women received back their dead, raised to life again" (11:35). But there were others who prayed as they witnessed the unrestrained rage of evil men against husbands and children. That called for a faith about which I know little.

Few things in my life have moved me as much as an event in 1969—a martyr's funeral in Kenya. People called him Evangelist Samuel. We knew him through Gladys, the woman who helped in our house. Along with many of the "saved ones," Samuel had refused to take the ancient oath of allegiance to tribal ancestors. He said he could not drink the blood oath because he had already drunk the blood of Jesus.

Infuriated by his adamant refusal, the oathers beat him mercilessly and left him to die in the forest, along with his wife and daughters. They survived, but he died. Within a day or two, a huge throng gathered around a simple corrugated-iron church for the funeral. To the surprise of all, his wife appeared. She had insisted that she must leave the hospital for the funeral. Silence fell on the crowd as she stood and forgave the killers. Spontaneously, a great song of praise erupted. The funeral was transformed into an experience of rapture.

The oathers are long forgotten. Samuel lives on, not only in glory, but in the memory of God's people in Kenya. And in my memory—for good!

*It is true, the world was not worthy
of people like Samuel.*

Jesus, the All-Worthy One

Destitute, persecuted and mistreated—the world was not worthy of them
(11:37-38)

A terrible calamity struck Jerusalem about a century and a half before Christ. The Romans enthroned Antiochus IV as the new king of Syria. In his lust for power he attacked Jerusalem in 168 BC. His goal was to destroy the Jewish religion and replace it with idolatry. His armies sacked the temple and removed all the sacred furniture. On the sacred altar he sacrificed swine flesh to Zeus and turned the temple rooms into brothels. He forbade circumcision, burned Scriptures, and ordered every Jew to eat pork. Those who refused were slaughtered.

A spate of bloodletting that defies imagination followed. The description in the letter to the Hebrews is as shocking as it is accurate. It was said that eighty thousand Jews met death at the hands of their tormentors and another ten thousand were sold into slavery. The Books of the Maccabees spare no details as the story of one martyr after another is told. King Antiochus destroyed everything the Jews had—everything but their faith.

The Jews arose from that dark hour more determined than ever to live for God. Six generations later, the true deliverer appeared. He too felt the cruelty of scourging and crucifixion. After three days he arose from the dead. He went through by faith.

Out of weakness we see the astounding life-giving power of God.

Lord Jesus, thank you for giving me
the privilege of knowing suffering,
triumphant saints who lived by faith.

Greater Faith When More Is Seen

**These were all commended for their faith, yet none of them received
what had been promised (11:39)**

None of them received what was promised. Yet their faith never wavered.

How about me? Why should my faith fail? I have absolutely no excuse. I have already received what was promised: fullness of life in Jesus Christ and the blessed infilling of the Holy Spirit. None of those "greats" knew what I know. None saw what I see. That puts their faith into sharp contrast with mine. They had faith in what was not yet theirs. I have the privilege of having faith in what is already mine.

If they believed without seeing, what keeps me from believing when I see so much more? I should have greater faith than Noah, who persisted in believing in the face of all odds; greater faith than Moses, who confronted Pharaoh with a shepherd's staff; greater faith than Jacob, who believed that his sons would form a solid foundation for God's covenant people.

I am humbled. I see my faith is but a candle before the noonday sun of the faith of these true believers. And they had but the promises, I have the fulfillment.

My mind broods over what the Spirit of God is saying. I begin to see it. Great faith is possible only if I walk with God, for I can hear from God only when I am walking in step with him. Revelation comes from hearing, and hearing is experienced in fellowship

> *So, Lord, how do I become more settled in my faith?*
> *The answer must simply be to walk closer with you.*
> *It is futile to have faith in faith,*
> *but I know that it is life eternal to have faith in you,*
> *the living God.*

Jesus Is Something Better

**God had planned something better for us, so that only together with us
they may be made perfect (11:40)**

Have I really heard these words: "something better for us"? Something better than what God planned for Abraham, Jacob, and Joseph? Something better than he planned for the renowned Moses and King David? Is that possible?

Not only is it possible, it is true. His name is Jesus Christ of Nazareth, Lamb of God, Son of God and Son of man, King of all kings, conquering Son, my Lord and Savior, and much, much more.

That reality excites the author of Hebrews. Jesus Christ crowns the efforts of all the saints. Jesus is better. Abraham envisioned a huge family of faith; Jesus brought into being the church, which is his bride, beloved and pure. Jacob dreamed of a nation of twelve tribes that would glorify God; Jesus is bringing into being a body of believers out of every tribe and nation. Moses saw by faith a redeemed, liberated people; Jesus has broken the power of Satan and has set the prisoners of sin free. Joshua envisioned a holy land where God's people would live together in peace and rest; Jesus opened the doors of heaven by his own blood so that you and I can enter this new land of peace and rest. David dreamed of a godly kingdom; Jesus is establishing the everlasting kingdom. I rest my eternal destiny on him.

Lord, you saved the best for last.
There is something better for us.
I want to know all of what that means,
Lord, for time and eternity.

Jesus Applauds Devotion

Therefore, since we are surrounded by such a great cloud of witnesses
(12:1)

The parade of faith of chapter 11 has passed before us. Each one, from Abel to the prophets, has a story to tell. I hear them all give witness to a single theme: walk closely with God and step out by faith when he asks you to do so. It all boils down to that.

Circumstances will differ, personalities will differ, but the refrain is common. The old hymn has it right: "When we walk with the Lord in the light of His Word, / What a glory He sheds on our way! / While we do His good will, He abides with us still, / And with all who will trust and obey. / Trust and obey, for there's no other way / To be happy in Jesus, but to trust and obey."

I am surrounded by a great cloud of witnesses who abandoned all and followed God. I hear not one sigh of regret from any of them. Imagine Moses saying, as he looked back over his life, "I should have refused to do what God wanted." David was sorry only that he had sinned so grievously, not that he obeyed God.

I hear the testimony of thousands of martyrs who gave to God their most precious possession: their right to live. As they gather around the throne of their Lord in glory, I hear only praise and thanksgiving, not a word of regret. This is the great cloud of witnesses that encourages me. I humbly take my place, at the rear of this glad procession, moving toward glory. Praise God forever and ever.

> *Lord, I am surrounded by saints and angels,*
> *on earth and in heaven, all singing with a loud, thankful voice,*
> *"Worthy is the Lamb who was slain*
> *to receive honor and glory and power*
> *forever and ever!"*

November 30

Jesus Fits Me for the Race

**Let us throw off everything that hinders and the sin that so easily entangles,
and let us run with perseverance (12:1)**

Amos lamented, "Woe to them that are at ease in Zion" (Amos 6:1 KJV). My faith in God compels me to run. Faith produces action and works. Noah built the ark. Abraham took his family out of Ur and pitched tents in a new land. Moses strode into the presence of Pharaoh to lead the Exodus. David slew the giant and expanded Israel's borders.

The faith God gives is active, not complacent. Dormant faith produces nothing at all. The writer of Hebrews says, "Let us run." This requires faith and effort. The Christian life is not a pleasant stroll, but a long-distance run.

I've worn out many pairs of jogging shoes in my lifetime. They have gone around the pyramids, the walls of Jerusalem, and many such places. I know that running calls forth every power in the body. Before running I remember telling my body, "Come on now, get ready, it's time to run." Something overcomes the body when it decides to run. It seems as if all the juices flow for that one thing. Is this not what the writer has in mind?

I am aware of at least two things when I run. First, I am only one of many runners. That is a huge encouragement. Second, I can run better if I can get rid of "everything that hinders." Hindrances are not in themselves bad, but they restrict my progress. Then there are some things that trip me. Hindrances simply slow me down; sin causes me to fall flat on my face. Jesus takes away sin. Run!

Praise God, the blood of Christ deals with both.
Thank you, Lord, for the desire and the energy
to keep on running.

December 1

Jesus, My Perseverance

Let us run with perseverance the race marked out for us.
Let us fix our eyes on Jesus (12:1-2)

I am encouraged by those who have lived by faith down through the centuries. I think of my great-grandfather, a beloved bishop in the church. As I run, I am reminded that he and many like him also ran and finished their course.

My friend Archbishop Janani Luwum of Uganda, who ran right into the lion's den of Idi Amin's terror, encouraged me. By faith he confronted the evil in that shocking regime. By faith, he is now among the Ugandan martyrs, a perpetual witness.

But they cannot give me the strength to keep running. That comes from Jesus Christ. He is my perseverance, my patience. So while in my peripheral vision I see my renowned great-grandfather, Moses, King David, Paul, and Janani, my attention is on Jesus, because he is the one who supplies my energy. They got their strength from God alone, and it is no different for me. I can hear them urging me on: "Do not look to us. You may glance in our direction now and again, but fix your eyes on Jesus. He alone is your strength and hope."

One reason to look to Jesus instead of a fellow runner is because the path of the race marked out for me is not the same as anyone else's. I am not competing with anyone. In this race we are all winners if we finish the course well. Furthermore, the race of life is not on a racing oval, but is marked through field and forest, mountain and desert. No two tracks are the same.

I do well to heed the encouragement of the saints. But I dare not stop to enjoy it. Their applause is pleasant, but I must keep my mind on the task—to run the race.

> *Lord God, give me grace*
> *to fix my eye on Jesus alone and run!*

December 2

Jesus, My All, A to Z

Let us fix our eyes on Jesus, the author and perfecter of our faith (12:2)

Where did Noah get the faith that kept him going for forty long years, despite public ridicule? Or Abraham, who risked everything when he stepped out of the familiar into a life of uncertainty and trial? How did these people sustain their faith?

According to what we have been learning, they did so because they received a call and a vision from God and because they walked with God every day, every step of the way. God does not inspire me with a vision and then leave me to my own wits to get on with it.

Moses, for example, needed as much faith the day he stepped into the daunting sea as he did when God spoke from the burning bush. Perhaps Moses' greatest test of faith came when God said he could no longer walk with the children of Israel because he might break out in wrath and destroy them all. He told Moses to go on without him. This devastated Moses, who knew his faith would wither into nothing in an instant if God were not with him. Moses depended entirely on those moments with God in the tent of meeting, his personal chapel in the wilderness. Moses feared walking alone more than any other thing. So should I. In order to keep running I must fix my eyes, not on myself or others or the goal, but on Jesus.

> *My God and Father, I am sure you planted in me*
> *any faith that I have.*
> *And I am equally convinced that you*
> *"who began a good work in [me] will carry it on to completion*
> *until the day of Christ Jesus."*
> *You are the instigator and the source of my faith.*

Jesus, Our Endurance

Who for the joy set before him endured the cross, scorning its shame
(12:2)

Jesus Christ was the most sensitive person who ever lived. He felt more deeply than I will ever feel. I crave acceptance. So did he. I appreciate the applause of people. So did he. I need to belong. So did he. I need the comfort of friends. So did he. I need the Father's approval. So did he. I want to be considered respectable and good. So did he. I want people to see my good works and express gratitude. So did he. I dread rejection. I cringe under mocking and ridicule. Jesus felt all that and much more. He felt every insult and every lash of the violent, unfeeling scourgers. He felt it all, for me.

What, then, gave Jesus the stout determination to carry that cross and to be hanged on it until he died? He saw beyond the shame, the mocking, and the anguish. He knew he had to be named the scum of the earth in order to make sinners fit for glory. So, regardless of how he felt, he went to Calvary for me, knowing full well that "anyone who is hung on a tree is under God's curse" (Deuteronomy 21:23). The taunts were merciless. His tormentors could not see that the sins that curse us all were on him. Jesus knew exactly what he was doing and "for the joy set before him endured the cross, scorning its shame." That energizes my weak knees. Joy is mine as I keep running.

Soul, consider Jesus.

I see clearly, Jesus, that you endured it all so that your joy
in bringing me to your Father would be fulfilled
and that my joy would be complete.
I see you experiencing that joy as your Father welcomed you into glory
as his precious sacrificial Lamb.
Your atoning work sets my heart and all heaven singing. It was for me.

December 4

Jesus, Our Example

**Consider him who endured such opposition from sinful men,
so that you will not grow weary and lose heart (12:3)**

In chapter 11 we were dazzled as the parade of saints passed. The stalwarts of faith of all ages passed by as we watched. We reflected on their walk with God, which produced that faith. Now we pause in the presence of the "better one."

The writer of Hebrews exalts Jesus, the eternal reality to which all other signs point. In order to impress this reality on Peter, James, and John, Jesus took them up the Mount of Transfiguration. They were astonished to see Moses, the peerless Jew, and Elijah, the beloved prophet. Both were men of outstanding faith. Among them stood Jesus. They all, including the three disciples, heard God's voice: "This is my Son, whom I love.... Listen to him!" (Matthew 17:5).

When the cloud cleared, Jesus stood alone, glorified before their eyes. Moses and Elijah surely said, "Amen. Listen to Jesus."

I admit that at times I hanker after law and order, as exemplified by Moses. At other times I wish I could see miracles all over the place, like those Elijah performed. Then by God's grace I am made aware that it is all in Jesus. He has enough law to last an eternity, and he can perform miracles that I cannot even imagine. The voice from heaven could not be clearer: Listen to Jesus.

When Peter, James, and John moved out to spread the gospel, they surely remembered that voice they heard so distinctly on the mountain. "Listen to him!"

*Jesus, tune my distracted ear to hear you only.
And to obey you sincerely. Forever.*

Jesus Is Unexcelled in Perseverance

**In your struggle against sin, you have not yet resisted to the point
of shedding your blood (12:4)**

Every problem I meet pushes me to consider Jesus once again. The Greek word used for *consider* means to "calculate," as in to weigh. I put Jesus on one side of the scale and my life with its demands and challenges on the other. Then I watch to see where the needle points. When I feel down or pressed, I get out my "atonement scales." I am always amazed that my light inconvenience carries no weight at all when put on the scales with Jesus Christ, who died for me.

So when I am distressed about something, I need to be reminded to consider Jesus. When I do that, things snap into focus.

As today's verse implies, we are all struggling against sin. It's allure is mighty. I freely admit it is a struggle. So what? When I am tempted to say, "It is enough," I turn my eyes to Jesus hanging there on the cross, shedding his blood because of my sin. I have not resisted sin to the point of the shedding of my blood, but Jesus did. I have maybe shed a drop or two of perspiration, because it is hard work, but not my lifeblood. Jesus went further; he shed his blood so that I might keep mine!

When I compare my temptations with the temptations of Jesus Christ, the Son of man, whose body, soul, and spirit faced the agony of the cross, I am embarrassed. I have not one foot to stand on. My "struggle against sin" takes on eternal meaning as I see Jesus, crucified, raised, and now with our Father in heaven.

Jesus, my soul considers your hope and joy. That's life!

December 6

Jesus Endured Discipline

My son, do not make light of the Lord's discipline (12:5)

This statement is designed to be an encouragement. But I do not relish the thought of being disciplined, and I am certainly not encouraged by it.

The encouraging part of it is that "the Lord disciplines those he loves" (12:6). The Lord does not waste time or energy, so to speak, on disciplining people who follow Satan, for they are not his children. He focuses all his attention on disciplining his own children so that they will be like him in all things.

As I view it that way, I see I should delight in the Lord when I am under his discipline, because that is sure proof that I am his favored child. And because he loves me, he will discipline me only to the extent to which I can respond.

I know a bit about this as a father. My wife and I soon learned that we have to discipline each of our four children differently. What might crush one is needed by another. I found myself frequently wondering how I could discipline my children with love, because they would probably see it as though I delighted in punishing them. I wanted to tailor the punishment to be the most appropriate for each child. Does Jesus not treat each of us differently? I believe he does but no child is left undisciplined.

> *I realize, Jesus, that you are so interested in shaping me*
> *to your likeness that you apply the most appropriate discipline*
> *to me personally.*
> *Even though I know this, I still squirm under discipline.*
> *Forgive me for that.*
> *Your desire is that I get to know you better*
> *and in so doing produce fruit that will bless others.*

Jesus Submitted and Rose from the Dead

**How much more should we submit to the Father of our spirits and live!
(12:9)**

I recall someone saying, "God had one Son without sin, but none without suffering."

As I travel about, I meet believers who insist that it is not God's will that any believer should suffer. They believe that the atonement fends off suffering. For them, suffering indicates a lack of faith. It may be so in some cases, but we need to be reminded that believers do suffer.

I might pray diligently that I may be spared suffering, thinking I know best. The writer of Hebrews reminds us that we probably thought that way when our earthly fathers disciplined us. As we look back, we are reminded that submitting was the right thing to do, because our parents did know best.

"How much more," then, "should we submit to the Father of our spirits and live!" The Hebrews letter abounds in "much more." This is an important one because it leads to life.

In my advancing years I am aware of the temptation to want my own way. In my earlier years I was probably more dedicated and more submissive than now. That concerns me, because many of the biblical saints, after experiencing youthful faith, later lapsed into catering to self. The youthful David slew mighty Goliath; the older David could not slay a moment of lust. The younger Noah built the ark; the older Noah collapsed into self-indulgence. The young Moses confronted Pharaoh; the older Moses became angry and struck the rock, contrary to God's command.

Lord Jesus, you submitted to the Father in all things.
Do that good work in me.

December 8

Jesus Focuses on the 'Later On'

**No discipline seems pleasant at the time.... Later on, however,
it produces a harvest of righteousness and peace for those
who have been trained by it (12:11)**

Discipline hurts! I have felt my heavenly Father's rod quite often. In all honesty, it is a painful thing and I feel wounded.

Discipline is not designed to make a person feel good. Its purpose is to remove some point of pride or something that is hindering the Holy Spirit from having full access into a person's life.

I have the choice when disciplined to doubt the Lord's love and wisdom or to repent of the thing God is trying to root out of my life, even if I do not know precisely what it is. I know one thing: the Lord does not discipline me for the fun of it, because I am sure he finds no joy in it at all.

I recall responding like this when a heavy discipline descended on me a while back. In my heart I felt him put his finger on an area of pride that resisted obedience. By his grace, he enabled me to repent. The blood of Jesus washed that resistance away, and even though I still hurt, I can bear it patiently. In hindsight, I can truly say, "That is exactly what I needed."

The phrase "later on" helps me. If I learn through discipline, the Lord will produce "a harvest of righteousness and peace" for me and for all those whose life I influence.

Lord, grant me faith while the hand of discipline is on me
so that I can press through it by your grace
and produce a harvest of righteousness and peace.

Jesus, Strength for Weariness

**Therefore, strengthen your feeble arms and weak knees ... so that the lame
may not be disabled, but rather healed (12:12-13)**

It does little good just to read the label on the medicine bottle, telling the benefits of the medication. For medicine to do me good, I must take it.

I have learned amazing things as I have pored over the letter to the Hebrews. But it will profit me nothing unless I act on what I have learned. Those breathtaking revelations do no good as ink on paper or as moments of insight in my heart. Jesus must spring to life and make all this real in my experience. At times, it seems my knowing is miles ahead of my doing.

So, after seeing Jesus in all his love, his power, his glory, and his wisdom, I am invited to do something about it. Our text is designed to stir me into action.

How? First, I can praise God that he has already strengthened my arms to bring peace and healing in the name of Jesus. My knees have already carried the gospel to others. Second, I am not entirely bereft of some strength, for which I praise God. Third, since my strength comes only from Jesus, I need to walk with him and love him dearly so that his strength is made perfect in my weakness. Fourth, I am not alone on this pilgrimage. I have brothers and sisters who are also walking this way, and they may be wearier than I am. I will pray that my friends who are wounded and tired may be healed. In Jesus I have faith that "the lame may not be disabled, but rather healed."

*Lord Jesus, keep on pouring your reviving, healing potion,
the blessed Holy Spirit, into my weak arms and knees.*

Jesus Removes Stumbling Blocks

Make level paths for your feet (12:13)

I have a responsibility to ease the way for brothers and sisters who are weak and wounded.

Jesus warned against placing stumbling blocks before weak pilgrims, saying, "If anyone causes one of these little ones who believe in me to sin, it would be better for him to have a large millstone hung around his neck and to be drowned in the depths of the sea" (Matthew 18:6). This is a doleful warning.

I am not sure what this means for me, but evidently I can inadvertently cause a little one to sin. The most obvious way to do this is to flaunt my freedom in Christ before fellow believers who are not as firmly grounded in grace. For example, a person who is near and dear to me almost destroyed his life by abusing alcohol. I must be extremely careful lest, by indulging in what might be for me quite harmless, I encourage him to slip back into his addiction.

But today's verse also points to something else. I am responsible for removing rocks that might cause me to stumble. Examples might be the stones of a critical spirit or of an unforgiving heart. It does little good to cry out to God to remove the stones for which I am personally responsible. I must deliberately take each one and remove it. There is no other way. God gives me the power to remove a stone; he will not do it.

God sent John the Baptist to clear for Jesus a path strewn with many stones. John taught that stones are removed by repentance and confirmed by baptism. We continue John's work by clearing the path to Jesus.

Point out those stones in my path
that need to be taken away, Holy Spirit.
Give me grace to name them and remove them.

Jesus Brought Peace by the Cross

Make every effort to live in peace with all men and to be holy (12:14)

Try as I might, perfect peace with all people eludes me. Thankfully, today's verse says, "Make every effort to live in peace," which implies that even though we try our hardest, our efforts might be frustrated.

The former owner of our house told me that his neighbor insisted that a disputed corner was his. Rather than quarrel with him, he gave the corner to him and had it registered. Every time I mow around that corner I am reminded of my own need to seek peace with everyone, especially neighbors.

However, it is good to remember that this world is hostile to Jesus. Just being a Christian and following Christ is itself an affront to many in our own culture. Western culture squirms when we confess Jesus' words, "I am the way and the truth and the life" (John 14:6). In their ears they hear only intolerance and bigotry.

Can I live at peace in this world? Will I deny my faith in Jesus just to make peace? My pursuit of holiness takes precedence over my pursuit of peace. Followers of the Lamb are out of step with the multitude marching headlong into ungodliness. Therefore, there will always be conflict. I wish everyone could understand that the way of the gospel is the way we were created to live. In the meantime, Jesus tells us to love our enemies. He promised to give us the power to do that.

> *Jesus, you showed the way. You loved sinners so much*
> *that you ate with them without compromising holiness.*
> *You touched the leper yet remained holy.*
> *You disputed with the Jewish authorities yet remained holy.*
> *You never compromised truth for a moment,*
> *no matter who you were with.*
> *Yet you liked to be with sinners.*
> *Teach me how you did that.*
> *It is where holiness and mercy meet.*

Jesus Hated Sin but Was Not Bitter

**See to it that no one misses the grace of God and that no bitter root
grows up to cause trouble and defile many (12:15)**

"Missing the grace of God" and the "bitter root" are linked. I have found that nothing stifles the free flow of God's grace like bitterness.

First comes the hurt I feel when my ego is miffed. If I simply try to shrug it off, it slowly but surely hardens into bitterness. If I do not own that bitterness as my responsibility and repent of it, slowly it produces bitter shoots that not only choke off the flow of grace in my own life, but also poison my environment, ultimately setting people against one another. Instead of living at peace with all people, I stir up feelings in others that result in quarreling, contention, and strife.

My tendency is to deny my own hurt feelings because I think I should be above that. My mind finds it absurd to carry that hurt, but my ego urges, "Hurt the one who hurt you!" My indecision results in doing nothing. The result is I drive the hurt underground where, like a root in darkness, it sprouts and spreads, contaminating the soil of my life and producing a hundred bitter shoots, each determined to poison the grace of God. And each getting ready to produce a whole tree of bitterness.

As a pastor and teacher I encounter people who are carrying hurt and bitterness. Some are chronically angry. I find families that are split and churches that are plagued by ancient family feuds. Grace will not flow until the roots are exposed. Through repentance grace will lay the axe to the root. Only then will the bitter root be severed in its entirety and the tree is free to grow taller once again.

Forbid, Lord, that I should miss your grace
by coddling hurt feelings.

The Way of Jesus Is the Pure Way

See that no one is sexually immoral, or is godless like Esau (12:16)

The rapid spread of HIV/AIDS in Africa is frightening. It is often spread through promiscuity. But another way it spreads is through the practice of levirate marriage, in which a man takes responsibility for a brother's widow. This includes honoring the deceased brother by having sexual relations with his widow. If the brother died of AIDS, of course, the widow infects her brother-in-law.

In a recent visit to Africa I heard someone say that it is good to live like a saved Christian even if you are an unbeliever. This does not only go for sexually transmitted disease but for all of life. A business friend of mine confided that he could hardly afford to live like a Christian because he competes by fudging the books to avoid paying taxes. I reminded him that Jesus did not create a world that prospers by cheating and lying. In business, as in anything, it is best to be Christian, because that is the way to cooperate with Jesus in his running of the universe.

Do not be like Esau, who did the ungodly thing of giving priority to his carnal appetites. In God's plan, the spiritual birthright takes priority. Esau chose the ungodly way and suffered the consequences. The writer of Hebrews uses Esau as an example of someone who considered his present desires and addictions to be more important than his spiritual inheritance.

Lord, remind me daily that above all things
I must guard my life with you.

Jesus Is God's Way

**[Esau] could bring about no change of mind, though he sought the blessing
with tears (12:17)**

Now and again the writer to the Hebrews startles me with pointed warnings. Here is one of the sharpest. Isaac mistakenly gave Jacob the birthright. Esau pleaded with his father to reverse what he had done and to give his birthright back. His tears were of no avail. Esau was distraught.

If people persist in continually deciding to please self instead of obeying Jesus, they may very well end up crying their eyes out to no avail.

But, praise God, that is not the end of Esau's story. He matured; he accepted what had happened. His change of heart was revealed as he refused to harm Jacob when he returned to the land after twenty years away. As a loving brother, Esau welcomed Jacob with kisses and joy.

I am impressed that Esau carried no bitterness toward his brother. We do not read of how God brought Esau to this place of peace. But we do have Jacob's story. Having come to the end of himself, Jacob admitted that he was Jacob, the supplanter and repented. So God changed both Jacob and Esau.

One of the most touching scenes in all the Scriptures shows the reconciled brothers burying their aged father Isaac. In doing so they proved to all posterity that the grace of God is sufficient to abolish all grudges.

Lord Jesus, you died forgiving your enemies.
Forgive me for carrying grudges.

Jesus Is Touchable

**You have not come to a mountain that can be touched and that is burning
with fire (12:18)**

Welcome to Sinai, a mountain of terrifying mystery. Mark its moods. Now it is a Vesuvius of blinding fire. Now heavy darkness falls over it, followed by smashing storms, convulsions of nature. What is happening? It is the justice of God on full display. Who dare approach such a mountain? It is a place of dread and death.

As the mountain shakes, a trumpet blasts, announcing the reason for the spectacular display. God speaks. "I am the LORD your God, who brought you out of Egypt, out of the land of slavery. You shall have no other gods before me. You shall not make for yourself an idol.... You shall not misuse the name of the LORD your God.... Remember the Sabbath day" (Exodus 20:2, 7, 8). Do not lie. Do not commit adultery. Do not take something that is not yours. And so on. Each statement heaps on the quaking Jews guilt on previous guilt.

This became unbearable for the trembling multitude. They "begged that no further word be spoken to them" (Hebrews 12:19). God continued to speak, declaring that if even an innocent animal inadvertently touches the mountain, it must be stoned to death on the spot. And "the sight was so terrifying that Moses said, 'I am trembling with fear'" (12:21).

Many of us come to this mountain first. There we see the wrath of God against sin. And there we recognize that we stand condemned. Sinai is bad news for sinners.

> *Praise God, there is another mountain,*
> *a mountain where truth and grace*
> *flow down as a single stream.*
> *It is called Mount Zion,*
> *the heavenly Jerusalem.*
> *Lead me, Lord, to that hill.*

Jesus Reigns in Zion

But you have come to Mount Zion (12:22)

I wish to tarry at this mountain and ponder each gift of God's grace. It is the "heavenly Jerusalem, the city of the living God" (12:22).

No one was more disappointed with the earthly Jerusalem than Jesus himself. Tears of compassion flowed freely from his eyes as he prepared to ride into that ancient city of promise on Palm Sunday. After all that God did for that city, he expected justice to flow from it to all nations. Instead Jerusalem killed God's prophets. That city on which God heaped untold blessings had become the center of bigotry. Crushed by the sadness of it all, Jesus wept.

While weeping those bitter tears, I would like to think that Jesus glimpsed another Jerusalem, the heavenly one. What was about to happen to him in a few days would usher in a new era. By his poured-out life he established the basis for the church, a community of faith that by his grace and power will fulfill every prophecy regarding the earthly Jerusalem.

The earthly Jerusalem rejects Jesus; the heavenly Jerusalem welcomes him. The earthly Jerusalem boasts of its splendor; the heavenly Jerusalem boasts of its Jesus, the Lamb slain for the salvation of the nations. The earthly Jerusalem kills the prophets; the heavenly Jerusalem listens to them. The heavenly Jerusalem glorifies those who follow the Lamb, no matter where they come from or what culture, tribe, or language they represent; The earthly Jerusalem assails Jesus to this day.

> *Our blessed Lord Jesus,*
> *may you never need to weep over the church,*
> *the new Jerusalem, as you did over the old one.*
> *As a citizen of the heavenly Jerusalem,*
> *I embrace all who love you,*
> *everywhere and for all time.*

Jesus' Grateful Worshipers

**You have come to thousands upon thousands of angels in joyful assembly,
to the church of the firstborn, whose names are written in heaven
(12:22-23)**

An African proverb says, "Only witches eat alone." That is because they have something to hide.

Sinai was a lonely place, for there a person felt convicted and condemned, without any comfort whatsoever. It was the loneliness of a prison cell where one cringed, awaiting judgment. There is a better way, much better.

Jesus was never alone. He told his disciples that he lived, thought, and acted in fellowship with his heavenly Father. Only once, if I am not mistaken, was Jesus truly alone. It was during that dreadful moment on Calvary's tree when he became sin for us. He felt the aloneness every sinner feels. Our sin, which he willingly bore in his body, cut him off from his Father. In agony he cried out, "My God, my God, why have you forsaken me?" (Mark 15:34).

I hear eternal pathos in those words. Jesus experienced the pangs of loneliness, of separation from his Father, so that I need never experience that loneliness myself ever again. Praise God, afterward he was greeted in glory by the adoration and praise of countless men and angels. He is now eternally at one with his Father.

That is our inheritance. Get ready, heaven. The saints are coming.

> *Lord Jesus, I embrace this heritage.*
> *Because you died and rose for me, I will never be alone.*
> *Mount Zion, to which I have come by grace, is a joyful assembly.*
> *You are our common joy.*
> *You, God's special Lamb, are worthy to receive glory and honor*
> *   and praise forever and ever.*
> *Praise you, Jesus, because my name is written in the Lamb's book of life*
> *   along with the names of all those whose hearts were stolen*
> *   by your undying love and mercy.*

Jesus, Our Perfecter

**You have come to God, the judge of all men, to the spirits of righteous men
made perfect (12:23)**

The law scares people, including me. Shouldn't it be more sinner-friendly? For starters, how about, "When it is convenient, worship God." Or "most of the time, do not worship idols." That would help.

That is not to be. The Judge, God almighty, sits on Mount Zion. He continues to judge according to the law. He could not do otherwise, because the law is the expression of his character. Zion is not lawless. The good news is that Jesus has already received the condemnation for my sin and has satisfied the demands of the law totally. His atoning work affirms the validity of the law.

People who put their entire trust in him find that they can be near to God the judge without terror because of Jesus. Grace does not disregard the law but affirms it. All who receive God's grace in Jesus Christ embrace the law. We do well remember that under the seat of mercy was the law.

The notion that people who live by grace have no regard for the law is false. We elevate the law and maintain a high ethical code. We know that we are not pronounced perfect because we obey the law. Rather we are perfected by the atoning work of our beloved Jesus. We know that Christ has already borne our judgment, so we obey out of love and gratitude, not out of dread. We are eager to do good works with Jesus.

> *My God, give me a correct understanding*
> *of how law and mercy can coexist,*
> *how truth and grace can kiss.*
> *I recall the words of your beloved disciple:*
> *you are "full of grace and truth."*

Jesus Is the New Covenant

To Jesus the mediator of a new covenant (12:24)

Sinai represents the old covenant. It speaks loudly that I stand condemned. Furthermore I have no advocate who can plead my case, even if I think I have a reason to be acquitted. It is a place of terrifying loneliness, a holy mountain in a dry wilderness, a place of fear and dread, a place of death and hopelessness. Who can approach that holy hill? To save people from destruction, God commanded that a line be set at the base of that mountain beyond which no one dare pass, not even an innocent animal.

But, wait, that is not the whole story. The prophet Micah asks, "Who is a God like you, who pardons sin and forgives the transgression? . . . You do not stay angry forever but delight to show mercy" (Micah 7:18). The prophets foresaw a new mountain. It is called Mount Zion. As we approach Zion we see Jesus Christ of Nazareth, now exalted above every name. He is high and lifted up. That is what it is all about.

As I learn more of him, I ponder what brought him to live among us and pay the price to take away the judgment against my soul. I bow in holy reverence, as do all the spirits of righteous people made perfect by his atonement. The eyes of my heart flood with tears. I come to Jesus. That is heaven itself.

> *Jesus, as you marked the holy transition from the old to the new,*
> *mark that transition in my own soul*
> *so I can enjoy this new mountain of peace and joy,*
> *Mount Zion, heaven on earth.*

Jesus' Blood Speaks Peace

To the sprinkled blood that speaks a better word than the blood of Abel (12:24)

In a fit of rage, Cain killed his brother Abel. As Abel's blood gushed from his body, I imagine it crying out, "Cursed be Cain. He is not fit to live among people. May he be a pariah on the earth. Mark him with the crimson M for murderer. Out, Cain, get out! May all who see you taunt and mock you until you die." What a terrifying word!

In a fit of rage, evil people killed their brother Jesus. As Jesus' blood gushed from his body, it cried out, "It is finished, the price for salvation is paid; now you who were enemies of God, repent and believe in me. Do not fear, but come near. I will bless you and put within you a new heart. I invite you to enjoy intimacy with the Father as I do. Come to me all who are burdened and weary, and I will give you eternal rest. The Holy Spirit says come, and let those who know me say come. Enter into the joy of my salvation. I give you a new family, a new name, a new citizenship, a new hope. Come and tarry not." That is a "better word" than that spoken by Abel's blood.

How different is the language of Sinai from the language of Zion! Sinai cries, "Stay away!" Zion pleads, "Come near." We who believe know the terror of Sinai. For many it is reason enough to move to a better mountain, to Calvary, Mount Zion.

At the base of Mount Zion Jesus displays a sign, "Whosoever will may enter. Welcome."

> *Praise God for this mountain of joy and peace.*
> *That is where I want to spend time and eternity.*
> *There I hear a "better word."*

Jesus' Kingdom Is Forever

Therefore, since we are receiving a kingdom that cannot be shaken,
let us be thankful (12:28)

The writer of Hebrews makes a final allusion to the two mountains. At Sinai, God's voice shook the earth with a mighty quake, reminiscent of Haggai's prophecy of the Lord saying, "I will once more shake the heavens, and the earth, and the sea, and the dry land" (Haggai 2:6). According to the prophet, after the shaking, the kingdom of God will remain. When Sinai shook, it sent a wave of shock through the people.

When Jesus hung on the cross as the sacrificial Lamb, "the earth shook and the rocks split" (Matthew 27:51). There was darkness over all the earth. The curtain that separated people from God ripped apart, offering free access. Praise God for that far-reaching shaking! It must have taken the priests some time to sew the curtain again.

I first experienced that shaking as a teenager when God began to show me the difference between earthly values and heavenly values. That was the beginning; many shakings followed. A particularly severe one struck in graduate school when the Lord shook my confidence in human philosophy. Another battered me in Africa when God shattered my self-sufficiency. All things but God will be shaken.

> *You have taught me much, Jesus, in the shakings.*
> *Particularly you taught me never to place ultimate confidence*
> *in anything made on earth,*
> *but to trust in that which comes down from heaven*
> *and God himself.*
> *Earthly kingdoms and systems are marked for destruction.*
> *Your kingdom, Lord Jesus, which I am receiving, lasts forever.*

Jesus Is Forever

**Keep on loving each other ... entertain strangers ... remember those
in prison ... keep your lives free from the love of money (13:1-3, 5)**

People who live on Zion's hill love one another. They echo the welcoming voice of Jesus. They welcome all repentant sinners—male or female, king or pauper. Inhabitants of Zion do not discriminate against or judge one another, for all have cast their sin on Jesus Christ, rejoicing in the fact that salvation has come as a free gift of God's grace.

Zion is marked by love, for it is the mountain of God, and God is love. The banner over this city is LOVE, which means love for the people who do not yet know Jesus and love for those who have chosen to share this mountain with God's people. I have no option; I must love those for whom Jesus died. Jesus did not offer a suggestion when he said, "Love one another." It is a command.

This attitude of open-armed acceptance and love is intensely practical. Isaiah saw it precisely: "They will neither harm nor destroy on all my holy mountain, for the earth shall be full of the knowledge of the LORD as the waters cover the sea" (Isaiah 11:9). As saints love one another, so the knowledge of God will spread across the entire world.

The inhabitants of Zion entertain strangers, visit prisoners, and do not pursue riches. They are content with what they have, and they serve one another.

They allow the shakings of life to draw them closer to the One who cannot be shaken. Their city will endure through time and eternity.

Jesus, keep me secure on this holy hill.

Jesus, Guardian of Purity

**Marriage should be honored by all, and the marriage bed kept pure, for
God will judge the adulterer and all the sexually immoral (13:4)**

"Wake up. We are living in the twenty-first century, not the Dark Ages! Get with it, man!"

I cringe when I hear such statements, because I know the following argument is coming: "Our society once approved of racial prejudice, slavery, and restrictions against women. But that day is over. Our society now says that those things were wrong. Using this argument they then pose the challenge, "Is that not true of restrictions concerning sex? What might have been wrong in the past is not necessarily wrong today." This is the new reality, our culture claims, and we must learn to live with it. This is called the "new morality."

Where do followers of Christ stand on these questions? I believe that morality is based squarely on the character of God. Morality is not something determined by popular vote.

True freedom is found in discovering how God designed the universe and then living happily within those eternal principles. The atoning work of Jesus Christ liberates all aspects of life. In all areas of life we should always consider Jesus, who speaks the last word.

> *Lord Jesus, each generation seems to come up with*
> *a new way to refute your character.*
> *Give us who love you a single eye to see you at work*
> *and a single ear to hear you speak.*

Jesus, My Constant Helper

**"Never will I leave you; never will I forsake you." . . . The Lord is my helper,
I will not be afraid (13:5-6)**

Zion is home for those who cannot make it without Jesus. They have given up on every other name, for they have considered all other names and found them to be no help at all. Jesus, the sovereign Lord of Zion, ensures the welfare of every inhabitant of the holy hill. He will never abandon his own. Zion is his permanent home, among the saints, and he will never leave that assembly. Where could Jesus go?

Those who live in Zion fear only what their Lord fears, nothing more. One fear they need never have is that Jesus will abandon them. They place all their reliance completely and only on the Lord.

While living in East Africa, I woke up to the fact that I am hopelessly incapable of running my own life. This came as a shock to me because I was proud that I needed no one to lean on. I thought I could do most anything.

I was discovering something delightfully new. I am a mess on my own. I need Jesus more than I need anything else. Like Jacob, my hip broke as I wrestled with the truth about myself. I found that in my own strength I will always limp. My daily limp of weakness reminds me of the eternal grace of God. Furthermore God uses my weakness to pour out his strength.

> *Praise God for that insight.*
> *I will never run on my own again.*
> *I am helpless without you, my Jesus.*
> *You are my helper.*
> *I will not be afraid.*

Jesus—Yesterday, Today, Tomorrow

**Remember your leaders. . . . Jesus Christ is the same yesterday
and today and forever (13:7-8)**

Christian leaders are ordinary human beings. And most of them truly love the Lord and are walking with God. It is not clear if the writer is referring to leaders like those listed in chapter 11 or to his contemporaries. In either case, we do well to "consider the outcome of their way of life" (13:7).

For some it was martyrdom, for others a translation into glory. The important thing is that each had faith, and that is what should characterize *our* lives. Even though no human being is perfect, we do well to look back at our leaders and note their hope, assurance, and unshakable faith. The writer wants us to mark the way they died; those who held firm to the end are our heroes. We are to imitate them.

Having made that point, the writer reminds us that our leader is none other than Jesus Christ, who is the same yesterday, today, and forever. I have had to change often, because I learned new truths. That will never happen to Jesus, our authentic leader, because he is the truth.

Furthermore leaders might be tripped up by sin. That will never happen to Jesus.

> *Jesus, I love what you said to John*
> *in the opening scene of the Revelation:*
> *"Do not be afraid. I am the First and the Last.*
> *I am the Living One; I was dead,*
> *and behold I am alive for ever and ever!"*

Jesus Is Outside Our Camps

Let us, then, go to him outside the camp, bearing the disgrace he bore
(13:13)

Israel's national sin offerings—a bull and a goat—were taken outside the walls of Jerusalem and burned. So too Jesus is our red heifer and was taken out of the city, where he became our sin offering on the cross.

If we are to live with Jesus, we too must leave our camps, go to him outside, and bear "the disgrace he bore." Our life in him is "outside the camp."

This world is a mosaic of camps that promise security and a place to belong. Ethnic identity is one such camp. Nationalism is another. We hope for safety among our own people. That is not the way of the cross.

My Rwandan friend Israel Havigumana, a Hutu, reached out in the name of Christ Jesus to bring together leaders of the warring Hutu and Tutsi. This was extremely costly for Israel; his own people saw him as a dangerous traitor. The Tutsi on the other hand, questioned his motivation.

Israel knew that reconciliation is only possible when each antagonist goes to Jesus, for it is only at the foot of the cross that true reconciliation is possible. It will never happen when people stay in their camps.

In the first rash of killings in 1994, Israel was killed by his own tribesmen. It is risky to go outside one's own camp and make peace in the name of Jesus. But there is no other way.

> *Lord, this world is full of camps.*
> *Any identity that I have outside of you*
> *—my beloved denomination, my nation, my culture*
> *—can become a camp that hinders my fellowship*
> *with all believers.*
> *As grateful, redeemed sinners,*
> *we meet outside the walls of Jerusalem,*
> *on a hill called Calvary.*

Jesus, the New City

**For here we do not have an enduring city, but we are looking for the city
that is to come (13:14)**

What marks the old city? It is a city of ghettoes, divided by ethnicity, social class, gender issues, politics, wealth and poverty, and even religious and atheistic bigotry. Each "camp" pursues its agenda. The old city is a boiling caldron of unrest and fear. It promises security, yet each individual feels alone and helpless, like the little boy who, when asked how he liked his first day at kindergarten, replied, "I was alone in a room full of kids."

An uncaring mayor rules the old city. He encourages deception, fear, discord, self-centeredness, pride, man-made philosophies and religions, illusions of permanence without purpose, devoid of hope and peace. The old city is doomed.

What marks the new city? Jesus reigns as the Lamb of God. He draws us by his love, and love is the new mode of life. He puts into his children the desire to serve God and one another. He enables people of the new city to serve those in the old city, so that those under the rule of Satan can migrate.

But each must choose. In the days of Israel, Saul disqualified himself from being king, so God anointed David. Each citizen had to decide whether to live under the disqualified Saul or under David. We must do the same.

Lord, I have made my choice.
I have left the old city and seek the one to come.

Jesus Wants All to Reside in the New City

For here we do not have an enduring city, but we are looking for the city that is to come (13:14)

To some readers, the book of Hebrews deals too much with separation from the world and not enough on the responsibility believers have to help the unsaved world to manage itself better. But the followers of Jesus do not disengage from society, even though they know the nature of sin. They do the works of Jesus always. They will not abandon this world until Jesus does.

Many people whom we serve in the name of Jesus will remain in the old kingdom. Yet we continue to serve in Jesus' name. It is up to the Holy Spirit to bring people to the place where they move into the kingdom. As nonbelievers embrace Jesus, they are radically changed and move with joy to Mount Zion.

Jesus did not try to reform the Jewish religion or the Roman Empire. He came to establish a new covenant in his blood and calls out people from every tribe and culture to be salt and light and to take the gospel to the ends of the earth.

We do not abandon our cultures; we live in them as followers of Christ. We do not walk away from our unbelieving friends; we serve them, learn from them, and love them. We do not despair when we look at the deterioration of society, because we know the power of our Lord Jesus to save. Our eyes have seen the "enduring city."

> *Jesus, my Lord and Savior,*
> *so live in me that even though I live in two kingdoms,*
> *I serve only you.*

Jesus Loved His Father and Did Good

Through Jesus, therefore, let us continually offer to God a sacrifice of praise—the fruit of lips that confess his name. And do not forget to do good and to share with others, for with such sacrifices God is pleased (13:15-16)

I feel honored to be able to look back on a lifetime of walking with Jesus. Now I am trying to sort it all out. I have made my share of mistakes and have needed to repent often of hurting others. On the flip side, I almost burst with joy as I bask in the loving presence of Jesus. He was there in every phase of my life, from those days when I knew no limits to my youthful aspirations, through marriage, raising a family and serving in the trenches of spiritual warfare as a missionary. Then he gave me the opportunity to interact with hundreds of leaders in a ministry of leadership training.

The writer of Hebrews sums it all up for me. Do everything "through Jesus," who is the sure and trustworthy foundation. Let our first service be a continual sacrifice of praise of the One to whom we owe everything.

All the while, we give the Lord the right to ourselves, to do his good works through us among the believers and beyond. The sacrifice of praise and sacrifice of work complement one another. All are expressions of thanksgiving for what God has done for us.

So, Jesus, flood my being with a continual urge to exalt you in all ways,
whether it be through offering the glass of cold water
to a person in need or just praising your name
with the lips you have given me.

Jesus, the Good Shepherd

Lord Jesus, that great Shepherd of the sheep (13:20)

We are approaching the end of our reflections on the book of Hebrews. This coincides in a way with my own life, for I am now growing older and am reviewing my own walk with Jesus. I am certain of one thing; I have been cared for by "that great Shepherd of the sheep." I feel moved to do what King David did—imagine myself as a sheep.

With all the sheep and shepherds around me I declare, "Jesus Christ is my shepherd."

The world has many shepherds, all promising good things. But no shepherd looks after his sheep like Jesus does. I speak from experience. He provided me with green pastures and sparkling clean waters. His healing balms soothed and healed my wounds. He found me when I wandered off a bit and lovingly brought me back to his flock.

He went out ahead of me and the others who followed him and prepared just the right place for us to be near him always. He employed his rod to crack the head of our enemy, Satan. He never left me, no, not for a moment. He slept at the door of our pen at night, making sure that no one—strange shepherd or enemy—would come in to snatch us away.

Do you want to know the secret of the contented, fulfilled, happy sheep? It is Jesus, that great Shepherd of the sheep. My greatest joy is to declare that Jesus is my shepherd!

> *Surely goodness and mercy shall follow me*
> *all the days of my life.*
> *Thank you, Lord.*

Jesus, My Benediction

**May the God of peace, who through the blood of the eternal covenant
brought back from the dead our Lord Jesus, that great Shepherd
of the sheep, equip you with everything good for doing his will,
and may he work in us what is pleasing to him, through Jesus Christ,
to whom be glory forever and ever. Amen. (13:20-21)**

The message of this precious letter to the Hebrews is summarized in this gracious benediction. We are invited to leave the reign of Satan, which is marked by unrest, and to take our places in the new kingdom of God, which is a place of peace.

God can do it by applying the totality of the atoning work of Jesus to our lives. We have within us, as a gift of grace, the Holy Spirit, who makes available to us the power that raised Jesus Christ from the dead. What can we possibly need that Jesus cannot supply?

God is equipping us to overcome Satan, whose sole desire is to lure us away from the simple gospel. God is also gifting us to carry forth his work on the earth. A third of the world's population has not the slightest idea that Jesus died for them to take away their sins and to make them new creations. The great Shepherd will seek the lost until the day of his return. He equips his church around the world to spread the gospel in every culture.

Even so, come Lord Jesus.

*May our work please you, Lord, for we do it in your name
and by your resurrection power.
We are ordinary sheep, but you are the great Shepherd.
With you as Shepherd we will lack nothing
as we extend the kingdom of God from our doors
to the ends of the earth.
All praise and honor and glory be to our Jesus,
now and evermore. Amen.*

The Author

Donald R. Jacobs served as a missionary in Africa from 1953 to 1973. During that time he founded the Mennonite Theological College in Tanzania and later served on the faculty at the University of Nairobi. After his African ministry, Jacobs directed overseas programs for Eastern Mennonite Missions and then worked as director of the Mennonite Christian Leadership Foundation. His previous books include *A Gentle Wind of God* (2006) and *Pilgrimage in Mission* (1983). He holds a PhD in religion and culture from New York University.